Classical *and* Modern Narratives *of* LEADERSHIP

LESSONS FOR LEADERS
THE CLASSICS AND THE MODERN WORLD

A series of books on lessons from the classical world relevant to leadership skills. The series will offer creative applications of the wisdom of the ancients in the contexts and idioms of contemporary leadership training.

Classical *and* Modern Narratives *of* LEADERSHIP

Edited by
VIVIAN L. HOLLIDAY

Aylesworth Professor of Classics and History
and
Director, Leadership Program, The College of Wooster
Emerita

Preface by
HENRY LUCE, III
Chairman and C.E.O.
The Henry Luce Foundation, Inc.

BOLCHAZY-CARDUCCI PUBLISHERS, INC.
Wauconda, Illinois

General Editor
D. R. Bustion, II

Contributing Editors
Aaron E. Baker, Esq.
Albert M. Devine, Esq.

Cover Design and Typesetting
Charlene M. Hernandez

Part of the series
Lessons for Leaders: The Classics and the Modern World

© Copyright 2000 Bolchazy-Carducci Publishers, Inc.
All Rights Reserved

Bolchazy-Carducci Publishers, Inc.
1000 Brown Street, Unit 101
Wauconda, Illinois 60084 USA

http://www.bolchazy.com

Printed in the United States of America
2000
by Bang Printing

Hardbound ISBN 0-86516-478-9
Softbound ISBN 0-86516-479-7

Library of Congress Cataloging-in-Publication Data

Classical and modern narratives of leadership / edited by Vivian L. Holliday
    p.   cm. — (Lessons for leaders)
  A collection of 6 essays by professors of The College of Wooster.
  Includes bibliographical references.
  ISBN 0-86516-478-9 (cloth : alk. paper) — ISBN 0-86516-479-7 (pbk. : alk. paper)
   1. Leadership. 2. Executive ability. 3. Organizational effectiveness. I. Holliday, Vivian L., 1935- II. Series.

HD57.7 .C543 2000
658.4'092—dc21
                                          00-022251

Contents

Contributors vi

Illustrations vii

Preface ix
    Henry Luce III

Acknowledgments xi

Introduction 3
    Vivian L. Holliday

I. Rhetoric, Iconography, and Leadership in Classical Antiquity: Pericles and Augustus 11
    Vivian L. Holliday

II. Machiavelli and the Modern Narrative of Political Leadership 45
    Mark R. Weaver

III. *Julius Caesar* and *Coriolanus*: Testing the Mettle of Leaders 69
    Raymond G. McCall

IV. The Study of Gender and Leadership: Points of Departure 81
    Mary Kathryn Addis

V. Wandering in the Arabian Desert with George Bush: A Study of Presidential Leadership 103
    Eric S. Moskowitz

VI. An Odyssey in Black Leadership: Joseph Gomez, A Bishop in the African Methodist Episcopal Church 143
    Annetta Louise Gomez-Jefferson

CONTRIBUTORS

Mary Kathryn Addis
Spanish and Women's Studies
The College of Wooster

Annetta Louise Gomez-Jefferson
Emerita, Theatre and Black Studies
The College of Wooster

Vivian L. Holliday
Emerita, Classics and History
Former Director, Leadership Program
The College of Wooster

Raymond G. McCall
Emeritus, English and Theatre
The College of Wooster

Eric S. Moskowitz
Political Science
Director, Leadership Program
The College of Wooster

Mark R. Weaver
Political Science
The College of Wooster

Illustrations

Rhetoric, Iconography, and Leadership in Classical Antiquity

Figure 1   Plan of the Ara Pacis
Drawing courtesy of George W. Olson

Figure 2   Aeneas panel, west front, Ara Pacis
Photograph courtesy of Carl A. Peterson

Figure 3   Mars, Romulus, Remus panel, west front, Ara Pacis
Photograph courtesy of Carl A. Peterson

Figure 4   Processional relief, precinct wall, south, Ara Pacis
Photograph courtesy of German Archaeological Institute, Rome, neg. no. 72.2400

Figure 5   Processional relief, precinct wall, south, Ara Pacis
Photograph courtesy of German Archaeological Institute, Rome, neg. no. 72.2403

Figure 6   Interior detail, garlands and bucrania, precinct wall, Ara Pacis
Photograph courtesy of Carl A. Peterson

Figure 7   Exterior detail, florals and swans, precinct wall, Ara Pacis
Photograph courtesy of Carl A. Peterson

Figure 8   Earth, Sea, and Land Breezes, east panel, Ara Pacis
Photograph courtesy of Carl A. Peterson

Figure 9   Prima Porta statue of Augustus
Photograph courtesy of Alinari/Art Resource, NY, neg. no. AL6512

Figure 10 Detail of Prima Porta statue of Augustus
Photograph courtesy of German Archaeological Institute, Rome, neg. no. 62.1788

Figure 11 Gemma Augustea
Photograph courtesy of German Archaeological Institute, Rome, neg. no. 32.754

The Study of Gender and Leadership

Figure 1 Cartoon: Don Wright, "Ironing out Problems"
© Tribune Media Services, Inc. All Rights Reserved. Reprinted with permission.

Figure 2 Cartoon: Tom Meyer, "Shotgun Wedding of Ferraro and Mondale"
Tom Meyer/San Francisco Chronicle. Reprinted with permission.

Figure 3 Cartoon: Tom Meyer, "The Bride Carries the Groom over the Threshold"
Tom Meyer/San Francisco Chronicle. Reprinted with permission.

Figure 4 Cartoon: Oliphant, "The Ferraro Look"
© 1984 Universal Press Syndicate. Reprinted with permission.

Preface

When, in 1984, I suggested to President Henry Copeland of the College of Wooster that the college have a course in leadership, there were very few such in the country and many of those were in the nature of leadership training—in effect, drilling techniques.

So I was delighted by Dr. Copeland's enthusiastic response. We determined that the course was to be in leadership studies to give it an academic rather than vocational cast and, in fact, to intellectualize the field, something of which so little had been done, and which, in fact, was at the heart of the matter. As Tacitus said, "Reason and judgement are the qualities of a leader."

Since we began the course at Wooster, already fourteen years ago at this writing, leadership studies has become a real movement, involving hundreds of courses, a number of endowed chairs and even a couple of graduate schools. At my foundation it developed into a sustained and growing program with an interesting variety of projects.

Vivian L. Holliday, who took over the Wooster course after it had been launched by Historian James Hodges, did me the honor of asking me to give a lecture in her classroom, a challenge to which I happily responded. In the lecture I divided the subject into four categories: direction, skills, qualities, and behavior, and listed under them all the mechanisms relevant to leadership.

Leaders are, of course, widely studied in history courses. Typically, what is covered is what they proposed or attempted and the results thereof. But very little is said about why, as leaders, they decided what they did. It's wonderful, therefore, that Professor Holliday has now written, assembled and edited this book analyzing the performance of a great variety of leaders.

All too many books about leadership have been dry and pedagogical, to say nothing of sometimes being plain wrong. I'm glad to offer this book as an exception to that.

August 21, 1998

Henry Luce III
Chairman and C.E.O.
The Henry Luce Foundation, Inc.

Acknowledgments

As editor I acknowledge with gratitude the extraordinary assistance of several individuals in the preparation of this manuscript. First, Barbara J. Hampton, adjunct faculty and staff of the College of Wooster, has through her insights as well as her editorial assistance contributed immeasurably to this project. I am also indebted to Don Bustion and Lou Bolchazy of Bolchazy-Carducci Publishers, Inc., who have matched their rhetoric in support of multi-disciplinary approaches and responsible popularization of scholarship with personal commitment to this project. Finally, I thank James A. Hodges, Emeritus Professor of History, who launched the Leadership Program in 1986, and Henry Luce III and Stanley C. Gault, members of the Board of Trustees of the College of Wooster, not only for their support and encouragement of the Program but also for their direct participation on occasion as visiting instructors in the Seminar, "Leadership: Theory and Practice."

There are several groups of individuals without whose assistance the book, even if completed, would have been the poorer: the contributors of the essays specifically composed for inclusion in *Classical and Modern Narratives of Leadership;* those individuals who supplied or assisted in locating the illustrations; and colleagues, both at Wooster and other institutions, as well as the anonymous editors and evaluators of the manuscript for Bolchazy-Carducci. I thank you individually and collectively.

Classical and Modern Narratives of Leadership

INTRODUCTION

Vivian L. Holliday

"The ultimate impact of the leader depends most significantly on the particular story that he or she relates or embodies, and the reception to that story on the part of audiences (or collaborators or followers)," writes Howard Gardner in *Leading Minds* (1995, 14). Gardner identifies three categories of leaders: the ordinary, the innovative, and the rare visionary. "The *ordinary* leader . . . simply relates the traditional story of his or her group," while "the *innovative* leader takes a story that has been latent . . . and brings new attention or a fresh twist to that story" (10). Gardner's third, rare, *visionary* leader "creates a new story, one not known to most individuals before, and achieves . . . success in conveying this story effectively to others" (11). Gardner observes that most people do not look for visionary leaders in ordinary times, but only in times of crisis.

The six essays that follow explore the narratives of innovative, ordinary, and visionary leaders and leadership. Each, composed specifically for this study by a member of the College of Wooster faculty, is freestanding in terms of historical and cultural context, approach, and issues examined. Collectively the essays address a number of the major issues, theories, and models treated in contemporary literature on leadership.

In this Introduction, I suggest a reading of the essays with an emphasis on the creation and communication of effective narratives of leadership and on psychologist Howard Gardner's recent cognitive approach to leadership in *Leading Minds*. I also consider some of the contributions of three earlier writers on leadership whose work is basic to an understanding of present-day commentary on the subject: Max Weber, James MacGregor Burns, and John Gardner.

First, the sociologist Max Weber identified at the end of the last century three categories for "the structure of social authority"("three inner justifications" or "basic legitimations of domination"): "the charismatic order," "the traditional order," and "the legalistic order" (Weber 78–79; Wills, 1994, 102). Strictly and narrowly defined, the charismatic leader is a founding leader who establishes a structure of governance passed down to successors. Vladimir Lenin, as the leader who founded the structure of the USSR as it existed during most of the twentieth century, remains a charismatic leader as defined by Weber—even with the recent fundamental changes in the system he established. The Greek word "charisma," however, which originally meant "favor" or "grace" bestowed by the divine, has taken on the sense of distinguishing personal traits and characteristics: usually physical, spiritual, intellectual, or some combination of the three (H. Gardner, 35) . Therefore, if we elect its present-day connotation, a leader with charisma need not be a founding leader, and so numerous individuals who manifest charisma defined as an attribute of personality might be assigned to the category of charismatic leaders.

Weber's narrower definition of the charismatic political leader as a founding leader produces a limited list of modern and ancient leaders. In addition to Lenin, Mao Zedong and the Ayatollah Khomeini readily come to mind as examples of twentieth-century charismatic leaders as defined by Weber. Most students of ancient history would classify as charismatic leaders Alexander the Great, the founder of the Macedonian empire, and Augustus, the first Roman emperor. Both profoundly changed the governance of their societies, although both did so in very different ways and with different results. We might also place Pericles, a leader of Athens in the fifth century B.C., into Weber's category of charismatic leader. Although Pericles was not the founder of democracy in Athens, he was and is so strongly identified with the beginnings of Greek democracy and made such a significant contribution to its development that he arguably belongs in the narrowly defined category of charismatic leader. In our time, Nelson Mandela of South Africa has been identified so fully with the new constitution that he has become a founding or charismatic leader for South Africa.

Weber's second and third bases for the social authority of leaders are the "traditional order" and "legalistic order." "Traditional order" leaders inherit their authority, while leaders whose authority rests on Weber's "legalistic order" hold their positions through "agreement" with those who are led. The successors of Alexander the Great and the Roman emperors who held power after Augustus were leaders whose authority was based primarily on the traditional order. Modern governing monarchs base their authority, at least in part, on the traditional order.

"When tradition . . . ceases to bind," writes Wills in his summary of Weber, "then authority is established by agreement and becomes legalistic" (1994, 103). Weber's "legalistic order" best describes the basis for the authority of most modern political leaders. Agreement, however, need not mean election by the citizens as a whole or by a representative body of the group; agreement may be silent, or it may mean merely the lack of significant opposition. Peisistratus, a popular Athenian tyrant of the sixth century B.C. and, to some extent, Julius Caesar at Rome in the first century B.C. gained much of their power through extra-constitutional means. The basis of their authority, however, was primarily legalistic because of the absence of meaningful opposition, at least initially, and the tacit, if not open, agreement of the masses. At the time of his assassination, Caesar was accused by some Romans of planning to change the structure on which his authority was based. As we shall see, his successor Augustus profoundly changed that structure by maintaining the appearance of a continuation of the legalistic order while, at the same time, successfully fostering the notion of himself as a leader whose authority rested on the charismatic and traditional orders.

Howard Gardner adopts and modifies Weber's categories with his definitions of ordinary, innovative, and visionary leaders. Gardner's ordinary leader, who effectively embodies a traditional story to audiences and followers, is equivalent to Weber's traditional leader. As an example of an ordinary leader, Gardner cites Gerald Ford. Gardner's innovative leader (cf. Weber's legalistic and traditional categories) gains the support of an audience in the context of the traditional narrative, but "brings new attention or a fresh twist to that story." Margaret Thatcher, Charles de Gaule, and Ronald Reagan are identified as innovative leaders. The visionary leader, like Weber's charismatic leader, "not content to relate a current story or to reactivate a story drawn from a remote or recent past . . . creates a new story." Gardner cites as examples of visionary leaders of this century Mahatma Gandhi of India and Jean Monnet of France, "the chief architect of a united Europe." (H. Gardner 8, 10–11, and 14).

In leadership studies focusing on the American presidency, James MacGregor Burns combines Weber's emphasis on the relational quality of leadership and, to some extent, the current broader usage of the term charisma to define his two major types of leadership: transactional and transformational. As its name suggests, transactional leadership involves some sort of exchange between the leader and those being led; though some are self-appointed, many transactional leaders are hired, elected, or heirs to their positions. Transactional leaders are usually more concerned with short-term goals and successfully managing an institution or group than with producing revolutionary changes in its character and values. Burns' transformational leaders, by contrast, emphasize longer-range goals, especially those directed at motivating followers toward the essential elements of a shared vision for their group or institution. Transformational leadership at its best empowers a significant number of followers to assume leadership roles of their own and thus take the shared vision a step further. While all leadership must involve attention to the realities of its context and short-term objectives, most leaders who make a lasting difference for an individual or a society are transformational leaders. They are able to "recontextualize a situation" and "to recombine things" in such a way that others will embrace their new combination (Cronin 30).

John W. Gardner, another twentieth-century commentator on leadership, combines the theory and practice of leadership in a series of accessible, remarkably jargon-free and insightful observations. During the terms of six presidents of the United States, Gardner held major positions of leadership, including Secretary of Health, Education and Welfare, founding chairman of Common Cause, and president of the Carnegie Corporation and the Carnegie Foundation for the Advancement of Teaching. In a large body of writing on leadership, he has raised some of the same issues as Burns but with a different emphasis and in a broader context. Gardner treats what he classifies in his 1990 book, *On Leadership,* as "the issues behind the issues" in any meaningful discussion of leadership—namely "motivation, values, social cohesion," and "renewal" of society. In view of the vastness of the problems facing American society—drugs, AIDS, homelessness, contamination of the environment, to name a few, Gardner has questioned whether we as a society are any longer capable of being led. Have Americans lost confidence in any effective action to such a degree that successful leadership is impossible (xii-xiii)? Gardner, however, remains optimistic: effective leaders do exist and can be developed to a far greater degree if we recognize that today they too frequently are "servants of what is rather than shapers of what might be." They become "trained prisoners of the structure" in our society and of the present tendency to reward specialists who can no longer act or at times think independently of limiting structural constraints. Gardner emphasizes the need for leaders who can see beyond the limitations of their time and place and who serve as agents of rebirth for institutions and individuals (Gardner, *On Leadership, passim,* quotes from Cronin 26).

Weber, Burns, John Gardner, and more recently Howard Gardner similarly emphasize the importance of appropriate linkage or fit between leader/narrator and follower/audience: Weber in terms of the basis of the leader's authority, Burns in the exercise of that authority to maintain and/or transform the context in which it exists, John Gardner in the dialogue that must exist between leader and led, and Howard Gardner in the centrality of the story related or embodied by the leader. Leaders and followers offer, writes Howard Gardner, "a drama that unfolds over time, in which they—leader and followers—are the principal characters or heroes." He continues, "Effectiveness involves fit—the story needs to make sense to audience members at this particular historical moment, in terms of where they have been and where they would like to go" (14).

We invite readers to consider which of these and other complementary and inclusive or competing and exclusive models and theories contribute most to the analysis and interpretations discussed in the six essays of this text. Each essay can be read independently, but to profit from an interplay of analysis, themes, and approaches, all six should be compared one with another.

The essays are arranged in chronological sequence based on the periods of the leaders or treatise on leadership analyzed. Each essay has a focus, or in some cases a dual focus, as follows:

A. Narratives of a Leader
   (Holliday, McCall, Moskowitz, Gomez-Jefferson)
B. Creating a Narrative of Leadership for a Particular Segment of Society Restricted in the Past from Exercising Leadership
   (Addis, Gomez-Jefferson)
C. Models, Means, and Theories of Effective Narratives
   (Holliday, Weaver, Addis, Moskowitz)

I argue in "Rhetoric, Iconography, and Leadership in Classical Antiquity: Pericles and Augustus" that every age and society has its "media" which have been both used constructively and misused by leaders. Successful leaders have not only seized the media opportunities of their time, but often expanded the usefulness of media as vehicles for communicating their leadership stories. Leaders who have used most successfully the available media in the service of innovative and on occasion visionary leadership are not housed exclusively, or perhaps primarily, in the so-called media age in which we live.

The emphasis in this essay is on the narratives of two leaders from classical antiquity who were highly effective in their use of the media of their times: Pericles and Augustus. Their narratives have the potential of stimulating our thinking about ways to use media more effectively, and also to see beyond the limitations imposed by the myopia of our time and place. How can the media of our times contribute to the education of leaders and their audiences for more effective leadership in the twenty-first century?

Pericles, a leader and shaper of the fifth-century B.C. Athenian democracy, and Augustus, who held supreme power in the Roman world from the first century B.C. into the first century A.D., gave their names to the ages in which they lived. They used available media to create lasting narratives of leadership, and with the assistance of writers, thinkers, artists and architects, they created stories of transforming and visionary leadership.

To what extent did the political and cultural contexts of the Athenian *polis* (city-state) and Roman *imperium* (empire) respectively determine the leadership narratives of Pericles and Augustus? What was the nature of the audience of each and what responses did each seek from his respective audience? What techniques and strategies did they use? To what degree were the narratives framed in traditional cultural forms: that of Pericles with an emphasis on public ceremony and epitaphic oratory, and that of Augustus with an emphasis on public ritual and iconography? Where does each fit in terms of Weber's charismatic, traditional, and legalistic orders, Burns' transactional and transformational leadership, John Gardner's emphasis on leadership as renewal, and Howard Gardner's focus on the right fit of the leader's story at a particular "historical moment"?

In "Machiavelli and the Modern Narrative of Political Leadership," Weaver looks at Machiavelli and his place in our current narrative of political leadership. In the process he criticizes models and typologies of Kellerman, Grob, Burns, and Tucker, among others. Weaver's essay compares "the model of political leadership advanced in contemporary scholarship on leadership with an overview of Machiavelli's model of leadership." He argues against a simplistic, realist reading of Machiavelli and the "one dimensional caricature that has so often dominated discussion of his work."

Weaver maintains that in the final analysis Burns, Kellerman, Grob, and Tucker present "a crude, simplistic dichotomy between [realist, bad] Machiavellian and [romantic, good] Socratic/Platonic models of leadership." He sees in the recent accounts of political leadership in Hampshire, Miroff, and Wills "a more coherent account of political leadership in that they incorporate Machiavellian themes in rethinking the issues of political leadership." These themes emphasize the ambiguity of moral and political choices, the inevitable conflict between leader and followers, the contextualized rather than universal characteristics and constraints of leadership, and the deconstruction of leadership (or the resistance to the construction of leadership) as a redemption from the real world of politics and power. They also point to a "type of agonistic model," a more accurate balance between competing but not necessarily mutually exclusive concepts.

McCall in "*Julius Caesar* and *Coriolanus*: Testing the Mettle of Leaders" offers a study of leadership narrative through the literature of Shakespearean tragedy. While contemporary writers on leadership frequently use references to Shakespeare to reinforce the positive qualities that potential leaders must possess, McCall reminds readers that Shakespeare's exploration of leadership was more complex. In many of his plays, Shakespeare probed the "wide gap between the motives and tactics of leaders and . . . the consequences of the use of power on themselves and on society."

McCall suggests that in *Julius Caesar* and *Coriolanus* Shakespeare raises ideas that are particularly relevant to current discussions of leadership in the United States. While the leader in each play is motivated by his society's most cherished value—honor—that value proves a source of weakness as well as strength. For both Brutus and Coriolanus, their mettle, the very temperament that makes them leaders, is alloyed with egoism and becomes a self-destructive and socially destructive weapon. Ironically, the quality of honor that made them heroes and leaders in one situation ultimately restricts their range of ideas and self-knowledge and produces their downfall. Shakespeare's plays suggest that self-knowledge in a leader is a vital but elusive quality, a lesson that contemporary aspiring leaders would do well to appreciate.

Addis in "The Study of Gender and Leadership: Points of Departure" addresses questions related to the use of gender as an analytic category and analyzes a series of texts about political leadership that examine gender in different ways. She warns that investigations of the contributions of gender to leadership would not simply mean expanding the study of any group of people to include women.

Suggesting that Joan Scott offers a "two-part definition of gender that can be used to study the processes by which the meanings of sexual difference are created . . . and acquire fixity," Addis then examines different genres of political satire to explore the way in which gender exercises a legitimizing function in the sphere of national political leadership in the United States. She discusses the satiric editorial cartoons surrounding Geraldine Ferraro's nomination as the Democratic vice-presidential candidate. The historically- and culturally-grounded incompatibility between political authority and womanhood illustrated in the cartoons has its origins, Addis argues, in the past creation of divisions between private and public life.

Case studies presenting narratives of women in leadership roles are also flawed by the assumption that these leaders, because they are women, should share some basic traits. This perpetuates the idea of a natural opposition between women and men. In contrast, Addis maintains that a truly feminist study of leadership would explore a range of issues not generally considered to fall within the boundaries of leadership studies. These might include a reconceptualization of the emphasis on the individual leader and a consideration of collective and emancipatory social transformation.

"Wandering in the Arabian Desert with George Bush: A Study in Presidential Leadership" is Eric Moskowitz's exploration of themes articulated in literature on presidential decision-making. He argues that "the quality of the decision-making process must be included in a comprehensive evaluation of presidential leadership." Good leadership "entails more than the ability to influence the actions of others." It involves wisdom and morality as well as the use of "persuasion, authority and power to muster the necessary support for the decision." He focuses on President George Bush's decision-making before, during, and after Operations Desert Shield and Desert Storm. In his analysis he applies the criteria developed in the social sciences for measuring successful decision-making.

Moskowitz observes that a high-quality decision process (HQDP) is no guarantee that the outcome will be positive, but the probability of successful results is significantly enhanced. After defining HQDP, Moskowitz considers personal, organizational and bureaucratic constraints on the exercise of the process before moving to a detailed consideration of the Bush presidency in light of the decisions made during the Persian Gulf Crisis. He closes his consideration of decision-making in Bush's leadership with a brief assessment of Bush's effectiveness in persuading the international coalition, the American public, and Congress during the Gulf crisis.

Moskowitz concludes on the basis of the major criteria which he considers that "the effectiveness of both the decision-making and the creation of political support by the Bush administration" was mixed. One might also conclude that the effectiveness of the Bush narrative of leadership during Desert Storm was mixed.

For "An Odyssey in Black Leadership: Joseph Gomez, A Bishop in the African Methodist Episcopal Church," Annetta Louise Gomez-Jefferson, dramatist and biographer *(In Darkness with God)*, chooses the narrative of her father's leadership. Joseph Gomez was active not only as a spiritual leader but also played a major role in upgrading and rebuilding traditionally Black educational institutions and in organizing and serving as spokesman for civil rights.

No attempt is made in this case study to fit Bishop Gomez into any of the specific categories of leadership analyzed here. Rather, Gomez-Jefferson presents the reader with the building blocks of the leadership narrative of a middle-class Black leader who for more than a half century served in major leadership roles in the communities in which he lived and worked. The reader is provided with an impressive body of evidence for the impact of Bishop Gomez' leadership on the communities of Cleveland and Wilberforce, Ohio; Detroit, Michigan; and Waco, Texas.

It is fitting that "An Odyssey in Black Leadership" is the final essay in this volume, because it calls upon the reader to assist in analyzing the story of a leader who created and communicated a unique narrative of effective leadership for his time and place. Without the dedicated, transforming leadership of community leaders like Bishop Gomez, national and international leadership would seldom be transforming or enlightened. He was in many respects the outsider who became an insider and the shaper/narrator of the stories of leadership for the local communities he served.

WORKS CITED

Burns, James MacGregor. *Leadership*. New York: Harper & Row, 1978.

Cronin, Thomas E., "Thinking and Learning about Leadership." *Presidential Studies Quarterly* XIV.1 (Winter 1984): 22–34.

Gardner, Howard, with the collaboration of Emma Laskin. *Leading Minds: An Anatomy of Leadership*. New York: Harper and Row, 1995.

Gardner, John W. *On Leadership*. New York: The Free Press, 1990.

Garver, Eugene. "Machiavelli and the Politics of Rhetorical Invention." *CLIO* 14.2 (1985): 157–178.

Gomez-Jefferson, Annetta Louise. *In Darkness with God: The Life of Joseph Gomez, a Bishop in the African Methodist Episcopal Church*. Kent: Kent State University Press, 1998.

Grob, Leonard. "Leadership: The Socratic Model." Kellerman 263–281.

Hampshire, Stuart, ed. *Innocence and Experience*. Cambridge: Harvard University Press, 1989.

———. *Public and Private Morality*. New York: Cambridge University Press, 1978.

Kellerman, Barbara, ed. *Leadership: Multidisciplinary Perspectives*. Englewood Cliffs, NJ: Prentice-Hall, 1984.

Miroff, Bruce. *Icons of Democracy: American Leaders as Heroes, Aristocrats, Dissenters, and Democrats*. New York: Basic Books, 1993.
Scott, Joan W. *Gender and Politics of History*. New York: Columbia University Press, 1988.
Tucker, Robert C. *Politics as Leadership*. Columbia: University of Missouri, 1981.
Weber, Max. "Politics as a Vocation." (1921) in *From Max Weber: Essays in Sociology*, trans. and ed. H. H. Gerth and C. Wright Mills. New York: Oxford University Press, 1958, reprint 1972.
Wills, Garry. *Certain Trumpets: The Call of Leaders*. New York: Simon & Schuster, 1994.

Rhetoric, Iconography, and Leadership in Classical Antiquity
Pericles and Augustus

Vivian L. Holliday

The topic of political leadership was of considerable interest in Classical Antiquity, both in terms of individual leaders and theory. Major classical historians and biographers—Herodotus, Thucydides, Xenophon, and Plutarch on the Greek side, and among the Romans, Sallust, Livy, Tacitus, Suetonius and Ammianus—focus on individual leaders. At the same time, they and other writers of prose frequently go beyond individual political leaders to comment on broader issues of leadership. Some explicitly devote significant segments of their work to the qualities, values, and education of effective leaders and include deliberations on the theory as well as the practice of leadership. Plato and, to a lesser extent, Aristotle, as well as Isocrates and Cicero, treat the subject of leadership as a phenomenon which transcends the experience of the individual leader.

In this essay I focus on the structuring of narratives of leadership by Pericles and Augustus and the role of rhetoric and iconography in the process: by Pericles in the democracy of fifth-century B.C. Athens and Augustus in the Roman Empire of the first centuries B.C. and A.D.[1] I do so because both Pericles and Augustus were complex and intriguing leaders. Their stories have the potential to contribute to our understanding of the times in which they lived and the timeless human phenomenon of leadership. Also, a focus on Classical Antiquity offers an opportunity to look at leadership, especially political leadership, in cultures and times that are foreign, yet vaguely familiar. In selecting Pericles and Augustus, leaders separated by some 400 years and different, though related, cultures, I have made a commitment to look both at and beyond the historical and cultural context of each. Such an approach offers the potential of illuminating some of the core issues of leadership raised by Weber, Burns, John Gardner and Howard Gardner (see "Introduction") as well as providing insights into the leaders themselves.

The past two decades have witnessed significant interest among scholars of Classical Antiquity in bringing to bear on broad cultural themes, such as leadership, sets of evidence that call for the application of disparate and often non-traditional strategies and methods. Illustrative of cross-disciplinary scholarship especially germane to my focus are two recent studies of the Roman world with thematic emphases and successful application of cross-disciplinary methods: Paul Zanker's treatment of visual imagery in the time of Augustus and S. R. F. Price's examination of the cult of the Roman emperor in Greek Asia Minor.

Zanker in *The Power of Images in the Age of Augustus* explores art "pressed into the service of political power" (5) not just from the point of view of a professional classical archaeologist. As Andrew Wallace-Hadrill notes, he also "picks up the growing interest among historians in ritual, ceremonial and the symbolic aspects of the creation and reproduction of power in society" (158). S. R. F. Price's study of the cults dedicated to the Roman emperor in Asia Minor is most successful in bringing to bear on the dual themes of ritual and power disparate sets of evidence, especially anthropological and historical. Price briefly notes in a preface to his study that growing up in an "Anglican cathedral house" and receiving a classical education contributed to his realization that the imperial cult cannot be "dismissed as mere politics with no religious meaning" but is "comprehensible by seeing both religion and politics as parts of a web of power" (1986, xi). The complex narratives of leadership and power created and embodied by Pericles and Augustus call for a similar synthesis of approach and the application of a variety of evidence: historical, political, religious, artistic, and anthropological.

Pericles and Augustus are not presented as parallel or contrasting case studies, but rather as creators and embodiments of distinctive narratives. They defined and gave their names to eras in their respective cultures, and both have served as models for many ancient and modern leaders. Although both belong to Classical Antiquity, the political and cultural contexts for their leadership were very different. Because they lived in different cultures some 400 years apart, we must look at the leadership of each through different cultural frames while exploring our cross-cultural theme.

Pericles' leadership took place in the Athenian *polis,* the democratic 'city-state,' and Augustus' in the *civitas,* the 'commonwealth' of the vast Roman Empire. To what extent did the *polis* and the *civitas* respectively determine the leadership of each? What was the nature of the audience of each and what response did each seek from his respective audience? What techniques and strategies did each use? To what degree and how is the narrative of the leadership of each communicated through traditional cultural forms: especially in public ceremony and epitaphic oratory in the case of Pericles, and for Augustus through public ritual and iconography?

Polis and *civitas*, audience and response, epitaphic oratory and iconography, ceremony and ritual join Weber's charismatic, traditional, and legalistic orders, Burns' transactional and transformational leadership, John Gardner's emphasis on leadership as renewal, and especially Howard Gardner's focus on the leader's story in addressing our cross-cultural theme of leadership. I turn first to the leadership of Pericles.

The major ancient source for the leadership of Pericles is his contemporary, the historian Thucydides *(The Peloponnesian War*, Book I and Book II, especially sections 12–65). Thucydides, however, gives little information on Pericles the private man. For biographical detail we must rely on other sources, especially Plutarch, who researched and wrote his *Lives* during the first and second centuries A.D. Plutarch informs us that Pericles lived a simple life, was a relatively shy person, was interested in philosophy and the arts, and chose as his close friends intellectuals and artists. He is portrayed as a leader of integrity, although his integrity was called into question on occasion, primarily through his enemies' prosecutions of his friends and associates. Among the most frequently cited examples of such indirect attacks on Pericles are the charges of embezzlement brought against Pheidias, Pericles' sculptor-friend, and a threatened prosecution for impiety of his philosopher-friend Anaxagoras.

According to Plutarch, Pheidias, who supervised Periclean building activity on the Acropolis in Athens and sculpted the cult statue of Athena for the Parthenon, was prosecuted for embezzlement of gold intended for Athena's statue. On the advice of Pericles, Pheidias had designed the gold of the statue in sections which could easily be dismantled, so that he was able to rebuff Pericles' opponents when he disassembled the statue and weighed the gold. He, however, was later charged with impiety for his alleged representation of himself and Pericles on the shield of the cult statue and, according to Plutarch, died in prison. Pericles' friend, Anaxagoras, however, was more fortunate. With Pericles' assistance, he abandoned Athens when prosecuted for impiety and thus avoided the death sentence imposed in his absence (*Pericles* 31 and 32).

We turn to Thucydides as our major ancient source for an evaluation of Pericles the leader of the mid-fifth-century Athenian democracy. For many if not most ancient and modern scholars, Thucydides' account is a reliable history of the period and an accurate evaluation of Pericles.[2] J. S. Rusten summarizes well the impact of the Thucydidean assessment of Pericles: ". . . Thucydides' portrait of Pericles reveals a leader unique in the history of Athens. His combination of intellect, patriotism, persuasive speech and incorruptibility provides a standard by which all subsequent politicians can be judged and found wanting . . ."(20).

Thucydides' idealistic portrayal of Pericles and Periclean democracy—compared to other democratic leaders and periods—continues to hold sway in contemporary assessments of Periclean Athens. E. Badian, however, has presented compelling arguments for a more critical examination of Thucydides' history for its pro-Athenian and pro-Periclean biases. "It has . . . been the aim of this investigation," writes Badian, "not to 'discredit' Thucydides, but to show that he must not be followed in slavish adoration and treated like a provider of revealed truth. He was an Athenian of his time, trying to convey the strong feelings that he naturally held about Periclean democracy and its disintegration owing to the war" (235, note 61). Badian's strictures, though overstated, correctly advise caution in seeing Thucydides—or for that matter any other historian—as a totally objective presenter and interpreter of the facts.

Thucydides' analysis and interpretations of events and individuals are often couched in speeches attributed to leaders of the city-states involved in the Peloponnesian War (431–404 B.C.). It would be surprising had Thucydides not followed the older but contemporary historian Herodotus in making generous use of speeches in historical narrative. For these two ancient classical historians as well as their successors, speeches were, if not strictly historical documents, nonetheless significant tools for the communication of historical analysis and interpretation. Thucydides does not give us word-for-word transcripts of the actual speeches, but rather interpretations of the issues and the positions taken by individual city-states and their leaders. Especially memorable speeches heard by Thucydides or his informers may nonetheless be reasonably close to the words of the speakers. (For the debate on this point, see Badian et al.) The use of language to communicate and to persuade was central to leadership in Athenian democracy, and, through the speeches, Thucydides illustrates well what a necessary and powerful tool oratorical rhetoric was in ancient Athens. Along with other ancient sources, Thucydides attributes to Pericles extraordinary skill in the use of rhetoric to project a public persona and to achieve his military and political goals as leader.[3]

Thucydides selected a limited intensive presentation of Pericles' public persona. He presents the case for Pericles and for Athens under his leadership—in contrast to that of his successors—primarily through three direct speeches assigned to Pericles. As Rusten notes, the three are attempts "to 'sell'... his strategy for the defeat of Sparta." In Book I (140–144), Pericles addresses "the impossibility of saving Attica" and advocates a withdrawal into the city walls. The Funeral Oration (II, 34–46), the second speech, presents democratic Athens as a place worthy of the ultimate sacrifice of one's life, and the third and last speech (II, 62–64) is that of a leader whose popularity is at a very low point but who persists in advocating, not imposing, a strategy he believes to be that demanded of responsible leadership (Rusten 201).

The most famous of the speeches Thucydides assigns to Pericles is the Funeral Oration (II, 34–46). Its ostensible purpose is to continue the tradition (probably not as long-standing as Thucydides implies) of honoring those men who had during the previous year lost their lives on behalf of the Athenian city-state. Nicole Loraux, in a valuable study of the genre of the funeral oration in classical Athens, correctly stresses the oration as "an institution of speech in which the symbolic constantly encroached upon the functional, since in each oration the codified praise of the dead spilled over into generalized praise of Athens"(2). If Thucydides has captured in the Funeral Oration the essence of the style of Pericles as well as his policies, the Athenian leader tastefully and eloquently used the public ceremony as a rhetorical opportunity to build consensus for the war effort through an idealistic vision of democratic Athens. That he is presented as doing so within the confines of the fixed formulaic commonplaces of the genre and the ceremony of a funeral oration (see Loraux 222–223) is further evidence of the importance assigned to Pericles' rhetorical skills—at least by Thucydides—in the construction of his narrative of leadership.

I will not rehearse the arguments for or against the closeness of the Funeral Oration in content, diction, and tone to the actual speech. Whatever the authenticity of the Funeral Oration, it is an assessment of Pericles' leadership by a major contemporary historian and participant in many of the events described, as well as an indication of the role of rhetoric in fifth-century Athenian democracy. As such, it would merit our study in its own right, even if it is primarily a creation of the historian. As J. S. Rusten suggests, the speaker of the Funeral Oration in Thucydides is flanked on one side by the real Pericles and on the other by the historian who is both the reporter and commentator on the real Pericles. "Deciding to which of the two he [the real Pericles] is closer is as difficult and as subjective as mediating between the Platonic dialogues and the historical Socrates" (16).[4]

The historical setting of the Funeral Oration may not at first glance appear to the modern reader to be much of an opportunity to give a state of the democracy address. Athens and her allies have been at war for one year against Sparta and her allies. Pericles, who comes from an aristocratic family with a long tradition of public service, is the most influential leader of the Athenian democracy. Although he did not found the Athenian democracy, he made fundamental changes that resulted in more male citizens being able to participate directly in the governance of the city-state. Furthermore, he had made Athens openly more than the *de facto* head of the Delian League, an alliance put together earlier in the fifth century ostensibly to deter Persian aggression. By moving the headquarters of the alliance to Athens and using tribute from its members for Athenian projects, especially the buildings of the Acropolis, he had made Athens into the capital of an Athenian empire of increasingly unwilling allies. One, if not the only, cause of the Peloponnesian War was fear of Athenian power and economic expansion at the expense of other Greek states.

Pericles' strategy during the first year of the war, whose Athenian dead the Funeral Oration honors, had been to avoid engagement and to allow the enemy to attack the countryside outside of the city walls of Athens with little or no opposition. The Athenian navy would in the meantime make hit-and-run attacks on enemy territory when and if it was reasonably safe to do so. Athenians, crowded behind the protection of the city walls, were growing impatient with Pericles' policy of letting the enemy destroy their farms while he resisted suggestions for a negotiated settlement to the conflict.

Although Pericles' Funeral Oration is the earliest surviving example of this genre, there is no reason to question Thucydides' claim that the ceremony and oration have a history (II, 34–35). The public ceremony for the burial of the dead offered Athenian leaders an opportunity to exercise military as well as political leadership. Pericles' Funeral Oration honors those who gave their lives in war for Athens, yet little is said directly in the speech about the war or Pericles' unpopular strategy. Instead, much is made of the Athenian way of life, which is contrasted throughout, often implicitly, with the less desirable ways of life of others, especially the Spartans. Any assessment of the role of rhetoric in Pericles' exercise of leadership must begin by addressing the significance of the Funeral Oration in Thucydides' historical narrative of Books I and II. Would deleting just the Funeral Oration while everything else, including the other two Periclean speeches, was kept, make a significant difference in our understanding of Pericles the leader or in the overall structure of Thucydides' history?

W. Robert Connor (52–78) sees the Funeral Oration as part of "a carefully developed structure" (65) of Book II and one of three famous connected narratives in Book II: the Funeral Oration; the description of the plague that killed so many Athenians, including Pericles himself; and Pericles' speech to the assembly, the final speech before his death in the autumn of 429. "The two Periclean speeches surround a central episode, the great Plague, and at the same time evoke and contrast sharply with one another," writes Connor (65). He is persuasive in his observations on the contrasts in Pericles' tone as the "spokesman for civic values and attitudes" (65) in the Funeral Oration and that of the Final Speech in which he addresses an erosion of civic pride and confidence and a breakdown of acceptable civic behavior, the latter to a significant degree the result of the plague. Thucydides reinforces his portrayal of Pericles as a leader for all seasons in a laudatory epilogue on Pericles' ability to "respect the liberty of the people and at the same time hold them in check. It was he who led them, rather than they who led him . . ." (II, 65). When we reach the epilogue, "the leader," writes Connor, "appears in a new light. His effectiveness derives not so much from his ability to express the characteristics and attitudes of his people as from his ability to counterbalance some of their tendencies" (65).

The Funeral Oration eloquently presents Pericles as a consummate social architect, who draws those he leads as confident participants into his vision of present and future Athens. As an elected leader who continued and expanded the democracy established by his predecessors, he had authority based on what Weber called the legalistic order. For most subsequent generations, however, Pericles was the leader most closely identified with the rise of political democracy in the western world and was, therefore, first and foremost, a charismatic leader in Weber's sense of founding leader.

Pericles' reputation as the charismatic leader *par excellence*, both as defined by Weber and in popular usage, can be traced to the ideas about democracy presented in the Funeral Oration (II, 34–46). Pericles shows appropriate respect for but does not dwell on remote and recent ancestors who brought Athens to a position of power and provided for her freedom. He quickly places his tribute to the dead into a context that directs attention beyond the past and present toward a future worthy of those who have gone before, including the dead. "What I want to do is . . . to discuss the spirit in which we faced our trials and also our constitution and the way of life which has made us great" (36). These are the sentiments of a charismatic and transforming leader.

The Pericles of the Funeral Oration is a powerful catalyst for "motivation, values, social cohesion," and "renewal" of purpose and thus fits John Gardner's category of ideal leader (see Introduction). The Athenian system "does not copy" others but is rather a "model to others" (37). He defines the values of the Athenian system—which by implication are missing in other Greek city-states—that produce social cohesion and contribute to the requisite motivation for sacrifices by all, not only the dead being honored:

> Our constitution is called a democracy because power is in the hands not of a minority but of the whole people. When it is a question of settling private disputes, everyone is equal before the law; when it is a question of putting one person before another in positions of public responsibility, what counts is not membership of a particular class, but the actual ability which the man possesses . . . . And, just as our political life is free and open, so is our day-to-day life in our relations with each other . . . . We are free and tolerant in our private lives; but in public affairs we keep to the law. (II, 37)

Pericles stresses the free and open life offered to the citizenry of democratic Athens. Through festivals and the enjoyment of objects of beauty, both those created at home and imported from abroad (II, 38), they can renew their spirits and enjoy social solidarity. Athens has rejected the harsh system of military training employed by the Spartans and relies on courage that arises naturally among those defending a free society (II, 39).

What are the values of the citizens of democratic Athens? What makes an Athenian worthy of the democratic *politeia*? Pericles addresses this topic in what has been called "the most quoted passage in Greek prose" (Rusten 152). Some individuals engage in the pursuit of wisdom (intellectuals), some wealth (businessmen), and others public service (politicians), but all good citizens participate through careful debate and discussion in the "life of service to the city" (II, 40; Rusten 152–156). In a peroration that summarizes the strengths of the Athenian *politeia* and its individual citizens, Thucydides has Pericles put the finishing touches on this verbal monument to his leadership of the Athenian democracy:

> Taking everything together then, I declare that our city is an education to Greece.... Mighty indeed are the marks and monuments of our empire which we have left. Future ages will wonder at us, as the present age wonders at us now. We do not need the praises of a Homer, or of anyone else whose words may delight us for the moment, but whose estimation of facts will fall short of what is really true. For our adventurous spirit has forced an entry into every sea and into every land; and everywhere we have left behind us everlasting memorials of good done to our friends or suffering inflicted on our enemies." (II, 41)

> So and such they were, these men—worthy of their city.... I could tell you a long story.... What I would prefer is that you should fix your eyes every day on the greatness of Athens as she really is, and should fall in love with her. (II, 43)

In the speeches, especially in the Funeral Oration, Thucydides not only presented Pericles a social architect with a transforming vision but as a leader who successfully and fully employed public ceremony and rhetoric to communicate and often to persuade the audience to make that vision their own. It is through rhetoric, the major medium of Athenian democracy, that he communicated not only his vision but also those qualities most frequently associated with successful political leadership: "a sense of history," "morale building," "courage," and "ability to concentrate on achieving goals and results" (Cronin 28).

The Funeral Oration is an enduring example of a transforming leader's use of a specific historical moment to transcend the particulars that gave rise to the occasion itself. Garry Wills aptly observes in his convincing and eloquent treatment of the significance of President Lincoln's "Dedicatory Remarks" at Gettysburg, which we have immortalized as the "Gettysburg Address," that "it was the challenge of the moment that both Pericles and Lincoln addressed" (1992, 52). Through rhetoric, both Pericles and Lincoln transcended the limitations of a particular moment and place to convey to their fellow citizens, and, to some degree, to future generations, a vision that continues to challenge and inspire.

Artistic and architectural monuments, especially those of the Acropolis, are also part of Pericles' narrative of leadership in Athens. As impressive as these were and are, even in ruins, they alone would not have insured his renown as a transforming leader. Through his reputed rhetorical skills as demonstrated in public oratory and the skills of Thucydides in historical narration, Pericles' vision of democracy outlived him and even transcended the geographical and conceptual boundaries of the small *polis* with its slavery and its citizenship limited to free males. For women and men who value democratic leadership, Pericles remains to this day a revered narrator/embodiment of Athenian democracy. In the Funeral Oration, during a brief respite from military activities, he skillfully framed the ceremony of national mourning with a narrative of the political activities of peace. He exhorted his audience, who were in a sense imprisoned behind the city walls, to transcend that space and the moment of mourning and rejoice in the freedom of their democratic system. Rhetoric was essential to leadership in Athenian democracy, as well as the indispensable medium of the historian who would interpret and evaluate that leadership; both Pericles and Thucydides served Athenian democracy well through the exercise of their rhetorical skills in the creation and embodiment—in Pericles himself—of an inspired narrative of leadership.

Although Roman political leaders before Augustus had relied heavily on traditional rhetoric in their exercise of leadership, Augustus and his successors did not, and in fact could not, rely on rhetorical skills as the major means of communicating vision and policy and building a sense of community that would at least serve the multiple interests of the Roman Empire. Leadership in the Roman world of Augustus demanded an idiom that would be accessible to the peoples of an empire of widely diverse cultures and languages and that could be easily used to communicate the goals of the new central government.

In examining the leadership of the first Roman emperor, I will focus on the historical context and the means employed by Augustus in the exercise of leadership. For the first centuries B.C. and A.D., there is a diversity of ancient sources, not only histories and biographies, but also inscriptions, coins, monuments, visual arts, ritual, and ceremony. No leadership, therefore, lends itself more readily than that of Augustus to a multi-disciplinary, cross-cultural, and temporal analysis, whether in reference to sources or research methods and strategies.

Indeed, philosophers, writers, historians, artists, and politicians of Augustus' own time studied and drew inspiration and models from other cultures and historical periods of the Aegean and Mediterranean areas. Augustus and many educated Romans of his day, especially those who actively participated in the power structure, knew and admired Greek history, literature, philosophy, art, and architecture. They were aware of the accomplishments of Athens under the leadership of Pericles as well as those of Alexander the Great of Macedon, the empire builder and military leader of the fourth century B.C.

To what extent Augustus consciously promoted one-to-one associations between the achievements of his age and those of the age of Pericles, we can never know precisely. While scholars continue to suggest specific influences, especially architecture and art, it is not necessary to find one-to-one analogies to acknowledge properly the influence such famous eras as that of Pericles no doubt had on Augustus' efforts to restore and enhance Rome's position as the center of a great empire. Recently, however, we have begun to recognize more fully the significance of deliberate, but often subtle, differences, especially those in the sculptural reliefs of such monuments as the Periclean Parthenon and the Augustan Ara Pacis, "Altar of Peace" (Kleiner 27–52).

The features of the Altar of Peace, primarily the processional reliefs of the outer wall, that point to the 524-foot Panathenaic processional frieze of the Periclean Parthenon as a formal model, suggest as many contrasts as similarities. Kleiner notes that "most of the Athenian frieze is devoted to the representation of horses and horsemen, chariots and charioteers, pitcher-bearers, musicians, sacrificial animals, and seated gods and goddesses; none of these motifs appear in the precinct wall processions of the Altar of Peace" (28). Augustus and his associates, as we shall see below, stress the imperial family in the representations of the processional reliefs—not the generic representations of a traditional religious procession on the Periclean processional frieze. Augustus was primarily interested in suggesting cultural and artistic, not political and ideological, comparisons with the Periclean age; most Romans, whatever their political leanings, recognized Periclean Athens as an era of exceptional cultural and artistic brilliance. It is reasonable to assume that the intent of any suggested association with Pericles was with his inspired and culturally transformative era.

While Augustus may have been content to suggest subtle associations between the era he inaugurated and the cultural and artistic flowering of fifth-century Athens, he was more direct during the early years of his principate in suggesting a connection between his leadership of a mighty empire and that of Alexander the Great. E. S. Gruen offers convincing arguments that "Augustus in fact promoted public consciousness of the connection" (69) between his own accomplishments and those of the Macedonian world conqueror and founder of empire. In support, Gruen cites literary as well as material and historical evidence. Among historical texts, he notes Dio's account of Octavian's [Augustus'] visit, after his victory over Antony and Cleopatra, to the burial place of Alexander the Great in Alexandria, Egypt. Octavian had Alexander's body removed from the mausoleum, not only to view the body and to make a floral offering, but also, if we believe Dio, to touch the body. "Alexander," writes Gruen, "possessed distinctive importance and held particular symbolic value. Octavian obviously touched the body, indeed made a point of it; Alexander's nose broke off in his hand" (Gruen 52 and Dio 51.16.3–5). Gruen argues that Alexander is a key symbol for understanding *pax Augusta*, "Augustan peace," which from the context of "conquest, power, extension of Roman authority and control over the nations of the world—in short, empire" (52).

The same young Octavian [Augustus], who viewed and touched the physical relics of Alexander and, we are told, considered but rejected taking the name Alexander,[5] began early to assemble what was to become a standard iconography, not only for his leadership but also one that came to serve Roman imperial power for almost five centuries. In fact, significant parts of this iconography outlived the Roman empire and even survive today in the many ceremonies and ritual of the Christian religion and also, though in modified form, in secular political iconography. There was nothing routine or mechanical about Augustus' construction of his iconographic narrative of leadership. It was a rich, multidimensional and many-layered narrative that suggested not only similarities but also profound differences between earlier narratives of political leadership and that of the first Roman emperor. Augustus' successful use of image and symbol, especially after his defeat of Antony and Cleopatra, was the catalyst for a profoundly transforming— rather than revolutionary—political leadership.[6]

My focus on visual and material evidence for Augustus' leadership is not the result of a lack of written texts and documents; to the contrary, we have, relative to other historical periods of the classical world, an adequate number. It is reasonable to assume that Augustus and his associates understood that the heavy reliance on the rhetoric of the past could no longer support the leadership of a more complex empire. To a large extent by deliberate design, but certainly to some degree as a result of the circumstances in which he became the leader of the Roman world, Augustus adapted, transformed and created a very complex and sophisticated body of visual images to communicate his program for leading the Roman world out of chaos after two decades of bloody civil war. A brief review of the early context of his leadership and a few of the tasks confronting the future Roman emperor after Julius Caesar's assassination in 44 B.C. will illustrate the challenges he faced.

The Roman state in the last half of the first century B.C. witnessed the total collapse of the political system and the disintegration of traditional morality and values. A century of political and social conflict and a decade of bloodshed had preceded the collapse. The violent breakdown of the Roman political system was accompanied by widespread disregard for societal values and standards for which the ruling class had traditionally been the spokespersons. With the questioning, or in some cases, the abandonment of values associated with family and morality, came a rapidly growing cynicism and a self-indulgence of the magnitude seldom seen before our own century.

It was into this war-torn and devastated Roman world that Octavian, to be known shortly as Augustus, stepped as a boy of nineteen at the time of Caesar's assassination. From 44 to 31, he was occupied with consolidating his power, forcefully, and some would say ruthlessly. His sharing of power with Mark Antony ended violently in 31 at Actium off the coast of Greece, when his navy defeated the combined forces of Antony and Cleopatra, the Roman-supported ruler of Egypt. Before and after this victory, in a smear campaign of much greater intensity than in any American presidential election, Antony and Cleopatra were depicted as degenerate, power hungry, corrupt individuals. Augustus eliminated the remaining opposition and emerged as sole ruler of the Roman empire—an area scattered over three continents and roughly equivalent in size to the United States.

Both the ancient and modern studies of Augustus' leadership emphasize its transforming character. He came into a deconstructed world and, in the English equivalents of his own words, "restored," "rebuilt," "revived," and "recreated" the physical, political, economic and especially the spiritual components of that world. Augustus himself wrote a brief account of his achievements, to be inscribed on bronze and placed in front of his mausoleum in Rome and at other locations throughout the empire. In this memoir, *Res Gestae*, or "Things Done," he stressed his role as restorer of traditional Roman political, religious, and social institutions. Under his leadership, Rome transformed an empire—war-torn, devastated, and bankrupt, spiritually and politically, if not economically—into something thriving, prosperous, and more stable than many of its inhabitants had known previously.

Karl Galinsky (1996) sees as central to any evaluation of Augustan culture and Augustus his claim in the *Res Gestae* that he surpassed all in *auctoritas*, "which as Dio noted (55.3.5) is a quintessentially Roman and therefore untranslatable term . . . . It is moral in the larger senses of the word and connotes the power of ideas" (12). Galinsky discusses in some detail ideas associated with *auctoritas* that are relevant to our discussion: "*Auctoritas* is or denotes a quality that is inherent in and emanates from an individual" (12); it "is granted not by statute but by the esteem of one's fellow citizens" (14); "it is acquired less by inheritance . . . than by an individual's superior record of judgment and achievement" (14) and "*auctoritas* is not static but keeps increasing . . . by continued activity of the kind that merits and validates one's *auctoritas*" (14). As Galinsky points out, the senate undermined the *auctoritas* that it had possessed earlier because ". . . it became an *auctoritas* in form but not in essence. *Auctoritas* is not simply a given, but needs to be constantly reacquired and validated. . . . it is a part of the Augustan ethos that emphasized process and ongoing effort rather than fulfillment" (15).

The title of "Augustus," meaning respected, awesome, revered—often associated with religious ritual and persons—was bestowed on the young Octavian by contemporaries who in view of the devastating failure of recent leaders had every reason to be less than confident of his success and the empire's future. With the granting of "Augustus" and other titles and honors, they anticipated the success and transformative character of Augustan leadership, even in its earliest stages. Indeed, the total collapse of the old system gave Augustus the freedom to fashion a leadership whose authority was perceived by some to be divinely ordained and by many others to rest on one or more foundations for "the structure of social authority" comparable to those defined by Weber: the charismatic, traditional, and legalistic bases for political authority (see above, Introduction).

Most students of Augustan leadership would classify Augustus, the founder of a structure of governance passed down to his successors, as a charismatic leader as defined by Weber. At the same time, Augustus might claim, at least in part, what Weber defined both as a traditional and a legalistic basis for his authority. As the adopted son and heir of the slain Julius Caesar, a few might claim political power as part of his inheritance and thus a traditional basis for his authority. Augustus himself emphasized an authority based on agreement, Weber's legalistic order. He redefined agreement both by observing formalities of approval by legislative bodies and by successfully presenting his programs as a response to the public will. Through shifts of emphasis, redefinition, and reformulation, Augustus took political, social, and cultural traditions and structures and reshaped them into a new, more vibrant, and relevant tradition. With some justification, he could claim to have "restored" the structure of the authority that some have argued he actually replaced. Augustus' exquisite orchestration of multiple themes in his exercise of power contributed to his success as much if not more than any personal abilities or the context of his leadership. He was able to create an environment conducive to the development of new or at least transformed institutions in every part of Roman society, but especially in what we currently classify as "civil society," with its intermediate institutions or "private groups that thrive between the realm of state and family" (Zakaria 1).[7]

If we bear in mind the absence in the Roman world of the first century of many of our own distinctions between not only the public and private but also the secular and religious, we can see the state shaping society through intermediate institutions, especially through social, economic, and religious guilds. The reconstituted old and newly created intermediate institutions of the rich and diverse civil society that Augustus fostered served as stabilizing and revitalizing components of the restructured Roman political, social, and cultural world, not only the first centuries B.C. and A.D. but also for at least three centuries thereafter. These institutions may tell us much about the nature of Augustan leadership and the role they played in creating and transmitting Augustan iconography.

Few institutions of what we might classify as Roman civil society during the Augustan era—whether economic, social, or religious or some combination of all three—were totally untouched by Augustan iconography, and many disseminated or actually became established components of that iconography. Augustus and his contemporaries, however, were not the first Romans to express political power through iconography; they merely expanded and adapted a tradition of communicating status of both the state and individual through narratives of visual art and ritual. An excellent example of this long-standing tradition can be found in the death masks/busts the nobility proudly displayed in public and private festivals and religious rituals. These linked the ruling class not only to individual ancestors but also to their lengthy exercise of power in the state. Most Republican portraits that have survived stress the experience of the specific individual represented, but they do so within the context of the extended family of noble ancestors and the even more extended power structure of the Roman nobility.

In a speech assigned to Marius, Sallust—a contemporary of Julius Caesar and politician turned historian—illustrates the long-standing use of masks/busts of one's ancestors as icons of status and power among the pre-Augustan ruling class. In 112–111 B.C., Marius, a *novus homo* or "new man"—one who was not a member of a family whose ancestors had held the top political office (the counselship)—won a stunning victory over the old nobles in his campaign for election to the consulship, the highest political office in the pre-Augustan government. After his victory, he made a speech to the popular assembly in which he encouraged enlistment of the common man in the army he was raising; Marius emphasized his victory in the election and in securing the military command as proof that the nobles could no longer rely on an empty iconography of leadership:

> Fellow citizens, compare me, a newcomer to political leadership, to the haughty nobles. . . . I cannot gain your confidence by displaying busts or pointing to triumphs and consulships held by my ancestors . . . . [The icons of] my nobility . . . were not inherited but are spears, a flag, metals, and other military decorations and scars I gained with great personal risks and by my own efforts . . . .
>
> (*The War with Jugurtha* LXXXV)

Augustan iconography expanded a practice of some nobles in the late Republic of displaying, in addition to the busts of their attested ancestors, recently "discovered" ancestors from centuries before. Augustus, as Simon Price points out, "was particularly successful at incorporating the great figures of early Rome into his genealogy and thus at laying claim to the whole of Roman history" (1987, 65). It was on Aeneas, the most remote of these legendary figures, a Trojan prince and the reputed son of the goddess Venus, that Augustus focused. At a minimum, the emphasis on this remote ancestor of the Julian family enhanced the superior status of the Roman emperor that was implied by the title of *"Princeps,"* "First Citizen," granted by the Senate. Augustus' careful attention to identifying legalistic and traditional foundations for his authority provided the stable environment in which the same iconography supported the restored state and celebrated her "first citizen."

Attention to traditional institutions and titles—modified and redefined for the most part—and an emphasis on legendary and historical ancestry provided the political, historical, social, and even religious foundations upon which Augustus constructed his iconography of leadership. Augustan iconography observed dual principles, simultaneously and with remarkable consistency: continuity with the past and at the same time a flexibility consistent with the demands of leadership in a Roman world very different from that of the past. The imperial iconography created under Augustus and expanded by his immediate successors was flexible not only in adapting existing images to the needs of central power but also in being readily translatable to a variety of institutions, both at the geographical center and on the periphery of the empire.

I now turn to an examination of three of the surviving examples of Augustan iconography central to an understanding of his leadership: the Ara Pacis Augustae, "Altar of Augustan Peace"; the Prima Porta ("First Gate") statue of Augustus; and the Gemma Augustea, "the Augustan Gem," on which Augustus is represented enthroned in the fashion and with typical paraphernalia of the deity Jupiter (see *Figures 1–11*). I have chosen these examples not only because of their artistic merits, but also because they collectively illustrate the most important components of Augustan iconography as well as the principles of continuity and flexibility.

Our study of leadership demands that we attempt to look at Augustan iconography as much as possible through the eyes of a viewer of his era. This means setting aside temporarily prevalent twentieth-century assumptions and tendencies that lead us to dismiss political iconography as "just" propaganda. To view Augustan iconography only or primarily in terms of imperial propaganda is to ignore the tradition and culture out of which it was created. Such an evaluation leaves little room for the possibility that Augustus, like many other Romans of his day, sincerely believed in the ideology communicated by the iconography.

The Ara Pacis, the Prima Porta statue, and the Gemma also address issues that belong to the broad context of Augustus' leadership and go beyond their function in Augustan iconography. To what extent, why, and how successfully, for example, did iconography replace rhetoric, the primary discourse of leadership of the Roman Republic and of Pericles' Athens centuries earlier? What role did Augustus' program of iconography play in his efforts to lay claim simultaneously to what Weber centuries later identified as charismatic, traditional, and legalistic bases for social authority? At what audience(s) was Augustus' iconography directed? Finally, to what extent was Augustus' iconography of personal leadership directed toward an iconography of public morality and a collective worldview?

The art historian Ja Elsner in *Art and the Roman Viewer* reminds us that "the way people represent their rulers is a key to understanding how the positions of those rulers were conceived" (159). Elsner examines (157ff.) changes in ways

Roman rulers were perceived by looking at Roman images from Augustus to Justinian.[8] I explore below the development, historical context, and reception of three visual representations of the first Roman emperor and the contribution of each to an Augustan iconography of leadership. Each visual case study begins with an examination of its physical context and design. Next, I temporarily abstract the images from their specific viewing frames and explore the continuity and transformations of representations adopted from the past. After discussing each of the three, I return in the conclusion to the broader issues of the Augustan iconography of leadership raised above.

ARA PACIS AUGUSTAE
"ALTAR OF AUGUSTAN PEACE," IN ROME

The Senate commissioned the Altar of Peace in honor of Augustus' victorious return from Spain and Gaul. The eastern end of the Field of Mars was chosen as the site for the new Altar. Sacrificial ritual marked its foundation on July 4, 13 B.C. and the dedication of the completed monument on January 30, 9 B.C. The Senate also made provisions for yearly sacrifices at the Altar. Scholars generally agree that the architects of the Altar as well as the artists who decorated the monument drew from many sources (Kleiner 29). In its original site and orientation, which are not identical to those of the current reconstruction, the Altar was part of a grand architectural and iconographic context: the Altar; a Solarium with an obelisk brought from Egypt, which served the practical function of gnomon, or pointer, for the solarium or sundial of Augustus located on the pavement below; and the Mausoleum or sepulchre of Augustus located across from the Altar.

New leadership in the classical world, as in our own time, often suggested new political directions by redefining physical space through expansion or reorganization (Price 1986, 169). The building of the Altar of Peace next to the area dedicated to the deity of war strongly asserted the new direction of Augustan leadership. Associating the Altar and its sacrificial ritual with the Solarium and Augustus' Mausoleum presented a multilayered iconographic narrative in the service of a new leader and government. For some, this narrative was little more than an association between the moment of time, indicated by the Augustan Solarium with the Egyptian obelisk as gnomon, and the new leader of the Roman world who had emerged victorious over the Egyptian queen and her consort, his former colleague Mark Antony. A few may have noted that on September 23, Augustus' birthday, the shadow of the obelisk-gnomon fell over the center of the Altar. For others—especially some philosophers, historians, and, as P. J. Holliday (1990, 542–557) has noted, a large group of freedmen living in Rome at this time who came from Greece and the eastern provinces—the complex of the Altar of Peace, Solarium, and Mausoleum may well have been an iconographic embodiment of beliefs and fears associated with some philosophies and a view of history current at the time. These included notions of a cosmic cycle, cataclysmic destruction, rebirth, and the return of a golden age. Freedmen from the eastern states where many of these ideas originated, or were at least strong, could easily harmonize ideas about Rome's place in cyclical history. For many,

Rhetoric, Iconography, and Leadership in Classical Antiquity

such notions were useful in accepting the rise of Rome at the expense of their ancentral homes.

To what degree Augustus and his advisers themselves believed that human history was cyclical, we can never know, but it is likely that some who were conversant with the dominant themes of philosophy and history would be true believers. Whether or not they embraced theories of cyclical history, they were not unique in capitalizing on such views of time and history; other Roman leaders had used widespread notions of cyclical death and renewal in the form of a Golden Age to support their political objectives. The genius of Augustus and his associates was their ability to use the media available to place the new leader not only at the center of the new Golden Age, but to suggest that he was to some extent its creator through his transforming leadership (see Holliday 1990, 544).

Much of the iconography representing the vision of a new Golden Age and a new Rome employed techniques comparable to those used for centuries in the most effective political oratory. Two frequently found in Augustan iconography are suggested—but not explicitly stated—contrasts to be supplied rhetorically by listeners ("enthymematic antithesis") and the identification and encoding of widely shared cultural beliefs and values with one's position.[9] The purpose of these techniques was to lead the audience to identify with and subsequently support the speaker's position. Thucydides has Pericles use both techniques in the Funeral Oration: while presenting the Athenians as positive models he suggests the unspoken antithesis that all other people are negative models, especially the enemy, the Spartans; he attempts to win the audience over to his position by encoding into the Oration shared beliefs and a shared vision of what it means to be Athenian.

With the Ara Pacis, Augustus and his associates suggest a contrast between the cessation of hostilities in the present and the suffering of the immediate past. The old order of strife and bloodshed among friends and even members of the same family is over. He invites the viewer to participate in a new vision of the present and, through his inclusion of children in the procession on the north and south exterior walls, suggests a continuation of the new order into the foreseeable future. He has not only redefined space through positioning of the Ara Pacis in relation to other monuments in the area, but also has addressed in their decorative sculptural reliefs regeneration in the natural and human worlds and, through ritual, even in the divine sphere. As the successors to the traditional and legendary leaders associated with the rise of Rome, Augustus and his associates are both the creators and the creation of the rebirth. The spatial relationship of the Ara Pacis complex of monuments and its sculptural reliefs evoked, for many, shared cultural values and, for some, deeply held beliefs about the cyclical nature of human history, including ideas about the new Golden Age and its leader.

The Altar of Peace *(Figures 1–8)* is a modest monument, consisting of a decorated enclosing wall (approximately 34 feet, 5 inches on the north and south and 38 feet on the east and west) and inside, the Altar proper, resting on a podium, approached by steps and decorated with relief sculpture on its interior and exterior walls. The artistic details, the identity of figures represented, and the models and sources of the reliefs continue to be the subject of much debate. The designers of the Altar appear to have intentionally presented sculpture open in its details to multiple interpretations by the Altar's diverse audience. Nonetheless, there is little ambiguity in the overall message of the Altar's reliefs; through their carefully designed iconography, they invite the viewer to participate with the new leadership in political, social, and religious regeneration.

Few of Augustus' contemporaries, even in a cursory viewing of the Altar, would have missed the general significance of the decoration that included representations of legendary and contemporary persons and events. The better educated or more philosophical viewers no doubt focused on the more subtle, complex, and erudite interpretations of the details. Virtually all must have recognized the twelve bull skulls with fruits and sacrificial plates on the interior of the walls around the Altar *(Figure 6)* as signs of decay and regeneration. To the more sophisticated viewer, the number twelve may have also suggested other associations: to those who believed in the cyclical nature of time, with its pattern of rise, decline, death and regeneration for civilizations, twelve would have suggested the ending of the twelve *saecula* (generations) preceding the passage into the Golden Age; for some, the twelve swans of the scroll frieze of the lower section of the exterior walls *(Figure 7)* would have continued the leitmotif of the Golden Age through association with the twelve swans of Apollo, a deity cultivated by Augustus and especially associated with peace and the Golden Age; for still other viewers, twelve might well have suggested the legends of the twelve ships of Aeneas and the twelve eagles of Romulus, the legendary founding leaders depicted on the west wall of the Altar (see Holliday 1990, 545; *Figures 2* and *3*).

The figural reliefs on the exterior walls of the Altar, especially the Aeneas and Romulus panels on the west and the processional reliefs of the north and south, constitute the core texts of the iconography of Augustus' leadership. The reliefs of these panels address Augustus' simultaneous claims to social authority based on all three of the categories Weber would define as charismatic, traditional, and legalistic.

Those on the west exterior wall treat the two major founding legends of the Romans: the legend of the Trojan Aeneas' immigration to Italy and the founding of Rome by Romulus and Remus. The figural panel on the south side of the entrance on the west *(Figure 2)* treats Aeneas, mythical son of a Trojan prince and the goddess Venus. A refugee from the Greek destruction of Troy, he is represented with a small group—including his son Iulus—offering sacrifice in Italy at the end of his journey in search for a new home. Aeneas, like Augustus on the south processional wall *(Figure 4)*, has his toga pulled up on his head in the manner of a priest and is engaged in the ritual of sacrifice.

The figural panel on the north side of the entrance on the west presents the second founding legend of the birth of the twins Romulus and Remus to a princess and Mars, the god of war. The relief *(Figure 3)* represents the concluding segment of the legend that told of a wicked great-uncle's casting adrift the infant twins on the Tiber River (the uncle feared the twins because he had overthrown their grandfather, the legitimate king of a settlement near Rome that had been founded centuries earlier by Aeneas' son Iulus). The twins washed ashore and were nursed by a she-wolf, until their discovery and adoption by a shepherd. The panel is badly damaged, but represents the twins with the wolf and probably Mars and the shepherd. The viewers of the Romulus/Remus panel would have known well the sequels to the rescue of the twins, especially the eventual founding of Rome and the fratricide after a quarrel that resulted in Romulus' becoming the first king of Rome.

Most Romans living in the beginning of Augustus' reign probably knew the Romulus legend better than that of Aeneas. Some would have granted to the story, if not literal authenticity, a high degree of accuracy in its representation of early Rome as a stronghold of diverse groups of shepherds who were often in conflict over land and power. The Aeneas legend, while known among the educated nobility before the first century B.C., was elaborated and fully developed by Augustus' contemporary, the poet Vergil. Aeneas, with Venus as divine and a Trojan prince as human parent, offers a civilized, serene contrast to the crude, bellicose twins, with the deity Mars and an Italian princess for parents. As such, he was a ready-made icon for Augustus.

Through the composition of the reliefs of the exterior wall, the Altar of Peace makes clear Augustus' preferred linkage with the past via Aeneas rather than Romulus. The processional relief of the south precinct wall *(Figures 4 and 5)*, with Augustus and the imperial family as the focus, moves toward the Aeneas panel, while on the north precinct wall the Senators, a carry-over from the violent chaotic period prior to Augustus, move toward the panel with Mars and the twins. There was no better model for Augustus than Aeneas, who, loyal to family, homeland, and gods, led a band of fellow refugees, with much suffering and courage, from a devastated Troy to a new land and a bright future. While Augustus did not ignore the Romulus legend entirely, he gave Aeneas at least equal billing with Rome's founder, not only on the Ara Pacis but also by means of statues in his Forum.

Augustus, in the same priestly attire as Aeneas in the west panel, leads the processional relief of the imperial family, dignitaries, and attendants on the south side. The attending group is represented as participating in the ritual that accompanied the *constitutio* or "foundation" of the Altar on July 4, 13 B.C. Augustus, in the combined role of leader and priest, offers sacrifice on behalf of his family and the state. The processional reliefs represent the continuation of the leadership of legendary Aeneas, but they also clearly connect the Altar and its ritual to the historical moment of Augustus and the programs associated with his leadership. Even without the problem confronted by current viewers of an erroneous eighteenth-century restoration of some of the heads (Conlin 1997, 53–54), viewers contemporary with the construction of the Ara Pacis may have debated the identity of some of the figures in the imperial procession on the south; however, there is no room for misinterpretation of the processional friezes as a representation of a generic procession: the people are real people who are part of the historical moment of Augustus' leadership.

This historical moment—the ritual of sacrifice on the occasion of the foundation (or consecration) of the Altar—is not equivalent to a photograph of a modern groundbreaking ceremony. Agrippa, for example, who occupies a prominent place among the three groups of imperial family members, was deceased at the time of the consecration. It is highly unlikely, however, that viewers of the reliefs who were aware of such departures from historical accuracy would have been bothered. On the contrary, they would have correctly read the relief as part of the Augustan iconography of leadership that invited them to address issues that went beyond literal accuracy. Agrippa belonged in the procession because he was a major part of Augustan leadership; his inclusion invited viewer reflection on the role he had played and would continue to play through his sons, the grandsons of Augustus, who are probably among the children[10] represented in the procession. The designers of the Altar of Peace, here and elsewhere, deliberately play with the ambiguities among the "realities": the historical reality and iconographic reality of the Altar; there is an almost seamless blending of the two. This blending of contexts of the Altar of Peace tended—and still tends—to draw the viewer into the processions and the ritual depicted, even if only as an observer.

A few observations on the composition of the processional reliefs will be sufficient to illustrate how effectively the historical moment and iconography were blended in the service of social, political, and personal objectives of Augustan leadership. The first strong visual impression of the procession on the south wall *(Figures 4 and 5)* is of the three distinctive groups behind Augustus (see *Figure 4)*, who, like Aeneas in the panel on the west, leads the procession as the actual performer of the ritual of sacrifice. The imperial family is continued on the processional frieze on the north where they are joined by a group of senators. Each of the three family groupings contains at least one male, female, and child, while in the background are various officials and attendants of the priesthoods.

Possible male successors to Augustus appear to be placed in something of a pecking order by their positioning in relation to Augustus, but the major emphasis is on the imperial family unit. This emphasis is restated in the processional reliefs in many ways, including the representation, unusual on public monuments, of young children with their parents. A further distinctive feature of this inclusion is the realistic informality of the representations of the individuals in the groups, especially the depiction of active children looking away from the formal ceremony or pulling on the garments of an adult standing nearby *(Figure 5)*. Scholars have correctly seen the emphasis on family groups with small children as a deliberate linkage between the Altar and Augustus' social legislation designed to stem the decline of the noble family, encourage marriage, and increase the birthrate.[11]

The two remaining figural reliefs of the Altar of Peace—the fragmentary interior sacrificial procession around the Altar itself and the panels on the east— have often been passed over quickly as less significant or interesting than the Aeneas and Romulus panels on the west and the processions on the north and south. Elsner (199–210), however, has recently argued convincingly that these reliefs are essential to the overall theme of death/sacrifice and life/renewal and are designed to relate directly to the relief of the Altar proper. He sees the small interior processional relief of generic human participants and sacrificial animals as part of the longstanding Roman theology of renewal and rebirth through sacrifice and death. The panels on the east exterior wall continue the sacrifice/death and renewal/rebirth theme *(Figure 8)*.

The two upper relief panels flanking the east entrance at first glance appear to function primarily as decoration, with traditional female figures representing the Earth (or Pax or Italia) and Sea and Land Breezes on the south, and in the badly damaged panel on the north, Roma (or Italia) with weapons of war under her feet. While these panels are to some extent standard decoration of the period, they nonetheless fit well into a progressive development of the figural panels of the Ara Pacis. On the west there is emphasis on the mythic legendary sources of

Augustus' authority as leader. As one moves toward the east entrance through the processional friezes on the south and north, one sees myth and legend transformed into the flesh and blood of historical persons, who participate in the renewal of a relationship with powers outside history through the act of sacrifice. The figural panels on the east—Earth, Sea and Land Breezes, and Roma or Italia—emerge as abstract, ethereal symbols of the transforming power of both ritual and the exemplary leaders who carry out the appropriate sacrifices on behalf of their followers.

PRIMA PORTA STATUE OF AUGUSTUS

In contrast to the Altar of Peace, a public monument deliberately and fully integrated into the complex iconography of a public space occupied by three public monuments, is the Prima Porta statue of Augustus *(Figure 9)*. It was discovered in an imperial villa, located at Prima Porta above the Tiber, and thought to have belonged to Livia, Augustus' wife. The marble statue is larger than life-size and presents a young Augustus in military garb of decorated breastplate and cloak, with the body of an idealized fifth-century Greek athlete. Augustus makes the standard gesture of addressing an audience with his right hand, and in his left holds a spear (cf. Elsner 162 and Zanker 189). In the fashion of deities and heroes, his feet are bare, and instead of the usual support of a tree trunk, the Prima Porta statue features a dolphin ridden by none other than Cupid, son of Venus and half-brother of the Aeneas celebrated on the Altar of Peace as an ancestor of the Julian family.

Scholars still debate when the marble Prima Porta, now housed in the Vatican Museums, was sculpted and whether it is the original or a contemporary copy of an original, perhaps bronze, statue set up in a place in Rome more public than the garden of the villa. Most support a date shortly after 20 B.C., the date of the historical event depicted on the breastplate: the return of the Roman standards taken when the Parthians defeated a Roman army in 53 B.C. This event was a major accomplishment of Augustus' first official decade as *princeps*. Whether there was a now-missing original designed primarily for a public audience and set up at a site very accessible to the public, as in the case of the Altar of Peace, or whether the Prima Porta is an original intended for a more limited audience, the statue is an important component of Augustus' iconography of leadership.

Viewers of the Prima Porta move from an outer, one-dimensional to a more complex and multilayered iconographic narrative; they are gently enticed into an iconography that moves from periphery to center with increasingly more difficult decoding required. On the periphery, Cupid on a dolphin suggests Augustus' mythical family connections with Aeneas and Venus. Because of the convention of representing heroic and divine figures without shoes, Augustus' bare feet associate his image with statues of Greek heroes and perhaps even with divinity; his youthful and ideal athletic body-type suggests a new political order, the counterpart to the iconography of rebirth of the Altar of Peace; and his military attire hints at the stability he has achieved for the Roman empire. With the gesture of address, the viewer is invited to move in closer and focus on the central narrative contained in the elaborate iconography of the breastplate *(Figure 10)*. Without the breastplate, the iconography of the Prima Porta would be more decorative than substantive.

It is the breastplate that entices the viewer most strongly to contextualize or assimilate the image into the historical reality represented in its central scene.

At the center of the breastplate is the relief anchoring Augustus' leadership in history, while the figures representing the political, divine, and cosmic orders serve as an encircling frame for the central historical moment and suggest a leadership that reaches beyond that moment. The central scene around which the remaining iconography orbits is the return of the Roman standards by the Parthians, an accomplishment of which Augustus boasted in his *Res Gestae*. The Parthian king is presenting a standard to the Roman soldier (or Mars), who is accompanied by a dog (or she-wolf). From this firm central anchor in history, the viewer is drawn outward into a cosmic reality that is more abstract than the personifications of the panels on the east of the Altar of Peace. Directly below the return of the standards is Mother Earth with her cornucopia and two infants, and directly above, on the left, Sol, the sun god, rides in his chariot while on the right is Luna, the moon goddess, accompanied by Aurora, the personification of dawn. Slightly above and between Sol and Luna, Caelus or Sky holds his outspread canopy of the heavens. The two figures immediately below the historical center represent Apollo and Diana, two deities especially associated with Augustus and the coming of the Golden Age, while two mourning females to the right and left of the center probably represent, as Elsner (162) suggests, the conquered provinces of Gaul and Spain, from which Augustus (in the *Res Gestae*) mentions the recovery of standards previously lost in battle. As a seal and guarantee of the iconographic narrative of the breastplate of the Prima Porta, two sphinxes sit as sentinels on the shoulder straps (cf. Elsner 164; Zanker 192).

Through experience and knowledge of recent history, the Augustan viewer of the Prima Porta, Elsner persuasively argues, "is contextualised into the ideology of the Augustan Principate and is thus provided with a narrative through which to interpret the image into his or her subjectivity" (167–68). In the dual roles of contextualizer and contextualized, the viewer participates in the assignment of ideological meaning. Because Augustan iconography was sufficiently inclusive and flexible to accommodate a range of interpretations, it all the more effectively supported Augustus' leadership.

The Gemma Augustea

The Gemma Augustea, the "Augustan Gem" *(Figure 11)*, is a large double-layered, onyx cameo of two veins (height 7 1/2 ins. and width 9 ins.); the figures are carved out of the white vein while the artist, by removing the upper layer between the figures, uses the lower vein of blue as background. The Gemma, dated to early in the first century, is in the Kunsthistorisches Museum in Vienna.[12]

The Gemma is divided into two registers with an enthroned Augustus to the right of center in the upper register, and on the left a seated female personification of Rome, whose likeness resembles surviving portraits of Augustus' wife Livia. On the far left Tiberius, Augustus' designated successor, accompanied by a winged victory and holding a scepter in his left hand, disembarks from a chariot while a young Roman soldier—convincingly identified, on the basis of resemblance to other portraits, with Germanicus, Augustus' grandnephew and Tiberius' nephew—stands next to the chariot. Augustus himself, on whom all figures except Germanicus focus, is represented minimally clothed in the fashion of a hero or deity; in this instance an enthroned Jupiter is indicated by Jupiter's emblem, the eagle, under the throne. Augustus holds an augur's staff in his right hand and with his left he holds a scepter. Under his and Roma's feet are weapons of war while above, between Augustus and Roma and within a multiradial disc representing the Sun, the artist has represented Capricorn, the zodiac sign ascendant at Augustus' conception. On the right end of the upper register, moving clockwise, are personifications: *Oikoumene*, "the Inhabited World"—whose crenalated headdress represents the cities of the empire—crowns Augustus with a civic crown; Oceanus, the standard male personification of the Ocean, stands behind seated Tellus, "Earth" (or perhaps Italia), who holds a cornucopia (empty perhaps to suggest recent famine) and is accompanied by two children.

In contrast with the peaceful, ideal world order depicted on the upper register, the lower register is set in a world of conflict: the artist represents here the raising as a trophy the armor of the people who through revolt and warfare would destroy the world of the upper register. Some scholars identify the erection of the trophy with Tiberius' triumph for his victory over the Illyrians. Perhaps the artist has especially linked this scene with that event but has also suggested or predicted several victories associated with the future emperor Tiberius. Pollini, after noting that the left half of the lower register treats Tiberius' successes, suggests that the right half of the lower register "alludes to Tiberius' anticipated victories over the Germans" (271) who had ambushed and destroyed three Roman legions under the Varus' command in 9 A.D. The right half of the lower register would then serve as both an exhortation to future victory in the event of a German invasion and a generic promise not to allow revolts and threats directed against the predestined world order of the upper register to go unpunished.

Pollini links his analysis of the lower register with several noteworthy details of the upper register: Victory with "reins and whip in hand"; Germanicus in military gear and "left hand clasping the hilt of his sword," ready to accompany Tiberius on the campaign to avenge the slaughter of Varus' three legions; and the *bellator equus*, or war horse, behind Germanicus in a state of readiness (270). At any rate, whether set in one historical moment or representing the action to be taken should such moments arise in the future, the figures on the lower register make clear the Roman determination to support and defend the peace and prosperity over which Augustus presides in the upper register. The artist shows the fact that the defense of this new world order of the upper register is in the hands not only of the traditional Roman soldier but also in the able hands of the provincial soldiers who are now part of that order; these auxiliaries from the provinces—Zanker (232) suggests Spain and Thrace—are personified by the woman with spears and the man with the broad-brimmed hat.

We know less about the context and intended audience of the Gemma than those of the Altar of Peace and even the Prima Porta statue. We can reasonably assume that it was intended for a limited audience and may well have been a gift from an individual member or personal friend of the imperial family to Augustus or a member of the emperor's family. Augustus himself, Tiberius, and Livia—Tiberius' mother and Augustus' wife—are likely recipients of the magnificent cameo. We can also infer from the wealth of detail that the artist knew both the traditional Roman symbols of authority and leadership and the reputation of Augustus as a bringer of prosperity and stability to the Roman world. There is a degree of ambiguity in the representation of Augustus—partially clothed, with bare feet in the style of a hero or god, and with Jupiter's eagle under the throne—but such associations of leaders with the divine and their symbols have a long tradition. Within the highly complex iconography of the Gemma, Augustus is associated with Jupiter, not deified as Jupiter. Many of the contemporary and earlier leaders of the Greek East and later some Roman emperors were not content merely to associate their leadership with the divine, but insisted on being accorded honors of divinity during their lifetimes.

The Gemma is on one level of reading an iconographic narrative of the *adventus,* "arrival," of the future Roman emperor Tiberius to extend his formal *salutatio,* "greeting," to Augustus after his victory over the Illyrians. I agree with Pollini (269) that the Gemma probably does not represent the triumph granted to Tiberius for his victory of 12 A.D., but instead presents a formal *adventus*, "arrival," and *salutatio*, "greeting"; there are too many departures from the standard attire and symbols of the traditional triumph that the Senate and Roman people granted to victorious generals of the pre-Augustan era. Augustus adapted the traditional triumph to his purposes, primarily to reward success in campaigns which he had entrusted to members of the imperial family and to indicate a line of succession in the imperial family. A triumphal general, riding in a chariot, wore a special toga and tunic with which the statue of the Capitoline Jupiter was normally clad. The general carried an eagle-crowned scepter, "while a servus publicus standing behind him held the corona triumphalis over his head" (Guhl and Koner 587). As Pollini notes, "Tiberius is not represented here as triumphator . . . ." He does not wear the special toga and tunic, carry the appropriately decorated scepter, or ride in the traditional triumphal chariot (269). How then are we to read this formal return and this greeting that suggest the iconography of a traditional triumph but, as we see on closer examination, direct our attention beyond the ephemeral boundaries of the historical moment that they appear to celebrate?

As was the case with the Ara Pacis and the Prima Porta statue, the iconography of the Gemma addresses the ideology of Augustus' leadership. With the Gemma, however, Augustus, who has for forty years successfully presented himself and his ideology, is recognized as the unquestioned anointed leader of the civilized world. He does not participate in person in the conflicts to restore the peace, but sends his representatives, in this case Tiberius, his heir apparent. Augustus—with Jupiter's eagle and the augur's staff, indicating "that Tiberius' victory was won under the auspices of Augustus" (Zanker 230)—is the real triumphator. Surrounded by all of the symbols of the Golden Age of peace and prosperity of which his leadership is both the predestined agent and creator, Augustus is receiving the civic crown—not from Roma but from personified *Oikoumene,* "the Inhabited World."

All three examples of Augustan iconography examined here anchor their iconographic narratives in the present through the use of specific historical events and people. There is, however, a noticeable change of emphasis between the Ara

Pacis and the Gemma Augustea, whereas the Prima Porta statue, with its thematic emphasis on the recovery of the standards lost in the recent past, represents an intermediate stage. The emphasis in the Ara Pacis is on a concrete, specific event and persons involved in making possible the event: the dedication of the Ara Pacis on July 4, 13 B.C. The present is linked with a distant legendary past (legends of Aeneas and Romulus) and projected into the future, through the annual ritual to be enacted at the Ara and the visual messages of regeneration and rebirth. As we have seen, the designer of the Gemma also ties its narrative loosely to a specific event: the *adventus* and *salutatio* of Tiberius and, perhaps also, in the lower register, specific victories over challengers to the peace. The actual events, however, almost function as a generic backdrop for an emphasis on the timeless themes of Augustus' leadership: the new world order and provision for its continuation—in the present, by defending against military threats and, in the future, by providing for an orderly succession. In the Gemma, "the specific is overshadowed by the paradigmatic" (Zanker 232). We can see clearly in the Gemma Price's claim that "imperial images are not merely illustrations of ideology, they partly constitute it." He continues, "the images also became the focus of contemporary reflection about the emperor. They not only constituted their own discourse, they were the objects of discourse" (1986, 205).

We have moved from an iconography that represents Augustus' authority as grounded in the traditions of the legendary and historical past to an iconography of imperial leadership in which he is the central icon. Between the Ara and Gemma, there is an almost seamless transition from the notion of a continuation of the past to unmistakable imperial rule of one man. Augustus is presented in the Gemma as the pre-ordained leader and defender of a stable world (civic crown of *Oikoumene*). His leadership is endowed with a spirituality that has released it from the mundane constraints of history and tradition. We have moved from leadership at pains to stress a relationship with the historical and legendary past to one that strongly suggests a new world order established by Augustus as the model for the future.

My conclusions on the leadership of Pericles in Athens and of Augustus in the Roman world must, like the civic crown of *Oikoumene*, remain to some degree suspended. Another reading—perhaps through the eyes of a student who is meeting them for the first time or with a focus on other features—may result in new insights. Howard Gardner's statement (36) that "no leader is ever fully realized" is as applicable to ancient leaders as to his examples from the modern era. I would extend Gardner's observation to the stories of leaders, and especially those from centuries in the past. Too often in our study of historical leaders, we, in the name of historical perspective or critical distance, see them as abstractions whose stories were and remain fully realized. But however unrealized their stories, different the contexts (communities/audiences) of their leadership, and whatever its morality or lack thereof, our focus on the narratives of Pericles and Augustus suggests several significant defining features.

First, Pericles and Augustus used public oratory, ritual, and iconography most effectively to address their goals of reinforcing or creating communities of followers for the purpose of achieving short- and long-term objectives. Their respective communities (audiences/followers) were not necessarily completely voluntary, especially in the case of Augustus. There, however, is almost always some choice in the degree of cooperation of followers with effective leaders, even if the context is a community of interests; this is equally true of a leader and citizens of modern and ancient states. In the case of Pericles, the immediate objective was to contain the opposition to his unpopular policy in the conduct of the war. Yet the Funeral Oration is not a debate on the merits of his specific policies. If we accept Thucydides' overall assessment of his performance, Pericles skillfully used the traditional epitaphic oratory and ceremony of the public funeral to call on his fellow citizens to look beyond their immediate hardship and the occasion in honor of the dead to a vision of a community based on the timeless values he articulates. We do not know to what extent his speech followed standard topics for such an occasion. We can assume that to whatever degree it did so, he was successful in using to his advantage the traditional *topoi* rather than allowing them to dictate his message. Moreover, he enables his audience, past and present, to transcend the forms of the funeral ceremony and the specific historical moment in the life of the community in favor of a broader vision of a unique democratic community based on values worthy of all sacrifice. An emphasis on the leader's rhetorical skills in democratic Athens suggests that the building of community was a continuous process. The nature of democratic governance, then and now, requires successful leaders to identify, articulate, and reformulate democratic values into a coherent vision to be shared with the electorate of their place and time.

Augustus' task of community building was more complex than that of Pericles. In addition to bridging the chasms that had developed among various groups during the vicious civil wars, he faced the daunting task of creating a new rhetoric of leadership in a different Roman world for which the old rhetoric had proved to be inadequate. Not only did the new system of government call for new forms, but successful leadership in the Roman empire with its great diversity of languages, cultures, and ethnic groups required a rhetoric that transcended the language, culture, and ethnicity of any one group. His was the task of finding a vocabulary and forms for a new rhetoric of leadership that was portable and translatable throughout the vast empire.

Augustan iconography is no less than Periclean oratory a chosen rhetoric of leadership and exercise in community building. As we have noted in the iconography of the Ara Pacis, the emphasis is both on the past traditions and legends of Rome and on Augustus and his associates as the shapers and creators of a translation and rebirth of that tradition in a new political and cultural context. While Augustus could not have fully realized how long lasting would be the impact of his rhetoric of leadership, it would be naive to assume that he and his advisers accidentally stumbled on the idea of its utility in building communities, at least of mutual interests, throughout the Roman empire. Originally designed primarily with the short-term objectives of revitalizing the community at the center, Augustan iconography seamlessly combined the old traditions of Rome, the small, relatively insignificant city-state, with cyclical notions of world history that included an impending Golden Age, an idea especially widespread in the eastern part of the Roman empire. The result is history: the establishment of a political and a symbolic—indeed for some a spiritual—framework not only for the leadership of Augustus and his immediate successors, but for the Roman empire for some four centuries.

Both Pericles and Augustus had vision, but both were first and last practical politicians living and leading in the real world, not idealistic philosopher-kings of visionary Platonic republics. Pericles is too often presented as an eternal symbol of idealistic, visionary leadership. Augustus' long-lasting, evolving leadership,[13] on the other hand, with ample documentation supporting transactional and transforming activities, has been interpreted in two-dimensional terms to such an extent that students of his leadership from his own time to the present have tended to evaluate him as either an enlightened prince of peace or a manipulative dictator of self-serving propaganda. Whatever our individual evaluations of Pericles and Augustus as leaders—and few students of their leadership are neutral—we must conclude that both were consummate social architects who used available media to achieve their goals extraordinarily well.

NOTES

[1]My emphasis on the importance of a leader's creation of an effective narrative has benefited from Howard Gardner's brilliant study of the modern leader with an emphasis "on the particular story that he or she relates or embodies, and the receptions to that story on the part of audiences (or collaborators or followers)" (1995, 14). Gardner's work has confirmed the utility of this approach for the study of leaders and leadership in the twentieth century. He identifies as traditional his focus on the individual leader and the notion of leaders presenting messages. Distinctive or unusual features of his approach include "an emphasis on leadership as a cognitive enterprise, as a process occurring and recurring within—and between—the minds of leaders and followers"; different "kinds of stories and counterstories, competing with one another in Darwinian fashion"; and a "distinction between indirect leadership, through the creation of symbolic products and direct leadership, through storytelling and embodying" (296).

[2]Thucydides is an extremely valuable source, not only for the historical narrative of the period but also for his interpretation and evaluation of the events and leadership during the Golden Age of ancient Athenian democracy. Although Plutarch's *Life of Pericles* provides many biographical details missing in Thucydides, we would understand significantly less about Pericles' leadership if only Plutarch's account survived.

[3]I recommend that the reader place the discussion of Pericles in the entire context of Book II of Thucydides. To help readers who do not know ancient Greek to integrate passages quoted into a full translation of Books I and II, I use for quotations throughout the Penguin translation by Rex Warner (1972: reprint of 1954 edition). Its overall accuracy and easy availability recommend the Penguin translation. I note but have not had an opportunity to examine fully two more recent translations, those of Walter Blanco in 1998 and Steven Lattimore, also in 1998. For a full text and a translation of all other ancient Greek and Latin authors cited in this essay, consult under the individual authors the Loeb Classical Library (Cambridge, MA: Harvard University Press, various dates).

[4]Perhaps those of us who have become accustomed to the dramatization of history and biography and the reliance of contemporary leaders on sound bites have a better understanding than our immediate predecessors of the difficulties encountered by many in separating the real Pericles from the edited version of Thucydides' speeches, especially the Funeral Oration.

[5]See W. H. Gross, p. 35, note 40, for bibliography on the subect of Augustus' consideration of adopting the name "Alexander."

[6] The basic themes of my treatment of Augustan iconography were first developed in a series of lectures in the 1980s before I read Zanker's *The Power of Images in the Age of Augustus*. I recommend highly Zanker's extensive analysis of the use of images. More recently, Karl Galinsky's impressive *Augustan Culture* (1996) has made a major contribution to the interpretation of Augustus and his cultural context.

[7] The concept of "civil society" in the Roman world of the first centuries B.C. and A.D. differed in some important ways from the modern understanding of the term. Roman civil society was never as private or free of governmental direction and influence as current definitions of the term imply. Fareed Zakaria, for example, maintains that "at the heart of the [modern] concept of civil society lie 'intermediate institutions,' private groups that thrive between the realm of state and family" (1). He suggests that much of the current interest in promoting civil society is "the idea that culture and society shape the nature of government" (25).

[8] The exact dating and intended viewers of the Prima Porta and the Gemma are debated; however, along with the Altar of Peace, whose dates are certain, they shed light on how Augustus and his iconography of leadership were developed and received and the primary audience for which each work appears to have been designed.

[9] See James A. Mackin, Jr., "Schismogenesis and Community: Pericles' Funeral Oration," *Quarterly Journal of Speech* 77 (1991), 251–262 for a discussion of enthymematic antithesis.

[10] There is debate on the identification of two of the children as Gaius (next to Agrippa in south procession) and Lucius (next to Julia? in north procession), Agrippa's sons by Augustus' daughter Julia. Since the identification is not crucial to the analysis here, I will not present the specifics of the debate.

[11] See Kleiner for a recent discussion of the Ara Pacis and Augustus' social legislation.

[12] I recommend John Pollini's essay on the Gemma Augustea (see Works Cited) to readers interested in exploring in more detail than my focus permits what Pollini identifies as a "focus on the symbolic, ideological, and the rhetorical imagery, temporal aspects, and narrative possibilities of the Gemma Augustea" (see Pollini in Holliday, 1993, 260). A good example of the detailed exploration of narrative possibilities is Pollini's discussion of the "far-ranging symbolism"of Capricorn and Sol on the Gemma (280 ff.).

[13] See Galinsky's brief but excellent essay, "Leadership, Values, and the Question of Ideology" in chapter IV of his *Classical and Modern Interactions*. For his detailed treatment of the age of Augustus, see *Augustan Culture*.

WORKS CITED

Badian, E. *From Plataea to Potidaea: Studies in the History and Historiography of the Pentekontaetia.* The John Hopkins University Press, 1993.

Berard, Claude et al. *A City of Images: Iconography and Society in Ancient Greece.* Trans. Deborah Lyon. Princeton: Princeton University Press, 1989.

Blanco, Walter, and Jennifer Roberts, eds. and trans. *Thucydides: The Peloponnesian War.* New York: W. W. Norton, 1998.

Burns, James MacGregor. *Leadership.* New York: Harper and Row, 1978.

Conlin, Diane Atnally. *The Artists of the Ara Pacis.* Studies in the History of Greece and Rome, eds. P. J. Rhodes and Richard J. A. Talbert. Chapel Hill and London: University of North Carolina Press, 1997.

Connor, W. Robert. *Thucydides.* Princeton: Princeton University Press, 1985.

Cronin, Thomas E. "Thinking and Learning about Leadership." *Presidential Studies Quarterly*, Vol. XIV, No. 1, Winter 1984, 22–34.

D'Ambra, Eve, comp. *Roman Art in Context: An Anthology*. Englewood Cliffs: Prentice Hall, 1993.
Elsner, Ja. *Art and the Roman Viewer: The Transformation of Art from the Pagan World to Christianity*. Cambridge: Cambridge University Press, 1995.
Galinsky, Karl. *Classical and Modern Interactions: Postmodern Architecture, Multiculturalism, Decline, and Other Issues*. Austin: University of Texas Press, 1992.
———. *Augustan Culture: An Interpretive Introduction*. Princeton: Princeton University Press, 1996.
Gardner, Howard, with the collaboration of Emma Laskin. *Leading Minds: An Anatomy of Leadership*. New York: Harper and Row, 1995.
Gardner, John. *On Leadership*. New York: The Free Press, 1990.
Gross, W. H. "Ways and Roundabout Ways in the Propaganda of an Unpopular Ideology." *The Age of Augustus*. Ed. Rolf Winkes. Louvain: Art and Archaeology Publications, 1985. 29–50.
Gruen, E. S. "Augustus and the Ideology of War and Peace." *The Age of Augustus*. Ed. Rolf Winkes. Louvain: Art and Archaeology Publications, 1985. 50–71.
Guhl, E., and W. Koner. *Everyday Life of the Greeks and Romans*. New York: Crescent Books, 1989.
Holliday, Peter J. "Time, History and Ritual in the Ara Pacis Augustae." *The Art Bulletin*. 72,4: Dec. 1990. 542–557.
———. ed. *Narrative and Event in Ancient Art*. Cambridge: Cambridge University Press, 1993.
Kleiner, D. E. E. "The Great Friezes of the Ara Pacis Augusta: Greek Sources, Roman Derivatives, and Augustan Social Policy." *Roman Art in Context*. Ed. Eve D'Ambra. Englewood Cliffs: Prentice Hall, 1993. 27–52.
Lattimore, Steven, ed. and trans. *The Peloponnesian War: Thucydides*. Indianapolis: Hackett, 1998.
Loraux, Nicole. *The Invention of Athens: The Funeral Oration in the Classical City*. Trans. Alan Sheridan. Cambridge: Harvard University Press, 1986.
Mackin, James A., Jr. "Schismogenesis and Community: Pericles' Funeral Oration." *Quarterly Journal of Speech* 77 (1991): 251–262.
Plutarch. "Life of Pericles." Trans. Ian Scott-Kilvert in *The Rise and Fall of Athens*. Baltimore: Penguin, 1964.
Pollini, John. "The Gemma Augustea: Ideology, Rhetorical Imagery and the Creation of Dynastic Narrative." *Narrative and Event in Ancient Art*. Ed. Peter J. Holliday. Cambridge: Cambridge University Press, 1993. 258–298.
Price, S. F. R. *Ritual and Power: The Roman Imperial Cult in Asia Minor*. Cambridge: Cambridge University Press, 1986.
———. "From Noble Funerals to Divine Cult: The Consecration of Roman Emperors." *Rituals of Royalty: Power and Ceremonial in Traditional Societies*. Ed. David Cannadine and Simon Price. Cambridge: Cambridge University Press, 1987. 56–105.
Rusten, J. S. ed. *Thucydides: The Peloponnesian War: Book II*. Cambridge: Cambridge University Press, 1989.
Sourvinou-Inwood, Christiane. *"Reading" Greek Culture: Texts and Images, Rituals and Myths*. Oxford: Clarendon Press, 1991.
Wallace-Hadrill, Andrew. "Rome's Cultural Revolution." *Journal of Roman Studies* 79 (1989): 157–164.
Warner, Rex, trans. *Thucydides: The History of the Peloponnesian War*. Introduction and Notes, M. I. Finley. New York: Penguin, 1972.
Weber, Max. *Economy and Society*, ed. Guenter Roth and Claus Wittich. New York: Bedminster Press, 1968 and *From Max Weber: Essays in Sociology*, ed. and trans. H. H. Gerth and C. Wright Mills. New York: Oxford, 1946.

Wills, Garry. *Certain Trumpets: The Call of Leaders.* New York: Simon & Schuster, 1994.
———. *Lincoln at Gettysburg: The Words that Remade America.* New York: Touchstone-Simon & Schuster, 1992.
Winkes, Rolf, ed. *The Age of Augustus.* Louvain: Art and Archaeology Publications, 1985.
Zakaria, Fareed, "Bigger Than the Family, Smaller Than the State," Review of *Trust: The Social Virtues and the Creation of Prosperity* by Francis Fukuyama. *The New York Times Book Review* (13 August 1995) 1, 25.
Zanker, Paul. *The Power of Images in the Age of Augustus.* Trans. Alan Shapiro. Ann Arbor: University of Michigan Press, 1988.

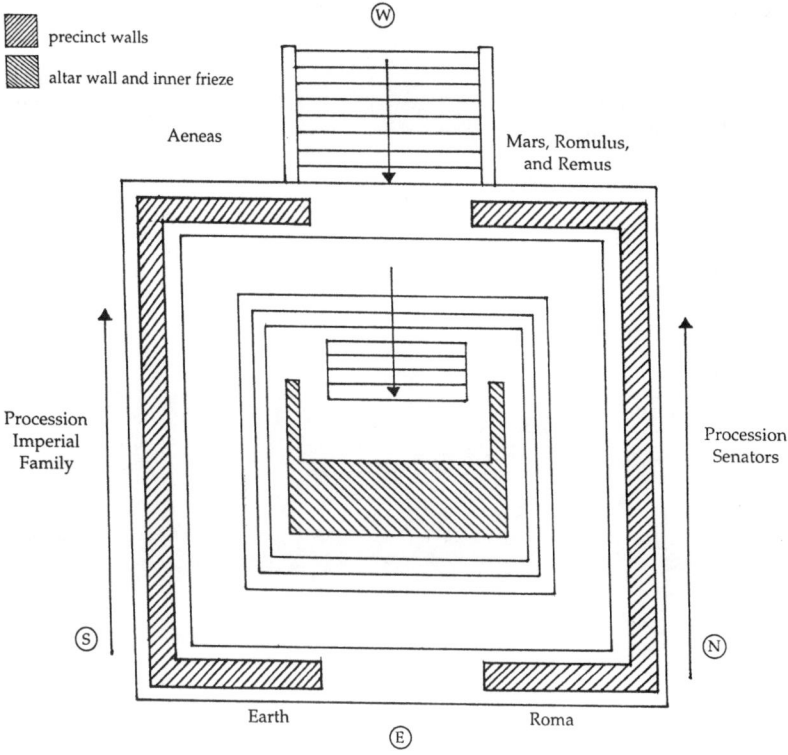

Figure 1   Plan of the Ara Pacis
Drawing courtesy of George W. Olson

Figure 2   Aeneas panel, west front, Ara Pacis
Photograph courtesy of Carl A. Peterson

Figure 3   Mars, Romulus, Remus panel, west front, Ara Pacis
Photograph courtesy of Carl A. Peterson

Figure 4   Processional relief, precinct wall, south, Ara Pacis
Photograph courtesy of German Archaeological Institute, Rome, neg. no. 72.2400

Figure 5   Processional relief, precinct wall, south, Ara Pacis
            Photograph courtesy of German Archaeological Institute, Rome, neg. no. 72.2403

Figure 6   Interior detail, garlands and bucrania, precinct wall, Ara Pacis
            Photograph courtesy of Carl A. Peterson

Figure 7 Exterior detail, florals and swans, precinct wall, Ara Pacis
Photograph courtesy of Carl A. Peterson

Figure 8 Earth, Sea, and Land Breezes, east panel, Ara Pacis
Photograph courtesy of Carl A. Peterson

Figure 9 Prima Porta statue of Augustus
Photograph courtesy of Alinari/Art Resource, NY, neg. no. AL6512

Figure 10   Detail of Prima Porta statue of Augustus
                   Photograph courtesy of German Archaeological Institute, Rome, neg. no. 62.1788

Figure 11   Gemma Augustea
                   Photograph courtesy of German Archaeological Institute, Rome, neg. no. 32.754

Machiavelli and the Modern Narrative of Political Leadership

Mark R. Weaver

Machiavelli's Model of Leadership

Machiavelli offers one of the most important analyses of political leadership in the Western political tradition. Yet, ever since his works were placed on the Index in 1559 and he was villainized in Elizabethan drama, Machiavelli's contributions have been underestimated because he has been commonly identified with a type of "realist" theory of leadership that completely separates questions concerning the use of political power from any and all moral considerations. According to this realist reading, Machiavelli advocates the use of any means, no matter how immoral or evil, to acquire and retain power. This realist interpretation of his theory has been sustained in part by a reading of *The Prince* as a set of aphorisms for political leaders in any time and in any circumstances. However, this simplistic realist reading of Machiavelli on leadership is hard to sustain through a careful examination of *The Prince*, and it becomes even more problematic when *The Prince* is considered in the context of Machiavelli's analysis of leadership in *The Discourses*.

The Prince is certainly a type of advice book addressed to those who are rulers and to those leaders who would be rulers. In particular, it offers advice on conducting foreign policy and on managing relations between rulers and the people or between leaders and followers. Many of his statements on these topics do invite a simplistic realistic reading. For example, he states that ". . . one must either pamper or do away with men . . ." (*The Prince*, chap. 3), ". . . it is much safer to be feared than to be loved . . ." (chap. 17), ". . . a prince must know how to use wisely the natures of the beast and the man . . ." (chap. 18), and a prince should ". . . keep the populace occupied with festivals and spectacles" (chap. 21).[1] In addition, he clearly praises the actions of rulers or leaders who used immoral means to accomplish their goals. In particular, in chapter 7 Machiavelli describes how Cesare Borgia used murder, deceit, and other immoral means in an unsuccessful attempt to consolidate his political power, and concludes:

> Now, having summarized all of the Duke's actions, I would not know how to censure him; on the contrary, I believe I am correct in proposing that he be imitated by all those who have risen to power through Fortune and with the arms of others.
>
> (*The Prince*, chap. 7)

It is also clear that Machiavelli makes several "realistic" claims and presuppositions about human psychology and social relationships. For example, he finds "[t]he desire to acquire is truly a very natural and normal thing . . ." (*The Prince*, chap. 3) and holds that ". . . people are fickle by nature; and it is simple to convince them of something but difficult to hold them in that conviction . . ." (chap. 6). Indeed, Machiavelli is quite explicit in setting his analysis of political leadership apart from the writings of idealists who base their theories on imagined "republics and principalities that have never been seen nor known to exist in reality . . ." (chap. 15). In contrast, by recognizing the immense gap between the ideal and the real, he intends "to write something useful for anyone who understands it . . .":

> . . . for there is such a gap between how one lives and how one ought to live that anyone who abandons what is done for what ought to be done learns his ruin rather than his preservation: for a man who wishes to make a vocation of being good at all times will come to ruin among so many who are not good. Hence it is necessary for a prince who wishes to maintain his position to learn how not to be good, and to use this knowledge or not to use it according to necessity. (*The Prince*, chap. 15)

Although scholars disagree about exactly where Machiavelli draws such lines, there is evidence in *The Prince* to demonstrate that it is not a simple matter of completely divorcing politics from morals as the simplistic realist reading requires. In the first place, Machiavelli specifically acknowledges, especially in chapter 8, that there is a distinction between what is efficient and effective in acquiring power and what is truly praiseworthy in politics:

> Still, it cannot be called skill to kill one's fellow citizens, to betray friends, to be without faith, without mercy, without religion; by these means one can acquire power but not glory.
> (*The Prince*, chap. 8)

He draws on this distinction in chapter 18, "How a Prince Should Keep His Word":

> And it is essential to understand this: that a prince, and especially a new prince, cannot observe all those things by which men are considered good, for in order to maintain the state he is often obliged to act against his promise, against charity, against humanity, and against religion . . . . long as it is possible, he should not stray from the good, but he should know how to enter into evil when necessity commands.
> (*The Prince*, chap. 18)

Certainly, much hinges on the interpretation of "necessity," but it is important to note that Machiavelli is not constructing a model of leadership that is meant to be appropriate to all times and places. *The Prince* is a book about the kind of leadership required of new princes or those leaders who are establishing or acquiring new principalities (chap. 3). Moreover, for all his observations that seem to invite quick conversion into political maxims, Machiavelli again and again emphasizes that circumstances are critical. For example, even on a more technical topic such as the utility of fortresses, he insists that there is no general rule and that one must pay careful attention to details (*The Prince*, chap. 20). This emphasis is particularly important because Machiavelli regards the circumstances of new princes to be atypical of political leadership in general. As he notes, ". . . there is nothing more difficult to execute, nor more dubious of success, nor more dangerous to administer than to introduce a new system of things . . ." (*The Prince*, chap. 6).

In sum, this quick overview of *The Prince* challenges the prevailing realist account of Machiavelli as the discoverer or proponent of a theory of leadership in which morals are rendered irrelevant to politics. In contrast, Machiavelli advances a model that acknowledges the conflicts, tensions, and ambiguities that are inevitable when leaders must apply moral ideals to practical political situations. Moreover, Machiavelli recognizes that the levels of conflict and ambiguity that leaders confront will vary depending upon their own historical and political circumstances.

This historical dimension of Machiavelli's argument is clearer in his *Discourses on the First Decade of Titus Livius*. Like *The Prince*, the *Discourses* focus on a variety of tasks of leadership, especially founding new regimes, maintaining established states, governing them effectively, and conducting foreign policy (see *Discourses*, bk. 1, intro.). However, this work seems radically different from *The Prince* in that Machiavelli's own republican sympathies are quite clear, and he emphasizes the "practical knowledge" that the study of the history of Roman politics and institutions offers to leaders interested in establishing and maintaining self-governing states (see bk. 1, intro. and bk. 1, chap. 2). He specifically rejects any notion that leaders should merely attempt to imitate the actions of the Romans or other successful historical leaders without attention to their own historical circumstances. Machiavelli argues that ". . . human affairs are always in motion, either rising or declining . . ." and that praise of and attempts to imitate ancient institutions are appropriate only given specific current circumstances (bk. 2, intro.).

Among the many complex factors to be examined, Machiavelli emphasizes that leaders must take account of the human "material" with which they must work. For, although human nature (centering in human passions or desires) is constant, human behavior (which is also, at least in part, the product of belief or consciousness) differs vastly among countries, cultures and historical periods (see *Discourses*, bk. 1, chap. 63). Machiavelli categorizes these differences in terms of a fundamental distinction between corruption and the common good. People are corrupt when there is no respect for or observance of the laws, religion, and morals and where individuals (both leaders and followers) always put private advantage above the common good (see bk. 1, chap. 2). A totally corrupt people is completely without a common understanding of or commitment to a common good and therefore simply incapable of any kind of self-government:

> For a people which is totally corrupt cannot live free for even a short time, as will be explained below; our discussions, therefore,

will deal with those peoples in whom corruption has not spread too much and in whom there is still more goodness than corruption.
(*Discourses*, bk. 1. chap. 16)

In the *Discourses*, Machiavelli is particularly concerned with the type of political leadership that is necessary in order to found a viable republic or to renew the institutions of a republic that has fallen into a state of partial corruption (see bk. 1, chap. 9, and bk. 3, chap. 1). Machiavelli maintains that those political leaders who reorganize a corrupt city so that it becomes a self-governing republic are deserving of glory, while those who use the existence of corruption to achieve tyranny deserve blame rather than praise (bk. 1, chap. 10).

This short summary of the *Discourses* and *The Prince* certainly does not resolve the numerous interpretive questions that divide scholars of Machiavelli's political philosophy, particularly the continuing debate over how the seeming differences between his political perspectives in these two works can be reconciled.[2] At the same time, this brief account should be sufficient to demonstrate that his model of political leadership is not the simplistic, one-dimensional caricature that has so often dominated discussion of his work. Yet, in current examinations of leadership, as illustrated below, the nuances of Machiavelli's model are largely ignored, and his name continues to be merely a label for a discredited ideology that celebrates the pursuit of power and severs the notion of leadership from any ethics of responsibility. The realistic account of Machiavelli remains pervasive, even in academic studies of political leadership where one might expect more explicit attention to the theoretical issues addressed by Machiavelli or a more sophisticated understanding of Machiavelli's contributions to the Western construction of political leadership. Machiavelli still frequently appears in such academic work on leadership, when he does appear at all, as merely an illustration or representative of an irresponsible and untenable "realist" model of leadership, which is contrasted with a superior theory of moral leadership.

MACHIAVELLI'S PLACE IN MODERN NARRATIVES OF LEADERSHIP

One of the most striking features of the recent literature on political leadership is its common use of a simplistic and reductionist portrayal of Machiavelli. A useful illustration of this standard treatment of Machiavelli is provided by the anthology *Leadership: Multidisciplinary Perspectives*, edited by Barbara Kellerman. Kellerman, one of the most important and most influential of contemporary scholars of political leadership, makes only one reference to Machiavelli in her introductory essay on "Leadership as a Political Act." Moreover, she considers Machiavelli's views on leadership for the first time in the context of the question "What makes good leadership?", which follows previous sections on "What Is Political Leadership?", "Who Leads?", and "Why Do We Follow?" (1984, 84).

For Kellerman, not only is Machiavelli irrelevant to such questions as "What Is Political Leadership?", but Machiavelli's view of "good leadership" becomes nothing more than a simplistic contrast model used to showcase a superior vision of "good leadership." She cites one quotation (concerning how the prince must know how "to act like a beast" and "learn from the fox and the lion") from chapter 8 of *The Prince*, in reducing Machiavelli's account of leadership to a "model" of "good leadership" which focuses solely on providing prescriptions as to "how *leaders* would succeed." In contrast, Kellerman offers the model of Plato's philosopher-king, which speaks to the "issue of how the *people* (followers) would fare best." Attempting to avoid "the moral aspect" featured in earlier discussions of political leadership, such as James MacGregor Burns' distinction between transactional and transforming leaders (80), Kellerman argues that Machiavelli and Plato addressed "the same general phenomenon," but "had different constituencies in mind" (84).

The significance of this *one-paragraph* treatment of Machiavelli and Plato becomes clearer as Kellerman uses this contrast to return to the "more narrowly practical" question "of political leadership in late twentieth century America" (84). Kellerman concludes her essay and her section on "good leadership" by offering a "partial response" to the practical question of finding good political leadership in contemporary American politics. She maintains that there are only three choices: 1) accepting authoritarian leadership; 2) awaiting the appearance of charismatic leadership; or 3) redefining "good leadership" to focus on the constituency of followers (à la Plato) rather than the constituency of leaders (à la Machiavelli): "Americans proceed to find themselves leaders who listen as well as orate, who respond as well as control, who facilitate, as well as dominate, and who inspire rather than conspire" (86). In short, Kellerman's argument is that in order to resolve the present practical crisis in American political leadership, we must redefine the concept of leadership in Platonic rather than Machiavellian terms.

This is the primary role or part that Machiavelli plays in the general narrative of the nature and possibilities of political leadership that is offered by recent American scholarship on leadership. It is clearly, at least on the surface, a minor role. There is only one other reference to Machiavelli's work on leadership in the remaining eleven essays in Kellerman's anthology, which are designed to summarize the contributions that various disciplines can bring to "Leadership Studies."

However, the bit part that Machiavelli is assigned in this contemporary narrative of the search for political leadership continues to be an extremely significant one. This is made clear in the concluding essay in the anthology, "Leadership: the Socratic Model," where Leonard Grob returns to the issue of establishing a viable model of "good leadership" for contemporary politics. In his philosophically oriented discussion of leadership, Grob also uses Machiavelli's prince, now equated with Hobbes' sovereign and Nietzsche's superman, as representative of a model of political leadership which collapses the distinction between the real and the ideal, and which insists that "moral considerations must be subordinated to the mechanics of a struggle for power" if order is to be maintained (1984, 264). In this account, Machiavelli is clearly identified as the central advocate and creator of what appears to be the dominant theoretical or intellectual paradigm of politics and political leadership in the Western political tradition. This paradigm of political leadership sets aside as irrelevant all distinctions between moral or immoral behavior and holds that "[g]iven the dictates of the circumstances at hand, the leader must be prepared to employ any and all means in the service of his sole end: the establishment, maintenance, and continued welfare of the state in his charge" (264). Moreover, Grob also portrays this paradigm as resting upon the assumptions that all human beings are motivated by the pursuit of power, and that leaders and followers are alike in their basic natures: "The Machiavellian prince is thus moved by the same passions as his subjects; his leadership consists in his superior ability to wield instruments of physical and psychological force in the process of establishing order among those who would otherwise destroy themselves as a political entity" (265).

Although Grob briefly acknowledges some minor differences among Machiavelli's, Hobbes' and Nietzsche's conceptions of the ideal leader, his short account of their positions merely serves to elaborate the same simplistic dichotomy between Socratic/Platonic and Machiavellian models of leadership found in Kellerman. Machiavelli again plays the role of the founder of a stereotypical, crude form of "political realism" Grob apparently finds dominant throughout the modern Western tradition of politics. He, again like Kellerman, responds to the apparent crisis in Western thought on political leadership by calling for a return to the superior Socratic theory of leadership which, in explicit contrast to Machiavelli, represents leadership "as a moral activity" (269), contrasts the true task of leadership with that "of the mere wielder of power" (271), and practises "leadership as dialogue," rather than relying on coercion and manipulation (273). In addition, Grob categorizes political leadership as continuous with all other forms of leadership ("Leadership in the political sphere is to be understood in the same manner as leadership in the school or home," 275), portrays the philosopher-leader as engaged in a continual self-critique "which prohibits coercion or force in any or all of its many guises" (275), and places the role and tasks of leadership within a larger philosophical context of determining a course of life and an "openness to truth-as-a-process" (279). Thus, Grob, like Kellerman, argues that the practical resolution of our present crisis of political leadership can be achieved by rejecting the amoral Machiavellian notion of leadership and returning to a Socratic/Platonic conception of leadership with a clear moral vision.

The Kellerman anthology, culminating in Grob's vision of the ideal political leader as a Socratic teacher who leads by engaging followers in Socratic dialogue, is illustrative of a narrative of crisis and redemption that is pervasive in recent discussions of political leadership. This narrative typically ends in a call for a highly romanticized conception of leadership, most fully visible in the figure of the Socratic teacher-leader explicitly championed by both Kellerman and Grob. Yet, this romanticized narrative of leadership is more fully typified by what is absent rather than by what is present, by its various exclusions, omissions, and repressions rather than by its explicit call for a return to the Socratic conception of leadership. In other words, these analyses of leadership are problematic not only because they tend to culminate in romantic idealizations of the nature of leadership, but also because they systematically exclude or gloss over several of the most critical moral and political dilemmas of leadership. Indeed, as constructed by Grob, ideal political leaders turn out to be apolitical because their dialogical interactions with followers are completely free of all coercion, force, ambiguity and conflict. In addition, Machiavelli plays a major role in this narrative which excludes, omits and represses several of the most problematic, contentious, and ambiguous dimensions of their call for a new political leadership with a clear moral vision.

The Kellerman anthology demonstrates that these recent academic models and typologies of leadership, like the treatments of leadership written for a wider audience and with a more explicit reformist political agenda (see, e.g., chap. 16 in Gardner), do constitute a particular narrative that functions to promote a particular politics of leadership and followership. As Murray Edelman argues in his attempt to assess the rhetoric of contemporary analyses of leadership: "The main function of 'leadership' as a sign is to displace from attention most of the structural influences, conflicts, unequal bargains, strategies, repressions, tensions, and failures characteristic of politics" (1988, 60). Although it would be unfair and inaccurate to characterize Kellerman's and Grob's essays in particular, or the anthology in general, as completely failing to address such concerns, their romanticized visions of leadership do function to repress the significance of these concerns as they bear upon systematic analysis of the nature and dynamics of political leadership. Furthermore, although recent academic work on political leadership is hardly monolithic, it does tend to share this common narrative of a decline in our conception of leadership, with Machiavelli playing the role of subversive villain, which Kellerman and Grob have illustrated for us.

More specifically, at the very core of Kellerman's and Grob's analyses of political leadership is a simplistic reading of Machiavelli with a strong rhetorical effect. Their account presents him as formulating a subversive "realist" doctrine of political leadership that completely divorces politics from morality, and that encourages leaders to look only to their own interests and advancement and to neglect the interests of their followers. Their alternative model of political leadership, the return to a Platonic or Socratic conception of leadership that reconnects leaders with followers and politics with morals, makes sense only against the background of this narrative. Their romanticized vision of Socratic/Platonic leadership can be presented as a solution to our practical political crisis only if Machiavelli and others have somehow subverted our theoretical understanding of the nature of true leadership.

Of course, current scholarship on political leadership cannot be reduced to its interpretation of Machiavelli. Moreover, the preceding summary of this scholarship has focused on the place assigned to Machiavelli and has omitted certain of the elements that Kellerman, Grob, and others would insist are crucial to understanding their contributions to developing a viable theory or understanding of political leadership. Yet, while Machiavelli plays a relatively minor part in terms of attention that is explicitly paid to his work, his actual role in the common narrative running through this literature is critical. Its basic narrative is one of recovering, revitalizing, and reconstructing a classical doctrine of political leadership by reaching back across the Machiavellian erasure of the core distinctions (such as real/ideal) underpinning this classical doctrine. In this account, Machiavelli is the principal founder of a "realist" theory of leadership that portrays politics as a pure struggle for power in which all moral considerations are set aside, and that focuses the theory and practice of leadership on success as measured solely in terms of the acquisition and maintenance of power and the protection and promotion of the interests of the nation-state or some other political collectivity.

As my opening summaries of *The Prince* and the *Discourses* suggest, I find this reading of Machiavelli (not to mention the collapsing of Machiavelli's, Hobbes' and Nietzsche's theories), which is so pervasive in recent discussions of political leadership, to be appallingly simplistic and crude by the standards of established scholarship on Machiavelli's political theory. However, my primary interest is not in "setting the record straight" by detailing how Kellerman and others have distorted central claims in *The Prince* because they did not consider how they are qualified by the context within which they appear. Also, I will not concentrate here on demonstrating that *The Prince* is easily misunderstood if taken out of the context of the rest of Machiavelli's writings, particularly the *Discourses,* or that his views on leadership in *The Prince* must be considered in the context of his republican beliefs. Finally, I am not primarily concerned here with the issue of whether or not Machiavelli "really" is a realist or with retracing the historical trail of the construction of Machiavellianism and trying to locate the "real" Machiavelli in this history. In contrast, I intend to focus on a comparison of a model of political leadership that is pervasive in contemporary discussions of leadership with an overview of Machiavelli's model of leadership. In particular, I will concentrate on two important academic contributions to the construction of this pervasive, modern model of leadership: James MacGregor Burns' *Leadership* and Robert Tucker's *Politics as Leadership.*

In general, I intend to show that modern studies and discussions of political leadership continue to advance a simplistic caricature of Machiavelli's views, and that this caricature of Machiavelli is a central part of a rhetorical strategy for repressing and excluding certain troubling questions about leadership. It is in this sense that contemporary discussions of leadership could benefit greatly by moving from a dismissive distortion of Machiavelli to a serious engagement with his perspective. In this path I follow the lead of R. B. J. Walker, who, in the context of a critique of the dominant tradition within international relations theory, argues that "to take Machiavelli seriously" is to confront "someone who can be read in ways to problematize the most basic assumptions on which claims about the tradition are based" (1989, 29). Similarly, I think that "to take Machiavelli seriously" requires the reexamination of a model of political leadership that can be read as a powerful challenge to some of the fundamental philosophical and conceptual presuppositions upon which recent scholarship on leadership has proceeded.

At the same time, although there is much to be gained from confronting Machiavelli's accounts of the dilemmas of political leadership, he clearly does not offer a definitive theory of political leadership, and his account of political leadership is problematic in several important areas. In particular, Machiavelli's account of leadership certainly does reflect and incorporate the androcentric and misogynistic biases of his political theory as a whole, as Hannah Pitkin has carefully documented, and such biases are not relatively superficial problems that can be readily detached from some set of deeper claims and assumptions.[3] Moreover, Machiavelli's own understanding of politics and leadership is linked to conceptions of "human nature," history, and society that are at best incomplete and at worst simplistic, and he certainly does not offer definitive answers to the difficult and problematic questions concerning political leadership that he raises.

James MacGregor Burns and Machiavelli on "Transforming Leadership"

James MacGregor Burns' *Leadership* and Robert Tucker's *Politics as Leadership*, two significant academic influences on current discussions of the problems of political leadership, offer accounts of Machiavelli that parallel those of Kellerman and Grob. Burns, for example, is very much concerned with tracing the origins of the modern crisis of leadership, which he presents as essentially an intellectual crisis (1978, 1–2). Thus, his account of Machiavelli's work is presented as part of a more complex, more detailed narrative that locates Machiavelli's views on leadership in terms of this search for the intellectual roots of our present leadership crisis. Yet, the picture of Machiavelli that emerges is only a more detailed presentation of the same one-dimensional portrait offered by Kellerman and Grob.

Like Grob, Burns specifically places Machiavelli in the same grouping with Hobbes and Nietzsche as the formulators of a traditional doctrine that reduces both politics and leadership to "naked power-wielding" (14–18). Moreover, he also contrasts this "realistic view of man's perversity and frailty" with an alternative view of "moral leadership" that he traces back to Plato. In short, the same dichotomy between the Machiavellian prince and the Socratic/Platonic teacher-leader becomes a central component of Burns' model of political leadership. Indeed, this formulation of a dichotomy between the amoral Machiavellian leader and the moral Socratic/Platonic leader is the foundation of his central conceptual distinction regarding political leadership. Burns argues that one of the central intellectual tasks that must be undertaken to resolve the current crisis of leadership is to distinguish between "transactional leadership" and "transforming leadership." Transactional (or Machiavellian) leadership is based upon merely an exchange relationship between leaders and followers and essentially consists of the exploitation of existing needs, wants, or demands of followers by leaders. In contrast, transforming (or Platonic) leadership is based upon a mutual relationship between leaders and followers and requires the type of leader who "looks for potential motives of followers, seeks to satisfy higher needs, and engages the full person of the follower" (4).

Burns' narrative of the search for responsible leadership in practical politics and the underlying theoretical crisis of thinking about leadership is much more detailed, but the central plot and Machiavelli's particular role remain essentially the same as in the shorter narratives constructed by Kellerman and Grob. Although he formally acknowledges the possibility of alternative readings of Machiavelli's intentions in *The Prince*, Burns contends that "none of the theories explain the strangest fact of all: Machiavelli's practical advice was not at all practical" (445). By severing the real from the ideal, the practical from the moral, Machiavelli offered a model of ruthless political leadership that could only succeed in the short run and is necessarily doomed in the long run. More specifically, according to Burns, Machiavelli's "realistic" doctrine is self-defeating because of two fundamental defects. First, Machiavelli mistakenly over-generalizes on the basis of the "half-truth" that "men are essentially selfish" (446). Burns counters that human selfishness takes many different forms in different social and historical contexts, and that some forms of selfishness are more "benign" than others.

The more basic error, according to Burns, is that Machiavelli makes universal claims about the practice of leadership and politics on the basis of an analysis of particular social and political circumstances. In Burns' words, Machiavelli falsely projects "notions that were only locally applicable at best into an ideology of ruthlessness and selfishness" (446). But Burns is not simply concerned with the empirical adequacy of what he takes to be Machiavelli's account of human behavior; he also contends that Machiavelli's conception of human nature incorporates an unacceptable ethical presupposition: "More than selfishness; at the core of Machiavelli lay the most pernicious and inhuman concept of all: the treatment of other persons, other leaders, as *things*" (446). In Burns' narrative, this is the central error that is taken up by the power school and becomes the core of the dominant, manipulative transactional model of leadership. In contrast, he proposes an alternative account of political leadership, transforming leadership, which counters the dominant Machiavellian notion of the leader as merely a manipulator of followers by reaching back to a classical doctrine of leadership in which the leader acts in the interest of followers through commitment to clear moral ideals.

What is particularly ironic about the account of leadership that Burns constructs upon this dichotomy between Machiavelli and Plato is that whereas Burns constructs a model of leadership that excludes Machiavelli's formulation of these issues, Machiavellian themes do emerge in his own analysis of the tasks of political leadership. In other words, the general image of leadership that Burns projects is a romanticized one which clearly ignores or represses the contestable political and moral terrain that the political leader must frequently negotiate. Yet, when Burns attempts to summarize the specific "characteristics of leadership," there are clear similarities between his model and Machiavelli's model of leadership (452).

The romanticized overview of leadership is particularly evident in Burns' concluding chapter, "Political Leadership as Practical Influence." The chapter begins with the narrative that places Machiavelli's *The Prince* at the center of the spread of a doctrine of transactional leadership that systematically conflates leadership and manipulation. According to Burns, Machiavelli and his imitators, including Dale Carnegie, "seek to train persons to manage and manipulate other persons rather than to *lead* them" (446). In contrast, Burns offers this vision of transforming leadership:

> The search for wholeness—that is, for this kind of full, sharing, feeling relationship—between "teachers" and "students," between leaders and followers, must be more than merely a personal or self-regarding quest. Fully sharing leaders perceive their roles as shaping the future to the advantage of groups with which they identify, an advantage they define in terms of the broadest possible goals and the highest levels of morality.... If they are to be effective in helping to mobilize and elevate their constituencies, leaders must be whole persons, persons with fully functioning capacities for thinking and feeling. The problem for them as educators, as leaders, is not to promote narrow, egocentric self-actualization but to extend awareness of human needs and the means of gratifying them, to improve the larger social situation

for which educators or leaders have responsibility and over which they have power. (448–449)

Thus, at the core of Burns' conception of transforming leadership is the same romanticized vision of the Platonic or Socratic teacher-leader that is stated in more philosophical terms by Grob. One of its core elements is the insistence that political leadership does not differ from other forms of leadership, particularly those of the philosopher and the educator. According to this notion, the proper definition of good political leadership is found in the same criteria that apply to all forms of leadership: the search for wholeness, the mutual nature of the relationship between leaders and followers, and the leader's capacity to know and pursue a moral ideal that is free of ambiguity and conflict. Moreover, the fundamental crisis of leadership is, according to this romanticized vision, ultimately merely a philosophical or intellectual problem of definition or conceptualization. As Burns argues, the basic problem is a failure "to distinguish true leadership from manipulation" (458). Our present crisis of leadership is rooted in our confusion about the nature of leadership, and this confusion "will continue as long as we fail to distinguish leadership from brute power, leadership from propaganda, leadership from manipulation, leadership from pandering, leadership from coercion" (452). The essential task of achieving good political leadership in practice is, at base, the philosophical or intellectual task of "clarifying the definition of leadership" (452). Burns' romantic reduction of the complex problematics of leadership to a task of definition or of rational conceptualization is essentially a return to the same Socratic/Platonic model of leadership explicitly championed by Kellerman and Grob. Burns, too, is calling for a type of teacher-leader whose purely dialogical interactions with followers and whose critical powers of self-reflection would eliminate the messy complications of conflict, coercion, force, manipulation, and deceit.

Yet, even as Burns constructs this idealized vision of leadership in contrast to his caricature of *The Prince*, his more detailed account of the characteristics of such leadership overlaps with Machiavelli at several points. One of the clearest is where Burns speaks of true or good leadership as "causative" (454). By this he means that "the most lasting tangible act of leadership is the creation of an institution—a nation, a social movement, a political party, a bureaucracy—that continues to exert moral leadership and foster needed social change long after the creative leaders are gone" (454). This is, of course, precisely the task of political leadership that preoccupies Machiavelli in *The Prince* and the *Discourses*: what is required of political leadership in order to found a nation or republic (see de Grazia, 157–193).

Ironically, Machiavelli is clearly in agreement with Burns' characterization of transforming leadership as "causative," creative ,and genuinely transformative. As he states in the *Discourses*: ". . . though one man alone is fit for founding a government, what he has founded will not last long if it rests upon his shoulders alone; it is lasting when it is left in the care of many and when many desire to maintain it" (bk. 1, chap. 9). Moreover, he claims that "the well-being, therefore, of a republic or a kingdom cannot rest upon a prince who governs prudently while he is alive, but rather upon one who organizes the government in such a way that it can be maintained in the event of his death" (bk. 1, chap. 11).

Certainly, Burns might well respond that this commitment is simply not enough because another of his essential characteristics is that "leadership is morally purposeful" (455). He insists that leadership must be "goal-oriented" in an ethical sense, quoting Philip Selznick's claim that "the problem is always *to choose key values and to create a social structure that embodies them*" (455). Indeed, this commitment to create social structures or institutions in pursuit of an ethical goal or ideal is for him at the core of the real test of practical leadership: "*The ultimate test of practical leadership is the realization of intended, real change that meets people's enduring needs*" (461). And it is on exactly this point that Burns finds the Machiavellian doctrine of leadership so deficient. He argues that Machiavelli's position assumes a constant self-interestedness in human beings, whether leaders or followers, and confines the goal of political leadership to the manipulation of human beings on the basis of such self-interest rather than calling for a transformation to a more viable form of mutual cooperation.

But, again, this insistence that good political leadership is morally purposeful is a part of Machiavelli's account of leadership. For example, Machiavelli's model of transforming leadership is "a prudent founder of a republic, one whose intention it is to govern for the common good and not in his own interest, not for his heirs but for the sake of the fatherland .. ." (*Discourses*, bk. 1, chap. 9). However, Machiavelli, in contrast to Burns' model of leadership, also recognizes that there are very real tensions, conflicts, and ambiguities confronting the political leader who would undertake such a transformation. In the first place, he acknowledges that all forms of government are "defective" in that the institutions or social structures introduced by the transforming leader cannot guarantee the continued pursuit of the common good by succeeding leaders. Indeed, Machiavelli posits a historical cycle of decline and reconstitution in which all the established forms of government (of one, few, or many rulers) decline when successive leaders neglect founding principles and put the pursuit of their self-interests ahead of the common good:

> . . . the principality easily becomes tyrannical; aristocrats can very easily produce an oligarchy; democracy is converted into anarchy with no difficulty. So that if a founder of a republic organizes one of these three governments in a city, he organizes it there for a brief period of time only, since no precaution can prevent it from slipping into its contrary on account of the similarity, in such a case, of the virtue and the vice.
> (*Discourses*, bk. 1, chap. 2)

Thus Machiavelli clearly places the task of transforming leadership within the limiting context of historical constraints. He does not, as Burns clearly does, idealize transforming leadership as an intellectual, creative, morally pure task of designing permanent institutions that will satisfy enduring needs outside of specific historical and social circumstances.

In addition, Machiavelli argues that the more corrupt the people whom such a leader would attempt to transform, the more difficult and problematic the task of transformation becomes. In the case of a "totally corrupt people," people who do not recognize or respect any notion of common good, but rather simply pursue their self-interests, the situation is almost impossible. If the transforming leader attempts a reformist approach, the end result is likely to be failure:

> ... for it takes a prudent man who can see defects from far off and in their initial stages in order to reform them gradually, and it is not common to find a man like this in a city; and when one is found, he may never be able to persuade others to follow what he himself understands; for men are accustomed to living in one way, and they do not want to change; and this is even more true when they cannot see the evil for themselves but have to have it explained to them by abstract arguments.
>
> *(Discourses*, bk. 1, chap. 18)

Thus it is precisely in relation to Burns' notion of transforming leadership that Machiavelli raises a set of problems concerning how the reformer will be able to communicate this new moral vision of a common good to a group of people who are locked into self-interestedness.

Indeed, Machiavelli believes that the obstacles to transformation through reform are so great that the transforming leader will be drawn to a more radical strategy: reform that is attempted "all at once," or what we might call revolution.

> As for reforming these institutions all at once, when everyone realizes that they are not good, let me say that this uselessness which is easily recognized is corrected only with difficulty; for to do this it is not enough to employ lawful means, for lawful methods are now useless; it is necessary to have recourse to extraordinary measures, such as violence or arms, and to become, before all else, prince of that city, in order to be able to deal with it in one's own way. But since the reforming of a city into a body politic presupposes a good man, and becoming prince of a republic through the use of violence presupposes an evil man—because of this fact we discover that it happens only very rarely that a good man wishes to become prince through evil means, even though his goal may be a good one; while, on the other hand, we discover that it is equally rare for an evil man who has become prince to act correctly, for it would never ever enter his mind to employ that authority for a good which he has acquired by evil means.
>
> (*The Discourses*, bk. 1, chap. 18)

From Machiavelli's perspective, this is the central problem of transforming leadership. In order to achieve the transformation Burns endorses, the establishment of institutional or structural changes aimed toward a particular moral vision, the leader may have to use manipulation, deceit, violence, and other means which are clearly evil by established moral standards.[4] As de Grazia states in his review of the various specific examples of transforming leadership examined by Machiavelli, "The prince new, the founder of religion, the legislator, the sweeping reformer, and 'the wise ordainer' have a common problem... To reform an entire country 'it is not enough to use ordinary means, the ordinary methods being [in this case] bad; but it is necessary to come to the extraordinary, as it is to violence and to arms . . . .'" (1989, 237). Moreover, de Grazia contends that Machiavelli establishes a conceptual grounding for making practical judgments concerning whether conditions are ordinary or extraordinary, when extraordinary measures become excessive, whether the transforming leader is actually dedicated to the common good, and what are the ethical limits which apply to these extraordinary methods (258–317).

Certainly, one can challenge Machiavelli's notion of transforming leadership as requiring that the prince must "learn how not to be good, and to use this knowledge or not use it according to necessity" (*The Prince*, chap. 15). But this is very different from simply dismissing Machiavelli, as do Burns and many scholars on leadership, Machiavelli as collapsing the distinction between good and evil, or as endorsing a notion of transactional leadership that encourages manipulation of one's followers without concern for any moral ends. As de Grazia summarizes Machiavelli's view of transforming leadership,

> We have further found that the prince new is good—were he not good it would not be necessary for him "to learn to be able to be not good"; that he works "to do good for the generality of men"; that he will have greater moral choices to make than most men; that among these choices there often will be those of administering strong medicine or of carrying out extraordinary measures. (276)

There is, in de Grazia's terms, the "recruitment" or "supply" problem of finding a good leader who is willing to use the kind of "extraordinary means" characterized above. But Machiavelli's account of leadership has the distinct advantage that it makes these political, ethical, and practical problems explicit rather than covering them over in some kind of appeal to the romanticized, Platonic vision of political leadership found in Burns' theory of leadership. As de Grazia recognizes, Machiavelli's model of leadership places these ethical dilemmas at the center of concern for new and prospective leaders, particularly those who would transform political institutions: "To tell a prospective new prince that he shall have to enter evil insures that he cannot deceive himself" (238–239). In contrast, by denying or repressing the possibility that the transforming leader will confront such difficult and ambiguous political and moral choices, Burns constructs a romanticized view of leadership that promotes exactly such self-deception among those who accept his account of the tasks of transforming leadership.

ROBERT TUCKER AND MACHIAVELLI ON REVOLUTIONARY LEADERSHIP

Robert Tucker perceives himself as offering a fundamentally different theory of political leadership, which he specifically contrasts with that of Burns. In particular, he argues that, by dichotomizing transactional and transformational leaders, Burns' attempt to define political leadership in such a way that dictators like Hitler and Stalin simply do not count as genuine leaders results in "serious problems of political analysis" (1981, 12). In the first place, Tucker maintains that Burns' model ignores the evidence that Hitler, Stalin, and other "wielders of brute power" did have willing followers. Thus Burns attempts to exclude, by definition, the very possibility of authoritarian or dictatorial leadership, a conceptual move that Tucker rejects. Even more fundamentally for Tucker, by focusing exclusively on the relationship between leaders and followers as the core of a theory of political leadership, Burns fails to address central issues, such as "what it is that leaders do, or how they function as leaders" (12). On the basis of this critique, Tucker begins to construct an alternative theory of leadership that centers in the notion of "leadership as activity," and proceeds to use the insights of social psychology to analyze how leadership gives direction "to a collective's activities" (15).

Yet, even though Tucker recognizes some of the central romanticized elements within Burns' account of leadership and specifically contrasts his theory of leadership with Burns' theory, Tucker's own view of leadership also advances a highly romanticized vision of political leadership. It is thus doubly ironic that Tucker, who attempts to offer a more "realistic" account in contrast to the idealizations he uncovers in Burns, ultimately offers a romanticized vision of leadership that is quite similar to Burns' theory. First, Tucker also constructs a romanticized, Platonic version of political leadership based on his rejection of a caricature of Machiavelli's views on leadership. In addition, he also contradicts his own Platonic/Socratic ideal model of leadership by readmitting Machiavellian themes through a back door in his own analysis of the tasks of transformational or revolutionary leadership.

Although he does not examine the intellectual underpinnings of the current crisis of leadership as does Burns, Tucker's account of leadership shares the basic narrative structure found in Burns and typical of recent discussions of leadership. In Tucker's formulation of the standard dichotomy between "Machiavellian" and "good" accounts of leadership, there are two fundamental views of "the essence of politics" (1). First, there is the view of "the power school" that conceives of politics as power and that has been dominant since Machiavelli's *Prince*, "a 'how-to' manual for the princely power-seeker and power-holder" (4). In contrast, there is "the leadership approach" to politics, which he characterizes as the classical conception of politics that traces its roots back to Plato, and which he also locates, at least in part, in the work of Max Weber and Burns. Thus, in Tucker's hands, "the leadership approach," an approach that places leadership rather than power-seeking and power-holding at the center of our understanding of politics, becomes the alternative to the dominant, traditional view of leadership and politics that has been pervasive since Machiavelli. This approach, as articulated by Tucker, rests on a different set of assumptions about politics and offers the resources for reconceptualizing our present political crisis.

Tucker's model is organized around what he perceives as the three central tasks of leadership: 1) diagnosing the present political situation, including the nature of the difficulties and the possibilities of correction; 2) prescribing the course of action that is best, given this analysis of the situation; and 3) mobilizing the support that is necessary in order to achieve real change and resolve the political problems (see chap. 2). As he fills out this understanding of the nature and tasks of political leadership, the romanticism of his vision of the leader becomes increasingly clear. This idealization is, as with all of the other studies of leadership examined here, most visible in its explicit endorsement of a return to a Platonic conception of leadership. The concluding section of *Politics as Leadership*, entitled "A Platonic Conclusion," expressly points to Plato's philosophy as providing the understanding necessary to reconceptualize leadership (150). Working from Plato's formulation that political leaders must become philosophers or philosophers must become political leaders, Tucker constructs two different versions of a modern "Platonic interim leadership strategy" for the bipolar world of superpowers which he saw in 1980 (153). His primary hopes seem to center in the possibility of "a Russo-American entente for human survival [in which] the two governments...would exert their influence separately and jointly on behalf of order and the arresting of further growth of the crisis syndrome" (154).

In reply to those who continue to see such a possibility as "quite utopian," Tucker argues that his Platonic solution appears idealistic only if leaders and nations continue to think in terms of the traditional paradigm of power politics. Of course, he proposes his superior, alternative leadership approach to politics, which "takes human freedom seriously. It holds that human beings and their leaders have the capacity to learn from history and past mistakes, to take accurate measure of present situations, and to take action inspired by a sense of the common good" (157). Like Burns, he is calling for a kind of transforming leadership modeled on Plato, rather than the standard transactional leadership represented by Machiavelli (although it should be noted that Tucker's dichotomy between power politics and leadership as politics eliminates Machiavelli by definition from all discussions of politics, and thus represents, in this way, an even greater idealization of leadership than Burns' account). Overall, like Burns, Tucker presents an account of leadership that parallels Machiavelli's at critical points but departs from Machiavelli by continually masking the political conflicts and moral dilemmas raised by this very call for transforming leadership.

As with the other studies of leadership we have seen, this romanticizing of leadership is not a kind of late addition to an independently existing base of typologies, definitions, and theories. Tucker's approach presents an idealized, incomplete, and implausible account of political leadership not simply because of its specific inclusion of the image of the Socratic/Platonic philosopher-leader as the model, but also because of its systematic exclusion, at the theoretical level, of the moral and political dilemmas associated with the Machiavellian model.

What makes this exclusion of the Machiavellian account of political leadership especially damaging to both Tucker and Burns is that they both are genuinely concerned with articulating a notion of transforming or revolutionary leadership that is appropriate to our present political crisis. Tucker certainly has the more global and radical diagnosis of the nature of the present political situation, which he calls "a crisis of human survival" (114). He provides an overview of "the crisis syndrome," which includes such diverse elements as world-wide overpopulation, depletion of natural resources, environmental degradation, and the threat of nuclear war. According to Tucker, it is one of the essential tasks of leadership to define "the collective situation," to come up with a corrective course of action, and to mobilize popular support for this global understanding of our problems and their solution (114).

It is clear to Tucker that the established political leadership, or what he calls "constituted leaders," are not up to the task: "While time is running out for humanity, the governments of the approximately one hundred and fifty nation-states now in existence try to do political business as usual" (115). Tucker's hopes for a new leadership center in a type of "antileadership" (123) or in "nonconstituted leaders" who operate through non-traditional political and social avenues (72). The tasks of these antileaders or nonconstituted leaders are essentially those of what Burns called transforming leadership and what Tucker calls "revolutionary leadership" (see 105). Revolutionary leadership redefines the "collective situation" and engenders a "fundamental reconstitution of society" (106). Tucker's account of these revolutionary leaders focuses on their capacity for such a vision and their role in bringing about a fundamental change in consciousness: "A revolutionary mind of great creative power will be one that forms or adumbrates a new concept of social living that may, if a revolution takes place, become the sustaining myth of a new society" (107).

Since Tucker clearly believes that such revolutionary leadership will not be provided by the traditional "constituted leadership" of governments, bureaucracies, corporations, and organizations, he must look elsewhere for such revolutionary vision. His hopes seem to center in what he calls "the party for humanity," a "scattered company of twentieth-century people who have acted as nonconstituted leaders of a still nonexistent community of men" (130). What differentiates this party of humanity from traditional political leaders is that it is a "leadership cohort" rather than a "power-seeking group," and that it is a "moral party" with a shared ethic called "reverence for life" (131). Its revolutionary project is the transformation of the consciousness of the world community, to redefine our political situation in terms of our common interests as part of the human species, in order to bring about a political and social restructuring or reorganization of the world.

What makes Tucker's account of such a revolutionary leadership so idealistic is not simply the utopian elements so pervasive in this vision of an alternative future. The most problematic element in this vision of a new global political leadership is the way that Tucker, like Burns and Grob, romanticizes his account by eliminating or repressing the many dangers, conflicts, and difficulties that such leaders will necessarily confront. For example, Tucker's account of revolutionary leadership faces the Machiavellian complications noted above in relation to Burns. If, in De Grazia's words, "existing leaders or the old princes are worse than useless," then the political situation that calls for the revolutionary leadership of the new prince is likely to demand the use of extraordinary measures (1989, 235). This is so because, as Tucker well realizes, the "sustaining myth" of a particular society "as a common enterprise" has declined, or has become insufficient for the political reality that the society confronts (see Tucker 1981, 99–100). This is why the central task of revolutionary political leadership is to formulate and propagate what might become "the sustaining myth of a new society." Of course, this notion of a new sustaining myth is very similar to Machiavelli's understanding of the collective view of a common good that constitutes the fundamental basis of a viable political community.

But what Machiavelli acknowledges and Tucker represses is that this lack of a sustaining myth makes the task of revolutionary leadership particularly risky and problematic. Without such a common myth or unifying common identity, political leaders cannot attempt to persuade potential followers rationally by appealing to the sense of common identity and purpose that the sustaining myth provides. Indeed, without this common sense of identity, there is a collection of corrupt, self-interested individuals rather than a community capable of rational discussion and decision-making. As de Grazia states, "Because of defects in their nature and condition, people in extraordinary times cannot be easily persuaded to the truth . . ." (296). But, of course, now we are back at the central problem in Machiavelli's account of revolutionary or transforming leadership: the kind of crisis situation Tucker describes calls for new leaders who will use extraordinary measures for the common good; such leaders are very rare; and it is more likely that the leaders who do seek and attain political power will be those who act upon motives of private gain rather than the common good.

Towards an Agonistic Model of Political Leadership

As noted above in the comparison of Burns and Machiavelli, it is possible to challenge Machiavelli's account of leadership for suggesting that extraordinary measures, including violence and deceit, will inevitably be necessary to the success of transforming leadership. But Tucker is not up to this challenge because he, like Burns, Kellerman and Grob, simply eliminates these difficult moral and political problems by setting up a crude, simplistic dichotomy between Machiavellian and Socratic/Platonic models of leadership. The largely implicit narrative of this dichotomy begins with some notion of a contemporary political crisis in leadership (although the nature and severity of this crisis vary among the different accounts). In addition, according to the common narrative of these recent models of transforming leadership, the current crisis is in large part an intellectual and moral one that calls for the intellectual leadership of philosopher/scholars in reclaiming a Socratic ideal of the teacher-leader that lies beyond the realist era of opportunistic leadership inaugurated by Machiavelli. Thus the dichotomy between good (Socratic/Platonic) and bad (Machiavellian) theories of leadership is grounded in a narrative of the loss and promised redemption of a universal vision of proper political leadership that is again unified with moral ideals. Although these recent leadership studies purport to be the product of the latest social scientific analyses of the phenomenon, they actually represent the resurgence of a romanticized account of leadership that has at its core the depoliticized image of political leadership represented by the reduction of leadership to the dialogical relation between Socratic teacher and students.

If my reading of these recent studies and analyses of political leadership is correct, the reduction of Machiavelli's account of leadership to this crude caricature of amoral realism is not simply a side issue of interpreting Machiavelli that concerns only the community of political theorists. Rather, the summary rejection of Machiavelli's model of leadership represses the complex moral and political challenges that are raised in any systematic analysis of the types of crisis situations that call for transforming leadership. One of the most dangerous consequences of this narrative of redemptive leadership is its glorification and idealization of the role and nature of political leadership. Even if this image of the ideal leader as philosopher/teacher provides some limited conceptual space for raising some of the theoretical questions about the relationship between leadership and democracy, it certainly masks or represses the central relations between leadership and power.

The rhetorical strategy of this image of the ideal philosopher-leader is again most visible when we consider critically the image of a new leadership that is vested with Socratic/Platonic knowledge and virtue and that leads through dialogue and education. Machiavelli's model of leadership does not simply divorce such a normative model from the realities of politics, but rather addresses the difficulties that arise when we consider this normative model in the context of the complex and ambiguous empirical world of political conflict and change. In particular, Machiavelli's model of leadership does not eliminate the moral dimension of leadership by characterizing all leaders as dominated by the same (self-interested) motives as all "average" citizens, as the prevalent narrative holds. This distortion of Machiavelli's model of leadership serves to promote an idealized Socratic/Platonic image of leaders who rise, intellectually and morally, far above the common world of common citizens. It is part of a rhetorical strategy that ultimately aims to reduce politics to a search for the kind of good (superior) political leaders portrayed in this romantic image.

In short, the romanticized models of transforming leadership advanced by Kellerman, Burns, and Tucker foster a view of politics as the search for leaders as heroes. Despite their claimed democratic and radical intentions, such models of political leadership tend to undermine democratic politics. In particular, they contribute to the popular tendency to look for answers to complex political, social, and institutional problems by simply electing "good" leaders who have the moral will to stand above the ongoing dismal battle of conflicting interests. In addition, these idealized visions of leadership encourage the popular tendency to subject all elected officials and candidates to the most detailed scrutiny because they make moral character and purity of intent the essential characteristics of "good" leadership. Of course, since such purity is possible only within fictional or Platonic/Socratic worlds, all existing leaders and candidates automatically and necessarily fail the critical tests of leadership.

Machiavelli's account of leadership continues to offer a powerful challenge to this romantic, depoliticized Socratic/Platonic model of leadership and to provide some important signposts toward the formulation of an alternative, agonistic model of leadership. Three important recent works on leadership illustrate the continued relevance of Machiavelli to this search for a more coherent account of political leadership, both because they incorporate Machiavellian themes in rethinking the issues of political leadership, and because they point to the type of agonistic model of leadership that I am calling for here.

First, Stuart Hampshire, in *Innocence and Experience*, uses Machiavelli's formulation of the problems of political leadership to challenge current moral theories that "have a fairy-tale quality" because they attempt to erase or suppress "the realities of politics" (1989, 12). After an impressive brief survey of central moments in the history of moral philosophy, Hampshire turns to Machiavelli's formulation of the problem of political leadership in his last chapter, "Morality and Machiavelli." He argues that Machiavelli offers "an unsurpassed account of the salient conditions of political action" because Machiavelli demands attention to the intense conflict between the contradictory demands of political leaders' commitments to a (Christian) morality of innocence and a competing morality of experience that pursues the collective good of some polity or group in a realm of disagreement and conflict (164). Drawing on his earlier arguments concerning such issues as the nature of moral reasoning and justice, Hampshire offers "A Reply to Machiavelli," in which he attempts to demonstrate that there is a "notion of minimum procedural justice," which can be used in assessing the "competing conceptions of the good" and the "conflicting moral claims" inherent in political conflicts (186).

Although Hampshire's analysis of Machiavelli's examination of the central moral issues of leadership makes an important contribution to the formulation of an agonistic model of leadership, it clearly does not provide such a model. Even if the conflicts between competing moralities of innocence and experience are at the center of any viable conception of political leadership, they do not exhaust the ambiguities, conflicts, and tensions that confront political leaders. In part, Hampshire omits such further dimensions of an agonistic model of leadership because his entire discussion of leadership is at a general (philosophical) level, and he never examines in detail the specific dilemmas faced by any particular political leader.

Two other recent works on leadership make a further contribution to the articulation of an agonistic model because they do provide several case studies of political leaders and attempt to develop coherent typologies for examining the multi-faceted dilemmas of leadership. In *Icons of Democracy*, Bruce Miroff analyzes the requisites of *democratic* political leadership by examining the leadership styles of nine American leaders, beginning with Alexander Hamilton and concluding with Martin Luther King, Jr. Although Miroff ignores Machiavelli, he does examine John Adams as an "inheritor of 'classical republicanism'" (1993, 50) and recognizes this republican tradition as one of the component parts of the complex "American tradition of leadership" (358). Thus Miroff acknowledges a Machiavellian strain in the American political tradition in which the primary role of the leader is to resist "corruption" and to maintain or restore "civic virtue." In this republican conception, success in leadership must be measured in terms of establishing and maintaining "a positive passion for the public good, the public interest, honor, power, and glory . . . in the minds of the people" rather than simply in terms of providing free markets and economic success (53). Moreover, Miroff draws upon this republican tradition when he advocates "the restoration of honor" to the political realm and to the political career as essential to the "revival" of viable political leadership in the United States (358).

Miroff incorporates central elements of an agonistic model of leadership in that he explicitly acknowledges the tensions and conflicts among competing visions of good leadership within the American political tradition, as well as even more fundamental tensions between leadership and democracy (358). For example, in his portrait of Franklin Delano Roosevelt, Miroff suggests that one of his major defects as a political leader, namely his failure to reform democratic political institutions, can be linked to his practice of a politics that relied on "secrecy and covert action" (252) and a leadership style that remained overly "ambitious, devious, or manipulative" (240). Thus Miroff suggests that, typically of transforming leadership, FDR failed to negotiate successfully the complex tensions between the demands of exercising effective power in a "real" world of political conflict and the moral demands of using that power to make American institutions more democratic.

However, the conceptual issues concerning the tensions among competing ideals of leadership and between the demands of political leadership and the requisites of democratic politics are insufficiently developed in both Miroff's case studies and in his overall typology of political leadership. For example, Miroff argues that, despite the criticisms summarized above, FDR is ultimately different from other leaders who practised deceit and manipulation because these "masculine" traits were balanced by a "feminine" side, "a capacity for nurturance" (240). He returns briefly to this formulation of a "feminine" side of leadership that works to nurture and empower followers in his analysis of the general theoretical issues of leadership in his concluding chapter (351–352). However, this characterization of good political leadership as demarcated by a balance of "masculine" (manipulative) and "feminine" (nurturing) dimensions of leadership remains underdeveloped and problematic. Even more fundamentally, Miroff's basic typology of American political leadership—aristocratic, democratic, heroic, and dissenting types—proves inadequate to a full examination of the conflicts among competing visions of *democratic* leadership and of the underlying tensions between leadership and democracy.

Garry Wills' *Certain Trumpets* is a third contemporary study that specifically acknowledges the continued relevance of Machiavelli to the issues of democratic political leadership and that points to a more agonistic model of such leadership. Wills presents an ambitious typology of sixteen different kinds of leaders and attempts to explore each type in a brief case study that incorporates an analysis of one of sixteen different thinkers whose theoretical work is most useful and relevant to that specific type of leadership (1994, 272). He argues that Machiavelli, Max Weber, and Clausewitz are "the most original and influential" leadership theorists and further notes that their "views have been the ones most often stretched or misapplied" (272). Wills examines Machiavelli's work in his own analysis of Cesare Borgia, whom he classifies as an "Opportunistic Leader," and the apparent puzzle of the republican Machiavelli's endorsement of Borgia (239–240).

Wills offers important contributions to the formulation of an agonistic model of democratic political leadership, particularly because he emphasizes that the relation between political leader and follower is necessarily one of conflict and tension:

> That is the way leadership works, reciprocally engaging two wills, one leading (often in disguised ways), the other following (often while resisting). Leadership is always a struggle, often a feud. (11)

Wills thus rejects the romantic, depoliticized Platonic/Socratic model of leadership and argues that there simply cannot be one unified model of leadership, because the qualities of good leadership must vary according to the specific situation and social context within which it is exercised (20). An important part of his deconstruction of this romantic view of leadership is his use of Machiavelli to challenge James MacGregor Burns' and others' attempts "to sanitize the term 'leader' by distinguishing it from words like demagogue or dictator or autocrat" (227). Wills' approach to leadership, like Hampshire's and Miroff's, restores the complex and problematic issues regarding the tensions between leadership and democracy, between leaders and followers, and between politics and morals.

At the same time, Wills' case studies and theoretical work on leadership are inadequate guides to an agonistic model of democratic political leadership. In part this is so because his case studies are simply too brief, and he does not systematically develop his theme of the tensions, conflicts, and struggles inherent in the leader-follower relationship. More fundamentally, it remains unclear how his typology of different kinds of leadership and his theoretical examinations of leadership are relevant to the problems of democratic political leadership. For example, it is not evident, given his argument that one model of leadership cannot apply across politics, business, religion and so on, which of his types of leadership remain relevant to political leadership. Moreover, even if it is taken as given that certain types are clearly relevant—such as electoral, radical, reform, diplomatic, constitutional, rhetorical, and opportunistic, among others—it is not at all clear how these different types of leadership might be fitted together in a larger analysis of democratic political leadership.

Despite the criticisms made here, the analyses of leadership by Hampshire, Miroff, and Wills mark a challenge to the persistent narrative of political salvation through a type of redemptive leadership that is removed from power and politics. Hampshire, Miroff and Wills follow Machiavelli in focusing critical attention on the tensions and conflicts that are inherent in political leadership and that are particularly problematic for leaders who attempt to bring about fundamental change. They have, by challenging basic tenets of the romantic Platonic/Socratic conception of leadership and by refocusing attention on the Machiavellian formulation of the problem of political leadership, opened conceptual space for the further development of an agonistic model of leadership. While many of the specific features of this model remain uncertain, it must follow Machiavelli in featuring the inevitable tensions between leaders and followers, the limitations imposed by political conflict and struggle, the moral ambiguity and moral dilemmas involved in critical political choices, and the constraints of historical, social and institutional factors.

Notes

[1] All quotations of Machiavelli, unless indicated otherwise, are from the Bondanella and Musa edition and translation.

[2] There is, of course, a vast literature on Machiavelli. See, for examples of the most important works which place Machiavelli in a republican rather than a realist "tradition," Pocock (1975, 1978), Skinner (1978, 1981), Hulliung (1983), and de Grazia (1989). In addition, see Green (1984), Garver (1985), Kahn (1990), and Wiethoff (1991), for discussion of Machiavelli's political discourse.

[3] See Cantor and Bernay (1992) for an account of contemporary political women as models of leadership. Also see Miroff (1993) who argues that successful democratic leadership requires what he terms "the balance of masculine/feminine" (1993, 354).

[4] For a systematic discussion of Machiavelli's formulation of this moral dilemma and how it challenges fundamental assumptions pervasive in ethical discourse within the Anglo-American analytic tradition, see Hampshire (1978 and 1989).

Works Cited

Bondanella, Peter, and Mark Musa, eds. *The Portable Machiavelli*. New York: Penguin Books, 1979.

Burns, James MacGregor. *Leadership*. New York: Harper & Row, 1978.

Cantor, Dorothy W., and Toni Bernay. *Women in Power: The Secrets of Leadership*. Boston: Houghton Mifflin, 1992.

de Grazia, Sebastian. *Machiavelli in Hell*. Princeton: Princeton University Press, 1989.

Edelman, Murray. *Constructing the Political Spectacle*. Chicago: Chicago University Press, 1988.

Gardner, John W. *Morale*. New York: W. W. Norton, 1978.

Garver, Eugene. "Machiavelli and the Politics of Rhetorical Invention." *Clio* 14.2 (1985): 157–178.

Greene, Thomas M. "The End of Discourse in Machiavelli's *Prince*." *Yale French Studies* 67 (1984): 57–71.

Grob, Leonard. "Leadership: The Socratic Model." Kellerman 263–281.

Hampshire, Stuart, ed. *Innocence and Experience*. Cambridge: Harvard University Press, 1989.

———. *Public and Private Morality*. New York: Cambridge University Press, 1978.

Hulliung, Mark. *Citizen Machiavelli*. Princeton: Princeton University Press, 1983.

Kahn, Victoria. "Habermas, Machiavelli, and the Humanist Critique of Ideology." *PMLA* 105.3 (1990): 464–476.

Kellerman, Barbara, ed. *Leadership: Multidisciplinary Perspectives*. Englewood Cliffs, NJ: Prentice-Hall, 1984.

Miroff, Bruce. *Icons of Democracy: American Leaders as Heroes, Aristocrats, Dissenters, and Democrats*. New York: Basic Books, 1993.

Neville, Robert C. "Value, Courage, and Leadership." *Review of Metaphysics* 43.1 (1989): 3–26.

Pitkin, Hanna Fenichel. *Fortune Is a Woman: Gender and Politics in the Thought of Niccolo Machiavelli*. Berkeley: University of California, 1984.

Pocock, J. G. A. *The Machiavellian Moment: Florentine Political Thought and the Atlantic Republican Tradition*. Princeton: Princeton University Press, 1975.

———. "Machiavelli and Guicciardini: Ancients and Moderns," *Canadian Journal of Political and Social Theory* 2.3 (1978): 93–107.

Skinner, Quinton. *The Foundations of Modern Political Thought*, 2 vols. Cambridge: Cambridge University Press, 1978.

———. *Machiavelli*. Oxford: Oxford University Press, 1981.

Tucker, Robert C. *Politics as Leadership*. Columbia: University of Missouri, 1981.

Walker, R. B. J. "The Prince and 'The Pauper': Tradition, Modernity and Practice in the Theory of International Relations." *International/Intertextual Relations: Postmodern Readings of World Politics*. Eds. James Der Derian and Michael J. Shapiro. Lexington, MA: D. C. Heath, 1989. 25–48.

Wiethoff, William E. "A Machiavellian Perspective on the Rhetorical Criticism of Political Discourse." *Quarterly Journal of Speech* 77.3 (1991): 309–326.

Wills, Garry. *Certain Trumpets: The Call of Leaders*. New York: Simon & Schuster, 1994.

Zoll, Donald Atwell. *Modern Age* (Summer 1989): 215–223.

JULIUS CAESAR AND *CORIOLANUS*: TESTING THE METTLE OF LEADERS
Raymond G. McCall

John W. Gardner's *On Leadership* analyzes the qualities that leaders must possess if they are to facilitate the release of human possibilities. Generally upbeat, his book offers hope to potential leaders and their constituents that moral and cultural excellence can be achieved in the United States. Defining leadership as "the process of persuasion or example by which an individual (or leadership team) induces a group to pursue objectives held by the leader or shared by the leader and his or her followers" (1), Gardner accentuates the positive on nearly every page in a laudable effort to combat cynicism and despair. He buttresses his case with historic and contemporary examples of good and bad leaders, summing up his insights in aphoristic fashion; for example: "If a bad leader rules because of our lethargy, we are collaborators. The fault is not in our stars" (71).

Gardner's use of Cassius' admonition to Brutus exemplifies the way he and many writers appropriate Shakespearean language to reinforce an idea. But if the allusion triggers thoughts of the totality of *Julius Caesar*, the reader may become uneasily aware of the wide gap between Gardner's inspirational rhetoric and Shakespeare's probing of the motives and tactics of leaders and of the consequences of the uses of power on themselves and on society. In *Julius Caesar* and numerous other plays, Shakespeare quizzically examines leadership as process or example, raising disturbing questions about the tensions between idealism and pragmatism, the mixed motives of leaders, and the manner in which objectives are defined.

Some Shakespearean leaders use their power to manipulate others for questionable ends. Duke Vincentio in *Measure for Measure* and Prospero in *The Tempest* both attempt to play God, the Duke in carrying out a risky social experiment (ceding authority to a seemingly upright but untested deputy) and Prospero in seeking revenge for the loss of his dukedom. But Vincentio loses control of his experiment and is rescued by the intervention of chance, while Prospero, who is more in command of events, acknowledges that virtue is the rarer action than vengeance and that he has failed to civilize his slave Caliban, whose "darkness" he can now recognize as part of himself. In *Troilus and Cressida* Ulysses succeeds in getting the egoistic Achilles out of his tent and back to fighting the Trojans by shrewdly reminding him that reputation rusts unless polished by fresh achievements. Ulysses, however, in so manipulating the warrior, subverts the chain of command that he himself proclaimed is vital in any military or civic enterprise.

The murderously ambitious Duke of Gloucester in *3 Henry VI* and *Richard III* is a virtuoso manipulator, throwing his rivals off guard by skillfully playing a variety of roles, such as loving brother of Clarence, bustling promoter of the public weal, pious churchman. A less flashy manipulator, Claudius in *Hamlet* deftly employs psychological tactics to puncture the rebellious intent of Laertes and to make the young man his agent in securing the death of Prince Hamlet. Early in the play, he not only effectively covers up his murder of King Hamlet but also defuses any objections to his marrying the king's widow by reminding his courtiers that their "better wisdoms" freely condoned the match. Ironically, this smiling villain *is* a capable executive, quick to respond to a threatened invasion of Denmark by strengthening defenses and exerting diplomatic pressure on Norway.

Charismatic leaders are scrutinized as intensely as devious ones. The valiant Hotspur in *1 Henry IV* rallies his troops in the face of great odds, but his obsession with personal honor blinds him to the double dealing of his uncle Worcester; his readiness to sacrifice his men is parodied by Falstaff's dismissal of his own recruits as "food for powder." In *Henry V,* Henry's motives for invading France are ambiguous, and his superb oratorical skills in arousing his soldiers are counterpointed by the unheroic conduct of Bardolph and Pistol. Furthermore, in his debate with one of his men on the eve of the battle of Agincourt, he dodges the crucial question: Is the king's cause just? And this seemingly self-confident warrior monarch reveals a troubled conscience when he desperately prays that during the battle God will not think on the crime committed by his father.

In several instances Shakespeare shows that the attainment or exercise of power is inextricably linked to what politicians call image building. In *1 Henry IV* Prince Hal calculates how to exploit his reputation as a playboy: when he reforms, his dazzling image will enhance his authority. In *Troilus and Cressida* when Achilles and his Myrmidons slaughter Hector, Achilles orders a press release to be issued at once:

> So, Ilion, fall thou next! Come, Troy, sink down!
> Here lies thy heart, thy sinews, and thy bone.
> On, Myrmidons, and cry you all amain,
> "Achilles hath the mighty Hector slain!"
>
> (V.viii.11–14)[1]

The most pervasive themes in the plays dealing with issues of leadership concern the costs to society and to the individual of the pursuit of power. Richard III and Macbeth leave bloody destruction in their wake and end isolated from any life-sustaining human associations. Henry Bullingbrook (in *Richard II, 1 Henry IV* and *2 Henry IV*), in the course of overthrowing Richard II and seizing the throne as King Henry IV, steadily retreats behind a mask as if his public persona were achieved at the sacrifice of individual identity.

Shakespearean drama, like all good drama, has the capacity for vivifying issues in ways that nobly intentioned books like Gardner's cannot do. Gardner supports his generalizations with relevant anecdotes; Shakespeare commands attention by repeatedly dramatizing the collision of generalizations with concrete particulars. A notable example concerns Angelo, Duke Vincentio's deputy in *Measure for Measure*. Committed to the strict enforcement of Vienna's laws, he exposes his unpreparedness for applying legal principles when he and his colleagues are obliged to adjudicate a tavern dispute. Angelo quickly tires of the rambling testimony and leaves, "Hoping you'll find good cause to whip them all" (II.i.137). He impatiently dismisses the legal problem embodied by Elbow, Froth, and Pompey; but can a magistrate claim to understand justice while holding himself superior to the specific and messy appeals made by citizens daily?

Julius Caesar and *Coriolanus*, although they focus on remote periods of history, are especially relevant to American readers concerned with issues of leadership because they deal with forms of government more similar to ours than monarchy. More specifically, they explore the pressures that can cause a republic to disintegrate into either anarchy or totalitarianism. For many generations *Julius Caesar* was a standard text in American high schools, its relatively simple plot and its appeal to republican sympathies making it an appropriate introduction to Shakespeare. The story centers on the noble Brutus, who, alarmed by Caesar's monarchical ambitions, heads a group of conspirators who assassinate Caesar. Instead of liberating Rome from tyranny, however, the act results in chaos, civil war, and the loss of republican government. After the assassination, Mark Antony, Caesar's friend, first stirs the Roman people to riot and then forms an alliance with Octavius Caesar that ultimately crushes the forces led by Brutus and Cassius. On the eve of the crucial battle at Philippi, the ghost of Caesar appears to Brutus, who, recognizing his failure to quell the spirit of Caesarism, later commits suicide after his troops are outmaneuvered.

Coriolanus, like *Julius Caesar*, is derived from North's translation of Plutarch. Less familiar to American students, it focuses on an earlier period of Roman history when the commonwealth was threatened by internal dissension (the hungry commoners' demand for food) and attacked by the Volscians. Coriolanus, after subduing the external enemy, is rewarded by his fellow aristocrats with the nomination as consul. Temperamentally unable to submit convincingly to the customary ritual of courting public favor, he plays into the hands of the commoners' representatives who arouse the people to demand his banishment. In exile Coriolanus joins with Aufidius, the Volscian chieftain, determined to gain revenge by destroying Rome. He is deflected at the last moment, however, by an appeal from his strong-willed mother, and he agrees to negotiate a peace. Aufidius, jealous of his partner and enraged by his backsliding, has him murdered.

Each of these plays has at its center a leader motivated by his society's most cherished value, honor, but that value proves a source of weakness as well as strength. The two plays do not endorse Edmund's cynical view in *King Lear* that men "Are as the time is" (V.iii.31), but they do demonstrate how the mettle of leadership in time of crisis can be forged into a weapon destructive of self and society.

Furthermore, the crises are dramatized in ways that complicate our responses to the leaders' motives and tactics. Coriolanus' military valor helps to rescue Rome from Volscian threats, but on the home front his contempt for the people widens the gap between patricians and plebeians and hands the tribunes the pretext for stirring the plebeians into violent action. Brutus sees Caesar as aspiring not only to kingship, but also to the status of a god. Caesar's abuse of power is chillingly indicated early on when Brutus and Cassius learn from Casca that Murellus and Flavius "for pulling scarfs off Caesar's images, are put to silence"

(I.ii.285–86). Yet this man, who greets fellow politicians in II.ii in a ward-heeler's gladhanded manner, has an aura of greatness, boasting that in public affairs he is "constant as the northern star" (III.i.60), has brought glory to Rome, and in his will demonstrates beneficence to her citizens. Brutus convinces himself that Caesar is a clear and present danger, but his tactics contribute to mob violence, the emergence of a dictatorial triumvirate, and civil war.

A key word in Shakespeare's characterization of Brutus is mettle. Used twenty-eight times in seventeen plays,[2] mettle, according to the *Oxford English Dictionary*, functioned interchangeably with metal in Elizabethan English, the chief meanings being substance and temperament or disposition. The homonym metal/mettle permits a play on both meanings. Thus Regan tells Lear: "I am made of that self metal as my sister" (*Lr.*, I.i.69), and Angelo pleads to the Duke: "Let there be some more test made of my mettle" (*MM*, I.i.48). A similar play occurs in Cassius' monologue after Brutus exits near the end of I.ii: "Well, Brutus, thou art noble; yet I see / Thy honourable mettle may be wrought / From that it is dispos'd" (308-10). Cassius' phrasing, as Arthur Humphreys notes, indicates his belief that Brutus is an exception to "the alchemistical idea that noble metal (gold, silver) cannot be transmuted into anything inferior."[3]

Brutus' mettle is compounded of honor and reason. The descendant of the man who drove the last Etuscan king, Tarquin the Younger, from Rome, he frequently refers to his honor in the sense of public spiritedness, of the capacity for knowing what is best for Rome. To Brutus an honorable man is by definition also a rational man. An appeal to his honor and a reasoned justification of the assassination of Caesar form the basis of his speech to the citizens in III.ii. His idealistic motives prompt Antony's eulogy that he was "the noblest Roman of them all" (V.v.68).

Cassius quickly sees, however, that Brutus' mettle is not pure but is alloyed with egoism. Brutus is indeed honorable, but he is also proud of his reputation for being honorable. Early in his initial conversation with Cassius, he asserts in an unconscious parody of Caesar's boastful manner:

> What is it that you would impart to me?
> If it be aught toward the general good,
> Set honour in one eye and death i' th' other,
> And I will look on both indifferently.
>
> (I.ii.84–87)

Believing that honor confers superior judgment, he jumps on others' flaws, starting with his stuffy claim that he is not "gamesome" like Antony, a remark similar to Malvolio's "I am not of your element" (*Twelfth Night*, III.iv.124) and a prelude to his grievous underestimation of Antony's abilities. Equally telling is his reason for overriding Cassius' recommendation that Cicero be included among the conspirators: "O, name him not; let us not break with him, / For he will never follow anything / That other men begin" (II.i.150–52). Confidence in his superiority moves him to dismiss Cassius' hard-headed urging that Antony be killed along with Caesar and—later—that Antony not be permitted to address the public after Caesar's death. His sense of honor is seen in the least attractive light when he tries to hold himself above the sordid difficulties of the revolutionary movement by demanding funds from Cassius, who, unlike himself, can raise money by "vile means" (IV.ii.71).

Brutus has meditated on the problem of Caesarism before the play's action begins, and his soliloquy at the start of II.i shows him making a rational case for assassination:

> It must be by his death; and for my part,
> I know no personal cause to spurn at him,
> But for the general. He would be crown'd:
> How that might change his nature, there's the question.
> It is the bright day that brings forth the adder,
> And that craves wary walking. Crown him that,
> And then I grant we put a sting in him
> That at his will he may do danger with.
> Th' abuse of greatness is when it disjoins
> Remorse from power; and to speak truth of Caesar,
> I have not known when his affections sway'd
> More than his reason. But 'tis a common proof
> That lowliness is young ambition's ladder,
> Whereto the climber-upward turns his face;
> But when he once attains the upmost round,
> He then unto the ladder turns his back,
> Looks in the clouds, scorning the base degrees
> By which he did ascend. So Caesar may;
> Then lest he may, prevent. And since the quarrel
> Will hear no color for the thing he is,
> Fashion it thus: that what he is, augmented,
> Would run to these and these extremities;
> And therefore think him as a serpent's egg,
> Which, hatch'd, would as his kind grow mischievous,
> And kill him in the shell.
>
> (10–34)

As many critics have observed, however, his case is a rationalization. He starts with the conclusion ("It must be by his death"), admits that he has no specific indictment, and appeals to analogy rather than evidence: Human ambition is like the serpent's egg and must be destroyed before birth. "Fashion it thus"—his self-command—betrays that the argument is one fabricated against a man who trusts him.

One can sympathize with Brutus' inner struggle but be appalled by his naiveté. He never questions Cassius' motives or the provenance of the anti-Caesar letters planted in his home; Cassius works his mettle as readily as Antony works the mettle of the crowd at the Forum. Brutus' naiveté is bound up with his penchant for abstract thinking. Intellectually, he can firmly grasp the proposition that "Th' abuse of greatness is when it disjoins / Remorse from power," yet in one of the play's major ironies he cannot relate that insight to a bill of particulars against

Caesar or to the potential for abuse in others. In IV.i Antony and Octavius, in their cool review of their hit list, vividly embody the disjunction of remorse from power. Wishing that he could destroy the spirit of Caesar without shedding blood—because "in the spirit of men there is no blood" (II.i.168)—he concedes that Caesar must bleed for his wrongs. Yet what he envisions is a nice, clean murder—Caesar sacrificially carved as a dish fit for the gods—followed by the respect owing to his honor. Significantly his first utterance after the assassination is the abstract "ambition's debt is paid" (III.i.83). Although he urges his fellows to cry "Peace, freedom, and liberty!" (III.i.110), he offers the Roman populace no specific plan for government beyond a passing reference to "the commonwealth," and into the political vacuum he permits Antony to enter and do his mischief.

The introspective Brutus is the polar opposite of the impulsive Coriolanus, yet both are driven by an inherited sense of honor. Coriolanus' mettle is akin to Hotspur's; he is an honor-obsessed warrior as eager to engage in Volscian-bashing as Hotspur was to risk his troops at Shrewsbury, crying: "Die all, die merrily" (*1 H4*, IV.i.134). Although presumably more mature than Hotspur, Coriolanus exhibits a similar impetuosity and a similar drive to win honor "Without corrival" (*1 H4*, I.iii.207). Coriolanus may also remind readers of General George Patton, a good man to have on one's side in time of combat, but poorly endowed for civilian leadership. Both won great victories and both were intemperate. Patton slapped a shell-shocked soldier he accused of malingering; Coriolanus curses his men for retreating from Corioli: "You souls of geese / That bear the shapes of men .... All hurt behind, backs red, and faces pale / With flight and agued fear!" (I.iv.34–35, 37–38). At the end of World War II, Patton let it be known that he was ready to turn his tanks against the Russians; after his initial triumph over the Volscians, Coriolanus carries a field commander's "shape-up-or-ship-out" attitude into peacetime dealings with plebeians who complain of injustice. But Shakespeare's play is not a treatise on the limitations or inadequacy of military leadership when applied to civic issues; nor is it merely a variation on the theme that pride must have a fall. General Patton may have been arrogant; it is unlikely, however, that he would have ever switched his loyalty to the enemy. Coriolanus, the champion of Rome, transfers his allegiance to the enemy. Why so?

Two characteristics of Roman society are stressed: the patricians' desire to maintain their authority in face of the populist declaration that "The city is the people" (III.1.199) and their honoring of valor as the supreme Roman virtue. In the first scene Menenius tries to placate the hungry plebeians with his fable of the body and its parts, a fable that equates benign patricians with the belly, the organ that nourishes the body. Intended to legitimize the patricians' dominant role, the fable neither answers the commoners' immediate request for food nor indicates where the brains of the state are supposed to reside. Menenius prefaces his gentle chastisement with a threat that reflects the patricians' idea of their state as an irresistible force:

> ... you may as well
> Strike at the heaven with your staves as lift them
> Against the Roman state, whose course will on
> The way it takes, cracking ten thousand curbs

Of more strong link asunder than can ever
Appear in your impediment.
                                             (I.i.67–72)

   The patricians' decision (made shortly before the beginning of the play's action) to allow tribunes to speak for the people represents not an effort to understand the people or to create a more just society, but rather a concession intended to be a safety valve. As in *Julius Caesar*, the commoners, when presented as individuals, are usually perceptive and witty. In the opening scene one of them observes that Coriolanus fought not for his country but "to please his mother, and to be partly proud, which he is, even to the altitude of his virtue" (I.i.38–40); with equal shrewdness another tells Coriolanus when he solicits support for the consulship: "The price is, to ask for it kindly" (II, iii.75). But as a group they are fickle and easily exploited. The patricians, by distancing themselves from the people's problems and by allowing tribunes to serve as intermediaries, actually intensify the threat to order. Brutus and Sicinius, tribunes as interchangeable as Rosencrantz and Guildenstern, are uncouth in patrician eyes, but they rapidly seize the opportunity to increase their power by exploiting the people's unrest. Masters of political tricks, they stage-manage the public protest against Coriolanus, skillfully orchestrating the voices that demand his banishment. Coriolanus' inability to act in a conciliatory manner contrasts with the theatrical talents of the pair. His mother, Volumnia, shows more political astuteness in arguing that there is no necessary divorce between honor and policy; on the battlefield, she tells her son, it is sometimes necessary to deceive the enemy in order to win—therefore, why not preserve honor in peacetime by dissembling? In *Julius Caesar*, Brutus encourages himself and his followers to assume the roles of actors, only to be upstaged by a more gifted actor, Anthony; Coriolanus, true to his nature, is an inept actor.
   Menenius at least attempts to provide a rationale for the status quo, but one is struck by the paucity of ideas on the part of the aristocrats. In the only debate on governance, Coriolanus vehemently argues against dividing authority on the grounds that it will promote instability, but his case is as much temperamental as intellectual: Yielding power to the people will "bring in / The crows to peck the eagles" (III.i.138–39). The eagles' status is not to be challenged because it has been ratified by their valor.
   Closely following North's Plutarch, Shakespeare has Cominius, a Roman general, declare: "It is held/ That valour is the chiefest virtue and / Most dignifies the haver" (II.ii.83–85). The text, however, consistently undercuts positive connotations of valor. Although courage in defense of one's country is laudable, valor has become a life-denying obsession in Rome. Volumnia, about to greet her son on his triumphant return from battle, utters a death-worshipping couplet: "Death, that dark spirit, in 's nervy arm doth lie, / Which, being advanced, declines, and then men die" (II.i.160–61). The couplet echoes her earlier praise of her son's "bloody brow" as he slaughters enemies "Like to a harvest-man [that's] tasked to mow / Or all or lose his hire" (I.iii.36–37). The harvest image—doubly ironic in that the people are denied the fruits of a real harvest—shows how killing has become naturalized for the Romans; the shedding of blood comes to seem as natural for men as the shedding of tears for women. Cominius, in referring to a

battle as "this feast" at which Coriolanus had "fully din'd before" (I.ix.10–11), gives a cannibalistic twist to valor. The perverting effect of valor is further seen in the ways the battlefield supplies more satisfaction than the boudoir. During the fight at Corioli Coriolanus greets Cominius:

> O! let me clip ye
> In arms as sound as when I woo'd; in heart
> As merry as when our nuptial day was done,
> And tapers burned to bedward!
>
> (I.vi.29–32)[4]

This attitude is mirrored by his mother's: "If my son were my husband, I should freelier rejoice in that absence wherein he won honour than in the embracements of his bed where he would most show love" (I.iii.2–5). The Roman matron Valeria's approving description of Coriolanus' pre-adolescent son tearing a butterfly's wings grotesquely parodies the pervasive acceptance of the destructiveness implicit in valor.

Imbued with valor, Coriolanus is "a thing of blood" as Cominius calls him (II.ii.109), a machine that harvests corpses. His single-minded concern for attaining honor by the shedding of blood fatally blinds him to his own limitations. Raised by a mother ferociously dedicated to the perpetuation of the Roman ideal, he is motivated as an adult by a desire to please her. Like a pampered athlete, he assumes that his success in war excuses immature conduct off the playing field. When Volumnia anticipates his being named consul, he tells hers "Know, good mother, / I had rather be their servant in my way / Than sway with them in theirs" (II.i.202–04). The juvenile stubbornness expressed in "my way" is of a piece with the boyish self-consciousness that marks his disclaimers of pride in his wounds. His resistance to counterfeiting humility in order to win the plebeians' approval as consul is a form of affectation that is shrewdly discerned by a Roman officer: "Now, to seem to affect the malice and displeasure of the people is as bad as that which he dislikes, to flatter them for their love" (II.ii.21–23). When expelled from Rome, he transfers his talents to the enemy as readily as a professional athlete signs a contract with a once hated team, but he does so with an unprofessional attitude, telling Aufidius that he will destroy Rome "in mere spite" (IV.v.82).

As a leader Coriolanus exhibits a restricted range of ideas and tactics. Killing the enemy and scorning the commoners are reflex actions for him; his solitariness measures his limited self-knowledge. When banished from Rome, he defiantly asserts that he will find "a world elsewhere" (III.iii.135), but he cannot see that world as a social construct; it is merely an extension of his ego. The Coriolanus who in the play's fourth and fifth acts turns his back on Rome, "th' city of kites and crows" as he calls it (IV.v.42), is the same Coriolanus who ran "reeking o'er the lives" of Rome's enemies (II.II.119). The same types of images that characterized him as a Roman commander recur to describe him as a leader of the Volscians. Volumnia's industrious harvest-man is mirrored in Cominius' report that Coriolanus will not spare his former friends:

> His answer to me was,
> He could not stay to pick them in a pile

Of noisome musty chaff. He said 'twas folly,
For one poor grain or two, to leave unburnt
And still to nose th' offense.

(V.i.24–28)

Cominius, who praised the victor of Corioli as "a thing of blood," announces that Coriolanus leads the Volscians "like a thing / Made by some other deity than Nature," adding that they follow him "with no less confidence / Than boys pursuing summer butterflies, / Or butchers killing flies" (IV.vi.90–91, 93–95).

Coriolanus' vulnerability, however, is intensified as he pursues revenge. He cannot see that the Volscians are as fickle as the Romans and that their leader Aufidius, who embraces him with the same erotic intensity that Coriolanus embraced Cominius, will prove to be a jealous rival. But he is most vulnerable in his persistent denial of his human nature. Defining himself as "a lonely dragon" (IV.i.30), he seems to will himself to become more like a beast. Aufidius acknowledges that he fights "dragon-like" (IV.vii.23), and Menenius tells Sicinius that he "is grown from man to dragon: he has wings, he's more than a creeping thing" (IV.iv.12–14). He wills himself to "Break all bond and privilege of nature" (V.iii.25) as he prepares to resist his family's plea for mercy on Rome and ratifies his solitariness:

. . . . I'll never
Be such a gosling to obey instinct, but stand
As if a man were author of himself
And knew no other kin.

(V.iii.34–37)

Yet in yielding to his true author, Volumnia, in responding to her plea to save his family and his state, he reveals that he is not exempt from human bonds. His eyes "sweat compassion" (V.iii.196), the first and only time he weeps in the play. His yielding gives Aufidius the pretext he has been waiting for; stirring up his conspirators in a scene that recalls the tribunes' goading of the plebeians, he sets the stage for a reenactment of the charge of treason against Coriolanus. What stings Coriolanus most is Aufidius' contemptuously calling him "thou boy of tears" (V.vi.100. The compassion that he had felt vanishes as his ego asserts itself again. "Alone I did it" (V.vi.115), he shouts in reference to his victory at Corioli just before the conspirators stab him to death.

In both *Julius Caesar* and *Coriolanus* the protagonists' strengths are bound up with their weaknesses, and those strengths and weaknesses in turn are influenced by particular social contexts. From his distinguished ancestors Brutus inherits a sense of honor that motivates him to rescue Rome from a potential dictatorship, but honor becomes a prize that he seeks, and he grievously underestimates the prize's cost to Rome and to himself. Coriolanus is shaped by a society that exalts honor achieved by valor and neglects justice. He cherishes honor won on the battlefield, but his victories become personal trophies; his pride in these trophies contributes to his contempt for the people and fuels his dangerous sense of self-sufficiency. Both Brutus and Coriolanus illustrate how elusive self-knowledge is, and that elusiveness is at the heart of Shakespeare's examination of the mettle of leadership. At the end of Act III of *Measure for Measure* Duke Vincentio soliloquizes:

> He who the sword of heaven will bear
> Should be as holy as severe;
> Pattern in himself to know,
> Grace to stand, and virtue go;
> More nor less to others paying
> Than by self-offences weighing.
> Shame to him whose cruel striking
> Kills for faults of his own liking!
>
> (III.ii.261–68)

In context the Duke is criticizing the conduct of Angelo, but he is also questioning the depth of his understanding of the pattern in himself. Gardner emphasizes self-knowledge in all leadership training programs. "Somewhere, somehow, with all the courses, the extracurricular activities, the lessons learned from contemporaries, the help from wise elders, the young person must gain the necessary knowledge of self" (170). Shakespeare's plays yield no easily paraphrasable lessons or readily transferable wisdom, but at the very least they can make aspiring leaders appreciate how difficult it is to know the pattern in themselves.

Notes

[1] All quotations from the plays are from *The Riverside Shakespeare*.

[2] *The Harvard Concordance to Shakespeare*, 817. Nine of the twenty-eight usages occur in the *Richard II–Henry V* sequence, plays that offer a variety of perspectives on leadership.

[3] Introduction to The Oxford Shakespeare edition of *Julius Caesar* 118. The alchemistic metaphor works both ways. Casca, enjoined by Cassius to assist in persuading Brutus, says:

> O, he sits high in all the people's hearts;
> And that which would appear offence in us,
> His countenance, like richest alchymy,
> Will change to virtue and to worthiness.
>
> (I.iii.157–60)

[4] Aufidius, the Volscian leader, uses similar imagery in accepting Coriolanus as an ally:

> Know thou first,
> I lov'd the maid I married; never man
> Sigh'd truer breath; but that I see thee here,
> Thou noble thing, more dances my rapt heart
> Than when I first my wedded mistress saw
> Bestride my threshold.
>
> (IV.v.113–18)

WORKS CITED

Evans, G. Blakemore, ed. *The Riverside Shakespeare*. Boston: Houghton Mifflin, 1974.
Gardner, John W. *On Leadership*. New York: The Free Press, 1990.
Humphreys, Arthur, ed. *Julius Caesar*. Oxford: Clarendon Press, 1984.
Spevack, Marvin. *The Harvard Concordance to Shakespeare*. Cambridge, MA: The Belknap Press of the Harvard University Press, 1973.

The Study of Gender and Leadership: Points of Departure

Mary Kathryn Addis

When I was asked to write a paper about gender and leadership, I suspected, I think correctly, that what was intended was a paper about women and leadership. I also suspected that anyone turning to this paper for suggestions on how to incorporate gender into a seminar on leadership would likely be looking for appropriate ways to talk about and study women in leadership roles. Though talking about gender does not, of course, mean talking only about women, what research on gender has done in the various disciplines in which it has gained a foothold has been both to make women for the first time visible, and to make them visible in entirely new ways. We have knowledge now, for example, of women's participation in social and revolutionary movements, their presence in labor history, and their creative achievements as writers, artists, and musicians. This new knowledge about women goes beyond simply correcting for women's omission from previous research and far beyond seeing women only as victims of sexist beliefs and institutions; it documents as well the historical agency women have always exercised, and it reveals the complexly gendered nature of conventional measurements of achievement, including, certainly, achievements in leadership.

How properly to use "gender" as a critical term is, nevertheless, currently at the center of debate within feminist theory. In what follows, I want first to address questions related to the use of gender as an analytic category in order to lay the groundwork for a discussion of a series of texts about political leadership that treat and talk about gender in different ways. As we shall see, using gender as a conceptual tool in the study of leadership does not have to mean simply reserving time and space on the syllabus in order to study the careers of leaders who are women, though this should certainly be a part of the study. Second and equally important would be an examination of the ways in which gender exercises a legitimizing function in the sphere of political leadership. That the political leader's role in the United States is socially defined as a masculine role helps explain why so few women have held positions of political leadership. Other avenues of inquiry are also valid and necessary. For example, a study of feminist leadership—leadership in advancing emancipatory social transformation and sexual equality, whether the leaders be women or men—would contribute directly to what Sandra Harding sees as the purpose of social science research in women's studies, which is to produce knowledge of theoretical and practical value to women (1987, 8). A fourth line of inquiry might be a study of the ways in which the women's movement has itself successfully redefined the very concepts of politics, power, and leadership.

Gender as an Analytic Category

The contributions that gender can make to the study of leadership will depend on the kinds of questions asked. Joan W. Scott, Sandra Harding, and others, however, warn against just expanding the study of any given group of people to include women. Simply adding women cannot explain why women were previously excluded, cannot account for inequality, and invites essentialism, especially if the goal is to discover women's "difference." A well-known study that for Joan W. Scott does look for women's "difference" and as a result universalizes and normalizes the meaning of the category "woman" is Carol Gilligan's 1982 book, *In a Different Voice: Psychological Theory and Women's Development*.

Gilligan set out to study the experiences of those who had been excluded from mainstream research in order to challenge the validity and inclusiveness, in this case, of a dominant theoretical model of human moral development in the field of psychology. She claims that after years of listening to the ways men and women talk about their lives and the moral choices they were forced to make, she began to hear two different voices that expressed differently the processes by which moral decisions are reached. Though she writes in her introduction that she does not seek to generalize about sexual difference and though she claims that the two voices are distinguished more by theme than by gender, it remains clear that she is comparing a "feminine" with a "masculine" mode of reasoning and thinking about the relationship between self and other. What her study seeks to accomplish is the construction of an alternative model of development that characterizes female development more accurately than does the dominant model, which, as she demonstrates, was constructed solely on the basis of male experience. Countering previous assertions that many women are deficient in the area of moral growth because their ways of resolving moral conflict do not fit the pattern of the dominant model in the field, Gilligan concludes that it is the model itself that is deficient and biased because it fails to take women into account.

According to Scott, Gilligan's reliance on the unproblematized categories of "women" and "experience" is both a successful and a limiting strategy ("Experience" 1992, 24). It is successful because it exposes the exclusion of women and so exposes as false the claims to universality of the dominant model. The strategy is limiting because to take the category of women as a given and to talk about women's experiences and lives without questioning the meaning of the word "women" effectively naturalizes and universalizes the category itself. In this case, women's nature is presumed to be inherent and unchanging, and other social identities (e.g., those that pertain to race or social class) that distinguish women are erased.[1] Scott also points to the problem of circular reasoning, or what she calls "a slippage in the attribution of causality": "the argument moves from a statement such as 'women's experience leads them to make moral choices contingent upon contexts and relationships' to 'women think and choose this way because they are women'" (*Gender* 1988, 40). Experience explains gender difference and gender difference, in turn, explains the divergent experiences of women and men. This circular reasoning only reaffirms the idea of unalterable sexual difference.

What Joan W. Scott reads as circular reasoning, Judith Butler characterizes as a conflation or confusion of the referent (women) with the signified (what the word "women" means). Too often, according to Butler, the referent and the signified are taken to be the same thing when, in fact, they are not. The meaning of the word "women" is not transparent, nor even necessarily shared. The meanings of the terms of sexual difference vary historically and across cultures, and those meanings are not, therefore, natural and fixed, but socially constructed and so subject to change. Nevertheless, for Butler, "what women signify has been taken for granted for too long and what has been fixed as the 'referent' of the term has been 'fixed,' normalized, immobilized, paralyzed in positions of subordination" (1992, 16). For Butler and Scott, research that takes for granted what women signify creates within itself a theoretical impasse that makes it impossible to imagine how change might occur. Efforts, like Gilligan's, to establish some kind of feminine specificity, to give a specific content to the category of women, can lead to undesirable consequences. "Immobilization" can occur, for example, when womanhood is identified with motherhood, when feminine specificity is defined as maternal. Research that makes this kind of claim, even when motherhood is understood as a social rather than a biological function, not only ends up excluding all women who for whatever reason are not mothers but also leaves in place a definition of women that can create, perpetuate, and justify forms of gender discrimination. The equation of womanhood with motherhood, for example, deeply structures welfare policies in the United States, and, for this reason, as Nancy Fraser has clearly demonstrated, these policies discriminate against women.[2]

Scott cautions that we be more careful "about distinguishing between our analytic vocabulary and the material we want to analyze" (*Gender* 41).[3] She offers a two-part definition of gender that can be used to study the processes by which the meanings of sexual difference are created and acquire fixity in the first place. Her definition also allows for an analysis of a range of topics that are not usually considered to fall within the scope of research on sexual difference. "Gender," she writes, "is a constitutive element of social relationships based on perceived differences between the sexes, and gender is a primary way of signifying relationships of power" (42). The first part of her definition refers to "the understandings produced by cultures and societies of human relationships, in this case of those between men and women" (2). This part of her definition stresses that gender does not "reflect or implement" physical differences between the sexes, but instead "establishes meanings about bodily differences" (2). There is, she explains, "nothing about the body, including women's reproductive organs, [that] determines univocally how social divisions will be shaped" (2). "Gender," in this part of the definition, is clearly social in origin. Social organization is not built upon or derived from biological difference. Instead, society determines the meanings of biological difference, and it is these meanings which must be explained (2).

Gender has at its disposal symbols that express sometimes contradictory meanings, as in Scott's example of Eve and Mary as symbols of woman in the Western

Christian tradition (43). Different symbols express, in addition, normative concepts of gender identity and, as the term "normative" suggests, these concepts attempt to establish and limit the meanings that can be attached to any given symbol (43). The normative content of a symbol, its "fixed" meaning, comes out into the open when that content is challenged. This has occurred, for example, in some literary texts written by women who seek to redefine the symbols that have traditionally named them.[4] For Scott, "to disrupt the notion of fixity, to discover the nature of the debate or repression that leads to the appearance of timeless permanence in binary gender representation" (43) should also be the goal of feminist research. Normative or conventional meanings of the terms "woman" and "man" and "feminine" and "masculine" erase history and thus the processes by which specific meanings come to be seen as the only or the "natural" meanings of these terms. Alternative meanings are for this reason difficult to imagine and often remain out of reach.

GENDER AND THE LEGITIMIZATION OF POLITICAL LEADERSHIP

The second part of Scott's definition, the part that designates gender as a "primary field within which or by means of which power is articulated" (45), connects gender to social life generally. It highlights the ways in which gender is used to signify or symbolize relationships beyond those established between men and women or within the family. Of particular relevance to the topic of leadership are Scott's insights into gender's function as a socio-semantic field for signifying and symbolizing such diverse phenomena as national or international political relations. According to French anthropologist Maurice Godelier, "[i]t is not sexuality which haunts society, but society which haunts the body's sexuality. Sex-related differences between bodies are continually summoned up as testimony to social relations and phenomena that have nothing to do with sexuality. Not only as testimony to, but also testimony for—in other words, as legitimation" (quoted in Scott 1988, 45). Claims to power and political authority have, in other words, been legitimized by symbolic reference to biological difference.

Gender can legitimize in different ways. In my own field of Latin American literature, scholars have illustrated the diverse ways in which ideologies of gender are elaborated in what have come to be called "foundational fictions," novels that sought to participate in the process of national consolidation in Latin America after liberation from Spanish colonial rule. Many of the first "foundational fictions" drew a simple analogy between masculinity and the state (political authority, the rule of law), and between femininity and the national territory (the land, nature) that the nation state had the task of bringing under its authority and control.[5] This analogy reaffirms the traditional hierarchy of power built into the binary opposition between male and female: masculinity is associated with dominance and femininity with subordination. It is in this fashion that gender becomes implicated in the conception and legitimation of political power. According to Scott, "the significations of gender and power construct one another" (1988, 49).

The Study of Gender and Leadership: Points of Departure 85

That gender exercises a legitimizing function in the sphere of national political leadership in the United States can be demonstrated by examining different genres of political satire. One of the most striking instances of the use of gender for political satire that I have seen in recent years is the satiric postcard, "Unofficial White House Photograph," that was reproduced on the front cover of the Winter, 1988, issue of the journal *Critical Inquiry*. *(Figure 1)* The postcard presents a mock portrait of Nancy and Ronald Reagan standing in front of a window in the Oval Office. The postcard works its satire and communicates its disparagement of the leadership of the former President by means of a gender role reversal. Reagan's weakness as a leader is depicted as femaleness. The postcard puts the President's face on Nancy's petite and very "femininely" dressed body and puts Nancy's face on her husband's much larger and business suit-clad body. Assuming the conventional male position of the protector, Nancy embraces the smaller figure of the President as a husband might embrace his wife in a family portrait. The effect of incongruity is similar to that produced by those mock photographs taken at carnivals and fairs where you stand behind the cardboard cut-out of some faceless person or animal and acquire a picture of yourself with an identity that is not your own.

By means of the gender role reversal between husband and wife in the "Unofficial White House Photograph," the postcard both states and exploits a cultural equation of masculinity and political authority. The role of the national leader, the head of state, is a masculine one. If it were not, the postcard would fail as satire.[6] Femininity in this representation signifies a lack or deficiency. Femininity and masculinity are defined reciprocally and in a relation of hierarchy, and femininity, the negative term, means the absence of masculinity, the positive term. To satirize the former President and his leadership, all the designer of this postcard had to do was to characterize him as feminine. There was no need to point to any policy blunders or failures in his administration. The "decapitation and transposition" of the two individuals featured in the mock portrait do not, in my view, "drain gender of its power—as a guillotine drains a head of blood and oxygen" (Stimpson 1988, 227).[7] The postcard does not, at least to me, suggest that Nancy Reagan is in any way qualified to lead the nation because she assumes the male position in the portrait. The postcard simply says that Ronald Reagan is unqualified, a point further emphasized by the blurred image of the Washington Monument that appears behind the figure of Reagan, which represents an obvious phallic symbol intended to remind us, surely, of the masculinity of the founding father.[8]

Lest the "Unofficial White House Photograph" be seen as a unique case of identifying political authority and power with masculinity, professors teaching courses on leadership might ask students to examine a wider array of political cartoons for insight into how our culture construes gender and how it "genders" leadership roles. Public figures who are men can be satirized without reference to their sexual identity. That is, the exploitation of gendered imagery is not a necessary element in cartoons depicting male leaders. An exploitation of gendered imagery seems almost inevitable, however, in cartoons that depict women who have a strong public presence or who exercise power.[9] Students can compare the kinds of imagery used to satirize figures like Ross Perot and Dan Quayle with imagery satirizing Eleanor Roosevelt, Hillary Clinton, or even, incongruously, Christa McAullife.[10] The breaking of the boundaries thought to separate women's sphere from men's, the boundaries between private and public life, usually constitutes the basis of satiric portrayals of women who have or seek power, though other kinds of gendered imagery are also sometimes used.[11]

This can be seen very clearly in the editorial cartoons surrounding Geraldine Ferraro's nomination as the Democratic vice-presidential candidate in the presidential campaign of 1984. As Elaine K. Miller has demonstrated, these cartoons consistently and relentlessly foreground Ferraro's femaleness, her "otherness" with respect to the sphere of national politics. Even in the very few cartoons that Miller interprets as having been supportive of Ferraro's candidacy, the kinds of images and language the cartoonists use still "sabotage," in Miller's view, the intended positive message. One seemingly supportive cartoon, for example, shows Ferraro being handed an iron, with which she might be able to "iron out" the problems "Southerners" (in this case) had with a woman running for high public office (figure 1). Though the Southern gentleman who gives Ferraro the iron is presumably the target of this cartoon's satire, the very fact that Ferraro is given an iron, the fact that the cartoon identifies her as someone who can iron and so identifies her as a woman, can still be interpreted as a put-down. Femaleness, or any identification with the feminine, signifies, in all of the cartoons Miller analyzes, unsuitability for high public office. There is, to borrow a phrase from Nancy Fraser, a "conceptual dissonance"[12] between the role of the political leader and womanhood. Miller concludes her study by saying that there is very little positive imagery available for depicting female experience (1993, 387). I would draw a different conclusion: images of femininity, at least in our culture, do not work as symbols of leadership potential. Femininity, in fact, invalidates aspirations to a leadership role.[13] Images of motherhood or domestic labor can, in the context of the home and family, signify something positive, but they do not signify in the same way in the context of national politics, unless, of course, they are used to characterize the wives or mothers of male politicians. In the latter case, the wife's or mother's "femaleness" bolsters the masculinity of her husband or son.

That the political leadership role is a masculine one is conveyed clearly in the explicitly negative cartoons about Ferraro's candidacy. These unvaryingly portray Ferraro in domestic, romantic, or sexualized settings, especially when the question of the nature of her relationship with Mondale is made an issue. Metaphors of courtship and marriage abound, but the courting or marital relationship is often caricatured by some form of a gender role reversal. In one cartoon, the joining of the two candidates is presented as a shotgun wedding with the bride (Ferraro), in this case, holding the gun (figure 2); in another, they are newlyweds heading eagerly toward the door to the White House, though it will be the bride who carries the groom over the threshold (figure 3); in a third cartoon featuring the Republican opponents, Ronald Reagan hands George Bush another dress to try on in an effort to copy the new "Farrow look" (figure 4). These cartoons convey several messages. First and most obvious is the message that women are not suited to hold high elected office. Second, men who associate with women who exercise power put their own masculinity (read "power") in jeopardy.[14] Third and more specific to the Mondale-Ferraro campaign is the message that

Mondale gave in to "special interest groups" (i.e., women) by selecting a woman. The third message expresses the idea that a man would not normally select a woman as a running mate and suggests that there must have been something extraordinary about the situation (e.g., NOW has acquired too much power and influence; pandering to special interest groups was a way for Mondale to get votes, etc.) that explains Mondale's choice.

In any case, the humor of most of the cartoons depends on a reversal in the conventional relation of power between men and women. Mondale is frequently depicted as powerless vis-à-vis Ferraro, caricatured members of NOW, and even his own wife.[15] Exceptions to this reversal still sexualize the relationship between the two politicians. Two cartoons, for example, portray Mondale's search for a female running mate in terms of a man in a bar looking to score. The cartoons focus only on Ferraro's sexual identity, not her qualifications or lack of qualifications for the job. The cartoons all exploit a historically—and culturally—grounded incompatibility between political power or authority and womanhood.

Joan B. Landes argues that this particular kind of incompatibility in the West originated in the late eighteenth century, at a time when the divisions between private and public life, and between women's and men's spheres, in the modern sense, were created. In the early efforts to theorize the bourgeois democratic state, a desire to emancipate women as well as men from the tyranny of absolute monarchy ran up against a deep-seated belief that women and men possessed fundamentally different natures. Women were thought to be weaker, physically and intellectually, and less rational and more emotional and sensitive in character. Because of their reproductive capacity, women were also thought to be closer to nature. Men, therefore, according to the binary logic that usually governs the social construction of sexual difference, were associated with civilization and soon came to be seen as better suited to exercise the rights and responsibilities of citizenship in the modern bourgeois democratic state. The perception of immutable sexual difference was, of course, further reinforced in the eighteenth century by the growing separation of private from public life as capitalism evolved and as production left the home. For this reason and especially among the middle classes, the sexes were increasingly segregated. It was argued that women found self-realization within the private sphere of the home and family while men's arena for purposeful activity was public life, the sphere of paid labor and politics. The necessary distinction between private and public life was, in fact, a fundamental and deeply gendered component in the theorizing of bourgeois democracy. Politics came to be understood as coextensive with the public sphere, and private life came to be valued, at least from the perspective of the male theorists, as a kind of haven in a hostile and changing world, "a reassuring anchor to the now rapidly disappearing comforts of a more traditional social structure" (Landes 1984, 22).

The solution to the problem of women's emancipation within the new capitalist order took the form of a theory of republican or social motherhood. According to Landes, republican motherhood "provided the metaphor ... for a domestication of woman on the eve of her emancipation into society" (21). Rather than achieving the status of citizenship in their own right, women—at least women of the middle and upper classes—were confined to the new interior of the nuclearized bourgeois home within which their sole political role was to produce and nurture the citizens of the future. Women's separate nature justified their confinement, but in this age of egalitarian values they could not simply be labeled inferior. A further justification for the notion of separate but theoretically equal spheres was found in the bourgeois exaltation of sentiment and love. To the extent that women were perceived to be more sentimental and loving than men, they were also considered to be morally and spiritually superior. Their appropriate social role was to provide moral and spiritual support to the other members of the family, and the family as institution came to symbolize the moral center of the new social order. The very definition of the new public and private spheres therefore denied women any status as political subjects. If a woman was to exercise any political leadership, it was to be by example rather than by authority. As Chantal Mouffe has observed, the construction of modern citizenship on the basis of a separation of public from private life acted as a very powerful instrument of exclusion for women (1992, 378–379).

WOMEN AS POLITICAL LEADERS

Despite women's eventual acquisition of many of the rights of citizenship in many nations of the world, female political leaders are rare and female heads of state are more exceptional still. This exceptional quality is the basis for a collection of essays edited by Michael A. Genovese and entitled *Women as National Leaders*.[16] The book contains case studies of seven women elected to the highest executive office in their respective countries,[17] and the editor states in his introduction that he expects the case study approach to serve "as a preliminary step in theory building on gender and leadership issues" (1993, x). What Genovese seeks to discover is whether or not "gender has a causal relationship to style or substance in decision making" (8). He wants to find out, in other words, if women lead differently from men. A second consideration is the question of "what effect a woman's tenure in office had on definitions of gender in her society" (9), suggesting that a female president or prime minister might, in herself, have some positive impact on the way a given society constructs sexual difference.

The different case studies provide detailed and very interesting biographies of the individual women heads of state, but no theory on gender and leadership and very little information about women and politics generally. The best and most valuable chapter is the last one, which assesses the book's methodology, tactfully calls it deficient, and outlines a different approach to the study of this subject. This chapter, written by Patricia Lee Sykes, examines the conclusions Genovese himself draws in the preceding chapter and finds it fortunate indeed that Genovese is able to make few generalizations about the connections between the leader's gender and her leadership. Regarding the question of style, Genovese concludes that "no clear pattern (certainly no distinctively 'feminine' leadership style) emerges" (1993, 215). Neither is a clear pattern detected on the matter of policy preferences: "overall [the women heads of state] have tended to be spread across the ideological spectrum" (215). Even for someone with only a passing familiarity with the women leaders selected for study, these would not be surprising conclusions. I would not expect Margaret Thatcher to have much in common with, say, either Golda Meir or Corazon Aquino. The countries they led and the problems they faced were very different. Why, then, should the fact that the national leader was a woman be significant?

The flaw in this study is the very assumption of a feminine specificity, the notion that these leaders, because all of them happened to be women, should share some basic traits. As I have already indicated, the assumption of a feminine specificity works to naturalize and universalize the category of women and so leaves intact the notion of a natural and fixed opposition between women and men.[18] If we consider how difficult, if not impossible, it would be to make generalizations about male leadership, then why would it not be just as difficult and impossible to make generalizations about female leadership?[19] Why would female leadership permit generalization when male leadership does not? It would permit this only if one assumed at the outset that being a woman constituted some kind of limiting factor, if one assumed that a woman's sexual identity had a direct and determining influence on her leadership in a way that a man's sexual identity does not. Genovese, in fact, implies as much in his introduction:

> For the successful woman, the strategies she has developed and her style will *inevitably* be shaped and influenced by her society's definitions and expectations of gender. She will have learned, *consciously or not*, how to cope effectively with, and even turn to her advantage, the fact that she is a woman in "a man's world." The results of her interaction with her gender will not be seen in each decision she makes, or even necessarily be evident in any particular case. But a review of a range of decisions or her entire tenure in office *should* illustrate the relevance of gender to this leader at this point in her country's history.
>
> (7, emphasis added)

In this passage, as elsewhere in the introduction, the term "gender" is synonymous with "womanhood," and therefore "women leaders," because of gender's determining influence, are assumed to be somehow necessarily different from "leaders" without the prefix.[20] This is a questionable starting assumption that, fortunately, is not born out or proven in the case studies themselves.[21]

In her concluding essay, Sykes argues that Genovese's adaptation of the approach traditionally employed to study male leaders is inadequate as an initial step in theory building about gender and leadership because it has little or no explanatory value. Genovese merely adds "gender" to all the traditional variables (context, style, psychology, career, and agenda) and this only demonstrates, according to Sykes, that "many traditional notions about leadership (derived from the performance of men) apply to the experiences of women leaders" (225). Sykes proposes instead the adoption of a feminist perspective in which, presumably, gender would not function as simply one variable among others, but as the central and guiding analytic category. This analytic category should, I would add, carry all the theoretical sophistication and explanatory power Joan W. Scott gives it. Sykes does not provide the reader with a clearly delineated feminist methodology, but she does suggest several lines of inquiry. One would be the study of feminist (and female) heads of state, women who are "transformational leaders" and who therefore "can shed light on the capacity of women leaders to depart from tradition" (220) and redefine the very dimensions of political leadership. Her two examples are Gro Harlem Brundtland of Norway and Many Robinson of Ireland, both of whom successfully championed feminist issues, the former campaigning, for example, for the liberalization of abortion laws and the latter promoting reproductive freedom and the reform of family law. Neither woman was immune from criticism for taking feminist positions, but both succeeded in implementing a feminist agenda. This stands in startling contrast to the women leaders Genovese studies, none of whom, Genovese concludes, "challenged, in any fundamental way, the patriarchal power structure of her society" (217).

Sykes's criticism of the Genovese study and the alternative lines of inquiry she proposes illustrate three ways of articulating a relationship between gender and leadership. The most narrow approach, exemplified by Genovese, considers only the gender of the leader and assumes that this gender, especially if it is female, will have some kind of impact on that person's leadership. This is not a very productive strategy because it can, as in the Genovese case and as a result of the traditional methodology he employs, lead one either to conclude that gender is irrelevant or to conclude the obvious, that it is more difficult for women than for men to be elected to high political office. Genovese's superficial description of a gender hierarchy, which is limited to such comments as women live in "a man's world" (7) and women "remain outsiders and second-class citizens" (217), tells us little about how gender hierarchies are constructed and sustained in the first place and nothing about how they are contested.

The second way to articulate a relationship between gender and leadership is to examine the genderedness of the leadership role. My example was the political cartoon, a cultural product that both reflects and helps shape deeply gendered assumptions about legitimate and illegitimate political authority and power. Sykes also suggests inquiry along these lines. She suggests we query, for example, the gender implications of the term "Iron Lady," which the media used to characterize Margaret Thatcher and which Thatcher subsequently used to characterize herself. In this instance, for Sykes, "perceptions of leadership style prove more important than any 'objective reality' " (225–226). Though Thatcher was apparently proud of this appellation, the term "Iron Lady" could in the case of other women leaders "[transform] strength and determination (so admired in men) into rigidity and insensitivity (perceived as flaws in women)" (225). Women leaders are at the mercy of the media because assertiveness or ambition can so very easily be transformed, for popular consumption, into negative traits. It is the socially-constructed genderedness of the leadership role, itself contingent upon the organization of sexual difference within Western societies, that facilitates this kind of transformation.

The troublesome case of Margaret Thatcher merits further consideration, especially in light of the third way of articulating a relationship between gender and leadership: leadership in advancing gender and sexual equality. Although Genovese, the author of the Thatcher case study, acknowledges that Thatcher was hostile to "women's interests" (215), he does not analyze this aspect of her career, nor does her "hostility" prevent Genovese from concluding that Thatcher, unlike most of the other women leaders selected for study, "successfully" exercised political power (216). This prompts the question, success for whom and in terms of what criteria? Genovese works with a very individualistic concept of success: success means being able to wield influence, prevail over opponents, and win reelection (209).[22] A gender-sensitive reading of Genovese's case study would, I believe, raise a number of questions. These would include Genovese's own uncritical acceptance and repeated use of the term "Iron Lady" to characterize Thatcher in what is for him a positive light. A gender-sensitive reading would also uncover some gender stereotyping of the worst kind, both in Genovese's comments and in the comments of those he chooses to cite. One example should suffice. Genovese concludes that "the gender factor helped Margaret Thatcher" for the following reasons:

> From her early political rise, when the Conservatives needed "a woman," to her tenure as prime minister, Thatcher used gender issues [sic] with skill and cunning. She used her gender, sometimes relying on feminine wiles, sometimes as nanny, sometimes as bully, sometimes to coax, cajole, and flatter, but always calculatedly. As Young (1990) notes, "Without discarding womanhood, she has transcended it" (p. 312) (207).

A "wile" is "a trick or strategem to ensnare or deceive" (*Webster's Third New International Dictionary* 1981, 2616). The term "feminine wiles" captures the cultural stereotype of women as deceptive and not trustworthy and suggests that women get what they want by tricking men. Genovese's language, and the language of those he cites, is degrading to women. Why else, one may fairly ask, would "transcending womanhood" be thought of as some kind of achievement?

A feminist study of Thatcher would yield a very different picture from the one Genovese provides. Thatcher's hostility to women's interests extended beyond a rejection of feminism as a social movement to a steadfast pursuit of policies that, had they been fully implemented, would have had a direct and adverse effect on a large number of women, especially older and poor women and single women with children. One way to assess Thatcher's leadership from a feminist perspective[23] would be to consider her social welfare policies in light of the "welfare wars" and the femininization of poverty that have emerged, at least in part, as a consequence of the fiscal crisis of welfare state capitalism (Fraser 1989, 144–145). Thatcher's policy goal of sharply reducing welfare spending (Genovese 1993, 193) would, if Nancy Fraser's analysis of welfare capitalism is correct, have negatively affected more women than men because more women than men are clients of the welfare state (Fraser 1989, 132). A summary of Fraser's complex and compelling analysis of the U.S. welfare system is beyond the scope of this paper. Suffice it to note that, in her view, this system is not gender-neutral but two-tiered and that it positions men and women differently. The former are positioned as paid workers and the latter as unpaid mothers (133). All welfare capitalism does for women, according to Carol Brown, is to mark a shift in the character of male dominance, a change "from private patriarchy to public patriarchy" (quoted in Fraser 132). Welfare benefits "are system-controlling ones that reinforce rather than challenge basic structural inequalities" (Fraser 1989, 145) between the sexes.

Fraser's complexly argued analysis of the "gender subtext" of welfare suggests that a feminist study of Thatcher's leadership could legitimately focus on her social welfare policies.[24] I will not attempt to undertake such a study here. I merely note its absence in Genovese. Genovese's objective was to correct for the androcentric bias of traditional research on political leadership, with its "tacit assumption... that leaders are men" (1993, ix), by carrying out a study of women leaders. His research is weakened as much by the absence of any critical social theory as by the pitfalls associated with a separate treatment of women.[25] Genovese treats these women as exceptions to the rule but never questions that "rule," especially as it operates as an instrument of exclusion. More important, Genovese does not sufficiently take into account differences among women, and for this reason gender functions reductively in his analysis. He works with what Fraser and Nicholson call "unitary notions of 'woman' and 'feminine gender identity'" rather than with "plural and complexly constructed conceptions of *social identity*" that would treat "gender as one relevant strand among others, attending also to class, race, ethnicity, age, and sexual orientation" (429, emphasis added). Genovese too often talks about the woman leaders he studies as if they represented all women when, in fact, they represent only the elite. As a result, what Genovese studies is "elite political behavior" (Sykes 1993, 219) and the lessons to be learned from his study, Sykes argues, apply only to a consideration of the importance of the leader's gender within this very narrow sphere of political activity.

WOMEN'S MOVEMENTS REDEFINE LEADERSHIP

A feminist study of leadership would probably proceed differently and could focus on a range of issues not thought conventionally to fall within the boundaries of leadership studies. It might begin by redefining or reconceptualizing the very notion of leadership, especially the emphasis in conventional scholarship on the individual leader and on the binarism of leaders and followers.[26] Because feminist social theory is elaborated with the practical intent of emancipatory social transformation (Fraser 1989, 7), a feminist study would also likely privilege feminist leadership and might consider collective as well as individual action. It would not have to depend upon any single issue or methodology. Given the richness and breadth that feminist scholarship has already achieved in different disciplinary and interdisciplinary contexts, I would expect its contributions to leadership studies to be equally rich, opening up rather than foreclosing new lines of inquiry.[27]

As a way of concluding, let me cite two studies that investigate other dimensions of the relationship between gender and leadership. One is a chapter in Garry Wills study, *Certain Trumpets: The Call of Leaders*, devoted to the church leader Mary Baker Eddy. In contrast to Genovese and his unproblematized and unitary concept of woman and of the woman leader, Wills recognizes the significance a dominant historical definition of womanhood has for explaining Mary Baker Eddy's rise and prominence as founder and leader of the Church of Christ Scientist (Christian Science). It was in large measure in reaction to the dominant nineteenth-century view of women as spiritually strong and physically weak that Eddy worked out a theology and a philosophy of health that encouraged individuals, and especially women, to take control over their lives and take responsibility for their own health. Like some of the other new spiritualisms of the nineteenth century, Eddy's theology emphasized the mind's power to cure a sick body (1994, 178-179). This defied the authority of the medical establishment, especially its belief that women were more prone to illness than men. It also defied, as Wills demonstrates, that establishment's healing practices with regard to women, which often aggravated rather than cured illness (176).

Eddy's emergence as a church leader must be understood, then, in terms of the social definitions of sexual difference in vogue during her lifetime. Her work in founding a church was at least partially supported by the social emphasis on women's spirituality. Her belief that individuals are responsible for their own health and well-being, on the other hand, defied the social definition of women as physically weak and therefore subject to medical intervention. According to Wills, Eddy was not alone in her efforts to redefine and reclaim womanhood:

> One of the most interesting developments of the nineteenth century was the way some women took the dark room they were sealed into and made of it a powerhouse. . . . If they were to be the more "sensitive" gender, they would become sensitive to sources of power men did not guess at. Women mediums and spiritualists used their gifts to recover health and competence on their own, in defiance of male medicine (176).

In this passage, Wills clearly identifies the gender subtext[28] of Eddy's leadership role. Other chapters in the book *Certain Trumpets* also hint at the gender subtexts of different forms of leadership, but never so explicitly as in the case of Mary Baker Eddy.[29]

A second study that investigates the relationship between a social definition of gender and a particular kind of leadership is Jean Franco's essay "Going Public: Reinhabiting the Private," published in the anthology *On Edge: The Crisis of Contemporary Latin American Culture*. Among other recent developments in Latin American political culture, Franco comments on the social movement of the mothers of the disappeared in Argentina. The mothers' public protest of the disappearance of their children was especially remarkable because these women acted, according to Franco, within the context of a culture of fear created by military dictatorship, a culture in which all public political activity had been banned and in which citizenship was officially and practically defined as unquestioning loyalty to the regime. By demonstrating in the public space of the Plaza de Mayo, "the symbolic center of the nation" (Franco 1992, 67), these women were able both to redefine citizenship and to erase the boundaries separating the private from the public in the following ways. They used their marginal status, Franco argues, "to reclaim the *polis* . . . . They created an Antigone space in which the rights (and rites) of kinship were given precedence over the discourse of the state" (67). Their struggle, Franco notes in another essay ("Gender" 1992, 112), was necessarily ethical, "an affirmation of life and survival" ("Gender" 116), and an attempt to restore meaning to individual lives in a climate of terror and violence and in a historical context in which the home could no longer symbolize for the middle classes a haven safe from the intrusion of the state.

Some scholars, Franco observes, have essentialized this mothers' movement by interpreting it as an example of "maternal thinking," as action, that is, in keeping with women's traditional roles as mothers.[30] But Franco argues that these women, on the contrary, "substantially altered tradition by casting themselves as a new kind of citizen" (67). Their effective use of symbols (e.g., blown-up pictures of family members who had disappeared) undercut the regime's proclamation of itself as the protector of the family and the nation by exposing how the military had destroyed the very private sphere that it claimed it defended. As individual testimonies demonstrate, women's participation in this social movement politicized them to a degree they had never known. By demanding that the government disclose information, the women claimed the right to be heard, the right to participate in political debate, and hence the rights of citizenship. The movement, a case of collective rather than individual leadership, was very effective. The mothers were the only group in Argentina that, during the dictatorship, was able to challenge military authority successfully, and it did so by drawing national and international attention to human rights abuses. The movement has also, according to Franco, permanently changed the way we think about culture and politics in Latin America ("Gender" 115). Like Mary Baker Eddy, these women were able to transform what has traditionally been seen as weaknesses of womanhood into strengths. In the process, they became "women" in a different sense. They collectively established for themselves a new political identity and public role no longer predicated on the old separation of private from public life. Their example points to another dimension in the relationship between gender and leadership. It highlights the ways in which social groups excluded from power and from the decision-making processes of their society can contest the social roles to which they have been assigned and assume a new role of their own definition. The actions of the mothers of the disappeared had the effect of releasing the terms "woman" and "mother" from their old and fixed referents and resignifying them in such a way as to make "women" and "mothers" agents of political change.

NOTES

[1]By offering an alternative "feminine" model of development, argue Nancy Fraser and Linda Nicholson, Gilligan "invited the same charge of false generalization she had herself raised . . . though now from other perspectives such as class, sexual orientation, race and ethnicity" (1993, 427). Fraser and Nicholson regard Gilligan's work as important, but nevertheless cite it as an example of the ways in which "vestiges of essentialism have continued to plague feminist scholarship" (427).

[2]See pages 129–137 and Chapters 7 and 8 of *Unruly Practices*.

[3]All citations having to do with Scott's definition of gender as an analytic category are taken from her book, *Gender and the Politics of History*.

[4]Several of the Argentine writer Luisa Valenzuela's earliest short stories deconstruct, through irony, traditional symbols of woman. See, for example, "Trial of the Virgin," published in *Open Door* (1988, 172–79).

The Study of Gender and Leadership: Points of Departure 95

⁵See the essays by Mary Louise Pratt (1990) and Doris Sommer (1986).

⁶It is likely that the satire does fail for those viewers who recognize its disparagement of women.

⁷This is Catharine R. Stimpson's interpretation of the image in an essay that appears in the same issue of *Critical Inquiry*. The portion of the essay in which she refers to the postcard addresses the issue of the representation of women in our culture. She discusses the often vicious and misogynistic portraits of women found in the media, literature, history, medicine, and so forth, arguing that one of feminism's tasks is to change the cultural representation of women. Doing so, she suggests, "can change politics, even if that change seems marginal and unpredictable" (1988, 227). She refers to the postcard as a "different" representation, but she does not explain or provide evidence for this assertion except to say that the postcard was one feminists liked to send to each other. I doubt Stimpson speaks here for all feminists. As I have argued, the irony or satire of the image in question depends for its effect on a very stereotypical and misogynistic representation of gender difference.

⁸I should point out that the postcard image is not a photomontage. The faces of the two individuals do appear to come from photographs, but the rest of the picture is clearly a drawing made to look like a photograph. Hence the silly, overly-frilly blouse and the bow-adorned skirt to which Ronald Reagan's head is attached. This was not the apparel of the former First Lady. The business suit to which Nancy Reagan's head is attached, on the other hand, is not a caricature. It is a conventional man's suit, one that any male politician might wear. The American Postcard Company, Inc,. which orginally printed and sold the "Unofficial White House Photograph" postcard, is now under new ownership and was unable to grant permission to reprint this satiric portrait.

⁹This point is made repeatedly in the book *Stereotypes of Women in Power* (1992), an excellent collection of essays that study the ways in which female power has historically been interpreted. The essays cover a wide range of subjects, from Aristophanes's portrayal of "political women" (an oxymoron in his comedies) to two twentieth-century murder cases in which evidence against the alleged female murderers drew, in one case, on the notion of women as domineering and scheming and, in the other, on the stereotype of woman-as-witch. In both cases, the stereotype invoked notions of female power, power that is almost by definition illegitimate and dangerous.

¹⁰In her study of political cartoons featuring Geraldine Ferraro, Elaine K. Miller also examines "joke cycles," a genre of social and political commentary that enjoys a greater freedom of expression than the political cartoon because of its anonymity. A study Miller cites (1993, 391 n 4.) of the joke cycle surrounding the explosion of the space shuttle Challenger on January 28, 1986, points out the particularly cruel ways in which Christa McAullife was singled out, partly because she was not an astronaut, but mainly because she was a woman. See Elizabeth Radin Simons, "The NASA Joke Cycle: The Astronauts and the Teacher" (1986).

¹¹See, for example, Pierre Saint-Amand's essay "Terrorizing Marie Antoinette" for a discussion of how "the fear of women in power" (1994, 379) gets translated into what he calls a language of infamy (379). Saint-Amand compares eighteenth-century French caricatures of Marie Antoinette—these were partly responsible, he believes, for sending her to the guillotine on 16 October 1793—with caricatures of Hillary Clinton. The similarities he discovers—immorality or lasciviousness, for example, as a means of usurping power—are startling.

¹²Fraser uses this phrase repeatedly in *Unruly Practices* to draw attention to the masculine subtext of different social roles.

¹³As a couple of case studies in the Genovese collection *Women as National Leaders* prove, there are some very special historical and political circumstances in which the

femininity of a woman presidential candidate can be exploited, to her advantage, in an electoral campaign. This was the case with the election of Violeta Chamorro and Corazon Aquino to the presidencies of their respective nations, Nicaragua and the Philippines. I maintain, however, that these circumstances are exceptional and that the promotion of the "feminine" identity of the woman candidate (e.g., her status as the wife of a slain opposition leader or a too-easy equation of womanhood with the values of peace and justice) does not significantly challenge notions of separate spheres or the identification of political authority with masculinity. For details on the two cases I cite, see the relevant chapters in Genovese.

[14]There is one cartoon that, like the "Unofficial White House Portrait," boasts a tall and smug-looking Ferraro dressed in a man's business suit and towering over a defeated-looking Mondale dressed in a woman's suit (fig. 17.18).

[15]One cartoon (fig. 17.17) pictures a sheepish-looking Mondale getting home late at night. His wife, in curlers and brandishing a rolling pin, suggests that his claim that he was out "offering some woman the vice presidency" would not make an acceptable excuse for his failure to return home at an earlier hour.

[16]I wish to thank Carolyn Durham, former Chair of the Program in Women's Studies at The College of Wooster, for bringing this book to my attention.

[17]The national leaders studied are Corazon Aquino (the Philippines), Benazir Bhutto (Pakistan), Violeta Chamorro (Nicaragua), Indira Gandhi (India), Golda Meir (Israel), Isabel Perón (Argentina), Margaret Thatcher (Great Britain).

[18]In her conclusion, Sykes makes the same observation: "The search for similarities among women as national leaders occurs [in this study] in the context of fundamental contrasts between men and women, which places women in opposition as "the other" (1993, 228).

[19]Sykes makes this point in her conclusion (224).

[20]In a book that examines critically the kinds of basic conceptual errors that too often characterize the construction of knowledge and that have the effect of excluding and/or devaluing whole groups of people, Elizabeth Kamark Minnich argues that the use of prefixes as in, for example, "women's literature," "homosexual life styles," or "Black music," often serves to designate the non-universal, the particular, and hence the "less good" and the "less significant" (1990, 43). In order to understand how such prefixes work, one need only consider those instances where prefixes are not used and would be strange if they were, as in, to cite Minnich's example, "the white male philosopher Kant" (43). The use of prefixes in other cases represents philosophers of the other sex, or of other races, as special categories that depart from the norm and so they "are improperly judged because they are placed against standards, closed within contexts and discourses, that not only did not include them in the first place but were founded by people who thought they *ought* to be excluded" (43).

[21]Donna S. Sanzone's "Women in Positions of Political Leadership in Britain, France and West Germany" is one study that finds that women in positions of political leadership do tend to promote legislation and initiatives whose goal is to advance women's legal rights. This study does not compare women and men, does not look for distinctive leadership styles, and examines careers of women who for the most part held cabinet-level positions in three Western European nations. Margaret Thatcher is cited as the significant exception to the rule. Karen L. Tamerius's "Sex, Gender, and Leadership in the Representation of Women" also argues that the leader's gender matters, at least in state legislatures and Congress, when it comes to assessing women's "feminist" impact on policy. This impact is measured in the areas of agenda setting and policy formation. It cannot be gauged by roll call voting. Tamerius finds that women legislators represent women's interests in other ways, in the areas of agenda setting and policy formation

[22]Genovese is thus able to end his chapter on Thatcher with the following remarks: "Margaret Thatcher was a revolutionary leader, not simply because she was a woman, not simply becaue she was a powerful woman, but because she was these things and more. She governed for a dozen years, won almost all of her major policy goals, and vanquished her opposition. . . . She used her opportunities wisely and well, and seized power. As Webster (1990) says, there was 'not a man to match her' " (1993, 209).

[23]An assessment of Thatcher's leadership from the perspective of race and class would also be necessary in order to provide a more complete picture of the social impact of her tenure in office.

[24]Fraser, in fact, cites Thatcherism in her discussion of the contemporary debates over welfare (1989, 172–173).

[25]The danger of treating women as a separate category, as special cases, is that it can, according to Joan W. Scott, "serve to confirm [women's] marginal and particularized relationship to those (male) subjects already established as dominant and universal" (1988, 3).

[26]For a discussion of the ways in which the women's movement has itself redefined the concepts of politics (it includes the personal), power (empowerment instead of power over), and leadership (the movement's "emphasis on local control and autonomy," its "relating theory to practice," and its "discouraging forms of . . . leadership which make others feel inadequate or uninvolved") [Wainwright 1984, 181], see, for example, Hilary Wainright's "Beyond Leadership."

[27]For a feminist review of literature on leadership that focuses on this literature's inattention to gender, see Duerst-Lahti and Kelly's Introduction to *Gender Power, Leadership, and Governance*. Except in the introduction, this book does not look at the leadership of heads of state but instead at the level of U.S. state legislatures and Congress.

[28]I borrow the phrase "gender subtext" from Nancy Fraser (*Unruly Practices*).

[29]Often the gender subtext is only implicit. For example, though Wills never talks about military leadership as masculine, his otherwise consistent use of the inclusive "he and she" elsewhere in the text breaks down in the chapter on military leadership. The military leader is always referred to as a "he," though, interestingly, a follower at one point is referred to as a "he or she" (85). The masculine character of military leadership is derived from what Mary Louise Pratt (1990, 50–52) and Nancy Fraser (1989, 126) call the "soldiering" component of the citizen role. Fraser discusses this component to argue that citizenship itself is bound up with masculinity: "the soldiering aspect of citizenship," she writes, explains "the conception of the citizen as the defender of the polity and the protector of those—women, children, the elderly—who allegedly cannot protect themselves" (126). Pratt similarly argues that the modern nation-state is androcentrically "imagined": "military service and electoral politics, domains originally limited to males, have been central apparatuses for producing the imagined community " (50). Women had to struggle to obtains the rights of citizenship. One right that they have rarely claimed, however, is "the right to die for one's country" (52). Pratt explains this by observing that in Latin America "women's political and social engagement became heavily *inter*nationalist, and often *anti*nationalist" (52). In the European context, Virginia Woolf's *Three Guineas* remains a classic expression of this internationalism/antinationalism.

[30]An example of this kind of interpretation of the movement, one that Franco cites, is Sara Ruddick, "Maternal Peace Politics and Women's Resistance: The Example of Argentina and Chile."

Works Cited

Butler, Judith. "Contingent Foundations: Feminism and the Question of 'Post-modernism'." Butler and Scott, 3-21.
Butler, Judith, and Joan W. Scott, eds. *Feminists Theorize the Political*. London: Routledge, 1992.
Duerst-Lahti, Georgia, and Rita Mae Kelly, eds. *Gender Power, Leadership, and Governance*. Ann Arbor: University of Michigan Press, 1995.
Franco, Jean. "Gender, Death, and Resistance: Facing the Ethical Vacuum." *Fear at the Edge: State Terror and Resistance in Latin America*. Eds. Juan E. Corradi, Patricia Weiss Fagen, and Manuel Antonio Garretón. Berkeley and Los Angeles: University of California Press, 1992. 104-118.
———. "Going Public: Reinhabiting the Private." *On Edge: The Crisis of Contemporary Latin American Culture*. Eds. George Yúdice, Franco, and Juan Flores. Minneapolis: University of Minnesota Press, 1992. 65-83.
Fraser, Nancy. *Unruly Practices: Power, Discourse and Gender in Contemporary Social Theory*. Minneapolis: University of Minnesota Press, 1989.
Fraser, Nancy, and Linda Nicholson. "Social Criticism without Philosophy: An Encounter between Feminism and Postmodernism." *Postmodernism: A Reader*. Ed. Thomas Docherty. New York: Columbia University Press, 1993. 415-432.
Garlick, Barbara, Suzanne Dixon, and Pauline Allen, eds. *Stereotypes of Women in Power: Historical Perspectives and Revisionist Views*. New York: Greenwood Press, 1992.
Genovese, Michael A., ed. *Women as National Leaders*. Newbury Park, CA: Sage, 1993.
Harding, Sandra. "Is There a Feminist Method?" *Feminism and Methodology: Social Science Issues*. Ed. Sandra Harding. Bloomington: Indiana University Press, 1987. 1-14.
Landes, Joan B. "Women and the Public Sphere: A Modern Perspective." *Social Analysis* 15 (1984): 20-31.
Miller, Elaine K. "Politics and Gender: Ferraro in the Editorial Cartoons." *Feminist Theory and the Study of Folklore*. Eds. Susan Tower Hillis, Linda Pershing, and M. Jane Young. Urbana and Chicago: University of Illinois Press, 1993. 358-395.
Minnich, Elizabeth Kamark. *Transforming Knowledge*. Philadelphia: Temple University Press, 1990.
Mouffe, Chantal. "Feminism, Citizenship, and Radical Democratic Politics." Butler and Scott. 369-384.
Pratt, Mary Louise. "Women, Literature, and National Brotherhood." *Women, Culture, and Politics in Latin America*. Seminar on Feminism and Culture in Latin America. Berkeley and Los Angeles: University of California Press, 1990. 48-78.
Ruddick, Sara, "Maternal Peace Politics and Women's Resistance: The Examples of Argentina and Chile." *Barnard Occasional Papers* (Barnard Center for Research on Women, New York) 4.1 (1989).
Saint-Amand, Pierre. "Terrorizing Marie Antoinette." *Critical Inquiry*. 20.3 (1994): 379-400.
Sanzone, Donna S. "Women in Positions of Political Leadership in Britain, France and West Germany." Siltanen and Stanworth. 160-175.
Scott, Joan W. "Experience." Butler and Scott, 22-40.
Scott, Joan Wallach. *Gender and the Politics of History*. New York: Columbia University Press, 1988.
Siltanen, Janet, and Michelle Stanworth, eds. *Women and the Public Sphere: A Critique of Sociology and Politics*. New York: St. Martin's Press, 1984.
Simons, Elizabeth Radin. "The NASA Joke Cycle: The Astronauts and the Teacher." *Western Folklore* 45 (1986): 261-277.

Sommer, Doris. "Not Just Any Narrative: How Romance Can Love Us to Death." *The Historical Novel in Latin America*. Ed. Daniel Balderson. Gaithersburgh, MD: Ediciones Hispamérica, 1986. 47–73.

Stimpson, Catharine R. "Nancy Reagan Wears a Hat: Feminism and Its Cultural Consensus." *Critical Inquiry* 14.2 (1988): 223–243.

Sykes, Patricia Lee. "Women as National Leaders: Patterns and Prospects." Genovese, 219–229.

Tamerius, Karin L. "Sex, Gender, and Leadership in the Representation of Women." Duerst-Lahti and Kelly, 93–111.

Valenzuela, Luisa. *Open Door*. Trans. Horntense Carpentier et al. San Francisco: North Point Press, 1988.

Wainwright, Hilary. "Beyond Leadership." Siltanen and Stanworth. 176–182.

Webster's Third New International Dictionary. 1981 ed.

Wills, Garry. *Certain Trumpets: The Call of Leaders*. New York: Simon & Schuster, 1994.

Figure 1 Cartoon: Don Wright, "Ironing out Problems"
© Tribune Media Services, Inc. All Rights Reserved. Reprinted with permission.

Figure 2 Cartoon: Tom Meyer, "Shotgun Wedding of Ferraro and Mondale"
Tom Meyer/San Francisco Chronicle. Reprinted with permission.

Figure 3 Cartoon: Tom Meyer, "The Bride Carries the Groom over the Threshold"
Tom Meyer/San Francisco Chronicle. Reprinted with permission.

Figure 4 Cartoon: Oliphant, "The Ferraro Look"
© 1984 Universal Press Syndicate. Reprinted with permission.

Wandering in the Arabian Desert with George Bush: A Study in Presidential Leadership

Eric S. Moskowitz

Judgments about presidential leadership are often based on the notion that leadership is simply the ability to persuade others. By emphasizing the leader-follower dichotomy, political analysts all too often judge good leadership to be the ability to move followers in the direction the leader wishes. Richard Neustadt, in his justly famous treatise on presidential leadership, *Presidential Power*, argues that persuasion is the essence of presidential power. Kellerman and Barilleaux in their analysis of presidential leadership in world affairs stipulate that ". . . the issue is not whether our presidents are wise, clever or just. Rather, the focus is on their ability to get others to follow where they lead" (1991, vii).

Political power does have a role to play in the construction of our understanding of leadership, but good leadership requires more than the ability to influence the actions of others. Ultimately, judgments about good leadership must also take into account the wisdom and moral basis of the leader's action. Is the action based on a reasonable understanding of the opportunities and threats faced by the leader's organization? Is there a reasonable relationship between the costs imposed on some people and the gains made by others?

Conversely, a case where a leader made a wise decision, but then made an ill-conceived effort to gain the necessary support for implementing it would also fail to qualify as an instance of good leadership. A good leader must not only make the proper policy decision, but then appropriately and astutely use persuasion, authority, and power to muster the necessary support for the decision.

Recognition of this multifaceted conception of leadership can be found in some of the literature on foreign policy decision-making. For instance, Alexander George, in discussing the dilemmas of presidential decision-making, notes the tradeoff that exists between striving for high quality decisions which protect the national interest and striving for consensus and support for those decisions (1990, 1-4). Similarly, Greenstein and Burke, in their comparative analysis of decision-making on Vietnam in the Eisenhower and Johnson administrations, suggest that presidential leadership has two basic components: the substantive ability to analyze policy issues and the political skill to gain the support of others for the policy decision (1989-90, 572).

The essay that follows will build on the argument that the quality of the decision-making process must be included in a comprehensive evaluation of presidential leadership. The themes developed in the presidential decision-making literature will be used to evaluate the leadership of George Bush during the Persian Gulf Crisis of 1990. Toward this end, several preliminary tasks must be completed. First, one needs to consider requisites for a high quality decision-making process. What procedures need to be at least approximated for there to be a careful decision process? Second comes a consideration of the personal, organizational, and bureaucratic factors that affect the quality of the presidential decision-making process. Lastly, one needs to discuss briefly these relevant decisional factors in the personal and institutional presidency of George Bush. Only then can one move on to evaluate the leadership of Bush during the Persian Gulf Crisis.

Defining a High Quality Decision Process

A high quality decision process (HQDP) does not guarantee that the outcome of a decision will be satisfactory. Presidential decision-making takes place in a highly complex and uncertain environment. Important presidential decisions, of necessity, must be made without full information, and presidents do not control all factors necessary for a successful outcome. Nonetheless, an HQDP substantially increases the probability that the outcome will be positive. Pure rationality is not a requisite for an HQDP. Political scientists have long recognized that the standard for a perfectly rational decision is beyond the capacity of human decision-makers (Steinbrunner 1974).

A number of factors make this standard impossible. The decision-maker's value structure is too complex either to recognize all the values at stake in any significant political decision or to calculate precisely the tradeoff relationships among these many values. Furthermore, the situation will often be too uncertain. The decision-maker cannot be certain of the consequences of any of the options considered. There are simply too many unknowable variables involved. Even if all the necessary information about both the values and the environment could be gathered, the cognitive capabilities of human decision-makers are insufficient to handle so many data. Many of these factors are further exacerbated if decision-making takes place within a group rather than coming from a single decision-maker.

In place of these standards of pure rationality, analysts of political decision-making have begun to develop a more limited standard of effective decision-making. Irving Janis suggests several guidelines for an effective decision process:

1) extensive survey of goals and values at stake in a decision;
2) consideration of a wide range of options to achieve goals;
3) intense search for information relevant to the options;
4) careful risk/benefit analysis of the consequences of the options;
5) contingency planning for implementation under various conditions.

Tolerance, reconsideration, and flexibility are central to Janis' conception of effective decision-making. A wide variety of information and perspectives must be admitted to the decision process. Initially favored options and positions must be reconsidered. Decision-makers must strive to see the flaws in their initial choices. Contingency plans must be made for unexpected failures in the implementation of their chosen option (1982, 10 and 1989, 89–96).

Constraints on High Quality Decision-Making

Even these reduced requirements for effective decision-making can be quite daunting, particularly in complex and uncertain policy situations. Analysts of political decision-making have noted a series of personal, organizational, and bureaucratic constraints that limit the ability of government officials to achieve the standards of HQDM.

Personal Constraints

Because the institution of the presidency is dominated by a single person, the psychological dynamics of individual presidents can have a significant impact on the functioning of that institution. As a result, scholars often consider the impact of presidential psychology on the office. These psychological concerns can be broken into two broad categories—emotive and cognitive constraints.

A number of analysts have attempted to explore the impact of personality structure on the performance of policy makers, in general, and presidents, in particular. Decision-making is affected by the emotional state of policy-makers. James David Barber maintains that levels of self-esteem help shape presidential character (1992, 8–11). Only presidents with high levels of self esteem are regularly able to make effective decisions under a wide variety of circumstances.

More generally, Janis argues that effective decision-making can be constrained by emotional needs arising from fear, anger, frustration, shame, or guilt. "Whenever a person uses an emotive rule to make a decision, he or she, in effect, is allowing emotional reactions to play a guiding role in deciding what to do" (1989, 71). Emotion-based decision-making is even more likely under conditions of high stress where the problem has no readily available solution and where there is a high risk for personal blame with an ensuing loss of self esteem.

Janis describes a series of emotive rules that policy makers often invoke to relieve emotional stress during the decision-making process (1989, 70–80). Cognitive efficiency is lost as emotive rules of decision-making are employed to avoid the growing psychological pressure. Values, options, costs, and benefits are not carefully considered. Instead, the decision-maker may seek to avoid the pressure by procrastinating or passing the buck on the issue, by choosing the first option that superficially appears to respond to the problem, or by using gut reactions to dispense quickly with the problem.

In response to frustration or humiliation, the policy-maker may rapidly and excessively retaliate against the apparent source of the frustration. Decision-makers who pride themselves on being courageous may, in stressful situations, feel compelled to choose high-risk policy options to avoid the accusation of a lack of nerve. All these emotive rules or responses share the common danger that careful consideration of the decision is unconsciously constrained by the decision-maker in an attempt to meet his emotional needs.

The amount of information-processing required under conditions of complexity and uncertainty is simply beyond human capacity. Scholars have begun to explore the techniques frequently used by decision-makers to simplify complex cognitive tasks. While these cognitive shortcuts are essential for coping with the otherwise unmanageable burden of complex political decisions, they also can, on occasion, lead to faulty decision-making.

In his exploration of the cognitive approach to foreign policy-making, Alexander George focuses on two themes: the policy maker as either "consistency seeker" or "problem solver" (1980, 56–66). The problem solving approach views policy makers as naive scientists seeking to solve problems in a reasonable manner within the bounded limits of human information-processing capacity. The problem solver seeks: "(1) to discern the attributes of actors and social phenomena; (2) to infer the causes of salient events; and (3) to predict historical trends and the behavior of other persons." (57). However, in the attempt to accomplish these tasks, the policy-maker often uses a naive epistemology, ridden with flaws and biases.

The fundamental attribution error made by policy makers is a tendency to overemphasize situational variables when explaining their own behavior, but to use dispositional (personal) variables to explain others' behavior, particularly when the other's behavior is blameworthy. Another frequent attribution error is to overlook the non-occurrence of events when trying to explain situations or the behavior of others.

Researchers have also explored a number of heuristics or rules of thumb used by policy-makers to simplify the decision process. Policy-makers may simply adopt the first already-existing standard operating procedure that seems to satisfy the minimal requirements of the situation. Or similarly, they may adopt an incrementalist's approach by making only slight changes to existing policy in an attempt to respond to the most urgent symptoms of the current complex problem (Janis 1989, 35–40).

A variety of heuristics may be used by policy makers to judge the probability of various alternative outcomes. These probabilities are essential for calculating the costs and benefits of various options. The availability heuristic is the tendency to predict the outcome that seems similar to the most easily remembered past experience, affected by such factors as the vividness or recency of the experience. Jarring past events such as the appeasement at Munich or the Vietnam War will often be used as historical analogies for current decisions (Khong 1992, 19–46). Similarly, concrete information will tend to be weighed more heavily than abstract information.

The representative heuristic "refers to the tendency to predict the outcome that appears to be most representative of the salient features of the type of situation or person in question" (60). Policy-makers may rely on "surface commonalties" to judge that a current situation is part of a general category of events represented by a specific previous situation. For instance, United States decision-makers mistakenly saw the Vietnamese situation in the 1960s as similar to Korea in the 1950s, because of certain surface commonalties such as proximity to China, communist presence, divided North-South control of the nation, and aggressive behavior by the communist government (Khong 36).

A search for consistency further constrains the problem-solving capacity of government leaders. There is a strong tendency for decision-makers to assimilate new information to their already existing images and beliefs (George 1980, 61). The interpretation of new information will be filtered through the already existing beliefs raising the possibility that discrepant information will either be ignored (seen as irrelevant) or reshaped to fit the dominant beliefs. Though in a complex, uncertain world such drawing of inferences is essential, excessive consistency-seeking will cause a decision-maker to overlook important evidence which suggests that the decision should be reevaluated.

Bolstering is a frequently noted consistency-seeking behavior. It takes place after a decision has initially been made. Bolstering decision-makers disregard or minimize the disadvantages of the chosen option, while focusing on all its advantages. Though this behavior may be useful both for allowing the decision maker(s) to accept the decision and for building support among others for the decision, it impedes careful reconsideration, precise implementation, and the vigilant monitoring of feedback from the decision.

Organizational Constraints

In an attempt to compensate for the emotional and cognitive limitations of individual presidents, an institutional presidency has evolved to support the president. Several important lessons have been learned about the institutional presidency. First, different presidents construct different types of institutional presidencies. Second, presidents tend to construct advisory systems that are compatible with their own decision-making style. Third, no one advisory system is clearly preferable to all the others. The system must be compatible with the particular decision-making needs of individual presidents. Finally, no single system has been able to meet all the decision-making needs of the presidency.

Richard Johnson maintains that any attempt to manage the institutional presidency faces four important tradeoffs:

1) the optimal decision versus the doable decision;
2) conflict and conflicting information within the system versus cohesion to hold the system together;
3) the need to screen information versus the danger of distorting information;
4) increased time necessary to develop a comprehensive decision process versus reduction of time to enhance the responsiveness of the decision process (Johnson 1974, chap. 1).

Johnson concludes that modern presidents have used three basic types of management systems to organize the institutional presidency. His typology has come to dominate all analyses of the organization of the institutional presidency.

According to Johnson, Franklin Roosevelt used a competitive system that involved many highly competitive political advisors given overlapping tasks and high personal access to the president. The president personally settled the policy and political conflicts produced in this system. The major advantages of this management system were the generation of many innovative ideas, the sensitivity to political forces in the environment, and presidential involvement in the process. These advantages came at the cost of weak technical support of decisions, lack of careful coordination among policies, high strain on advisors, and an overloading of the president.

Johnson finds that several other presidents (Truman, Eisenhower, and Nixon) used a formal system of White House management. This management system was marked by a hierarchical form of organization with high levels of specialization, an intricate system of decision-making, and a premium on technical, neutral information rather than policy/political advocacy. Information and options were gathered at the bottom of the institutional pyramid and then passed through several layers of advisors before a final decision was made at the top. The formalistic system had several advantages. It gathered information from a wide variety of specialists and carefully considered the options based on that information. The hierarchical control also permitted better coordination among the various agencies within the federal government. Its costs included the distortion of information as it traveled up the pyramid, the cumbersomeness of the process, the isolation of the process from the political environment, the isolation of the president from hands-on policy experts and advocates, and the danger that the system could either be manipulated or short-circuited by its managers near the top of the pyramid.

The third management system identified by Johnson is the collegial. He sees this system in the Kennedy White House, though Ford and Carter were also said to have used the collegial system. This latter system sought to build a collegial team of generalists who together would solve the problems of the administration. Like the competitive, it was based on high levels of access to the president, considerations of political feasibility, and multiple delegations of tasks, but its team ethos softened the edge on the competitiveness. Its emphasis on careful problem-solving through teamwork approximates some of the optimal decision-making of the formalistic system without its cumbersomeness, presidential isolation, and danger of manipulation.

The costs of the collegial system come from the need for presidential management of the advisory team to maintain collegial relations. This requires a large amount of presidential time and a high degree of skill in interpersonal relations. Without proper presidential guidance, the collegial system has a tendency to drift. Moreover, as Janis notes, cohesive groups, such as a collegial White House, which are under high stress are susceptible to groupthink (1982, 243–248). Groups suffering from groupthink subconsciously overemphasize protecting the feelings of camaraderie within the group. Consequently, there is a desire to seek concurrence among the members to the detriment of high quality decision-making. The group members will overestimate the level of consensus within the group, exaggerate their own power and morality, and stereotype and demonize their adversary. The Kennedy administration's decision-making that led to the Bay of Pigs fiasco is often cited as a paradigmatic case of groupthink.

In the 1970s most scholars clearly favored the collegial management system. However, a new academic consensus was created in reaction to the difficulties of the collegial White House in both the Ford and Carter administrations and their midterm adoption of more formalistic systems with a chief of staff. The demands of a huge federal government, an ever more complex domestic and international environment, and a growing institutional presidency seem to require a more formalistic management system to provide a more systematic flow of information, coordinate administration policy, avoid excessive internal political conflict, and protect presidential time resources (Pfiffner 1996, 17–33).

Analysts now also recognize that Johnson's three-fold typology cannot adequately capture the nuances of decision-making behavior within the presidency. As both George and Greenstein and Burke note, decision-making has both formal and informal components. Johnson's categories focus primarily on the formal. For instance, Eisenhower's seemingly cumbersome formal system was enhanced by his active use of informal consultations with advisors. Furthermore, as George notes, formal organizational structures can be modified by the introduction of different decision procedures within those structures (1980, 139–146). George discusses the use of a devil's advocate, a formal options system, and multiple advocacy as potential procedures to enhance the different organizational structures.[1]

Finally, it should be reemphasized that the organization of the institutional presidency and the decision procedures built into it will be deeply influenced by the personality of the individual president. No one system will fit all presidents. George argues that there are three personality dimensions that are particularly important in fitting a president to an appropriate White House system (147–148). The first, cognitive style, refers to the various ways people prefer to gather and process information from their environment. Some prefer high levels of raw information, for instance, while others may prefer lower levels of synthesized information. The second dimension, people's sense of efficacy, has to do with skills and confidence in managing decision-making tasks. The third, people's orientation toward conflict, refers to their view of the necessity for political conflict and their willingness to participate in conflict.

For instance, Nixon had a high demand for information, but little sense of efficacy about managing the decision process and a distaste for personal conflict. He was unable to cope well with his original White House system, which was quite conflictual and required high levels of personal interaction. Nixon eventually created an information-based formal system with a chief of staff to manage the process and an on-paper decision-making procedure to shelter him from direct personal conflicts. While much of the literature has been premised on the constructing of an institutional presidency compatible with the president's personality, Hult suggests that systems should also be designed to compensate for presidential weaknesses (Hult 1993, 141). Nixon's highly sheltered, formalistic system may have merely exacerbated his own tendency to isolate himself from political forces in society and hence made the political blunders of Watergate more likely.

Bureaucratic Constraints

A relatively pluralistic government with multiple competing branches and agencies creates another constraint on presidential leadership and decision-making. Most of the studies of presidential leadership that have defined leadership in terms of persuasion have focused on this pluralism in American politics. In fact, pluralism is the basis of the argument that persuasion is required for leadership. In a polity with decentralized authority and multiple interests, command will be an insufficient basis to lead the government. Instead, successful presidential leadership requires that these independent political centers be persuaded to go along with the wishes of the president (Neustadt 1990, 29–49).

But independent bureaucratic interests and cultures create obstacles for high quality decision-making as well. The problem here is not excessive consensus in a small, homogeneous decision-making group (groupthink), but rather excessive dissensus in a larger, heterogeneous organization. Battles among self-interested bureaucratic agencies for control of national policy may degrade the decision process in many ways (George 109–119). Both the information and the options offered to the presidency may be shaped by the perspectives, histories, and interests of the participating agencies. This skewing of information and options may be inadvertent results of the agency's particular worldview and its repertoire of existing options, both of which developed over the course of the agency's history. On other occasions, the agency may intentionally manipulate the information available for presidential decision-making to protect its own bureaucratic interests. In either case, this distortion of information is most likely to be significant when there is a large disparity in the power and bargaining advantages among the bureaucracies. The skewed information of the dominant actor is less likely to be properly balanced by the opinions of weaker actors.

Bureaucratic politics can also inhibit quality decision-making because it obstructs decision closure. Incessant attempts by defeated bureaucratic interests to reopen a decision may cause confusion and delay within the decision process, not to mention making coherent implementation difficult. Finally, if bureaucratic battles become excessive, they will absorb much of the time and attention of the president, leaving him with fewer resources to apply to the policy decisions at hand. Presidential leadership requires recognition of the inevitability of bureaucratic politics and its dangers for high quality decision-making.[2] Presidents must both manage that conflict to keep it from spiraling out of control and use it to their advantage to gain a more comprehensive view of policy information and options.

THE BUSH PRESIDENCY

The quality of George Bush's presidential leadership was shaped both by Bush's personal style as well as the institutional arrangements he created in the White House to meet his decision-making needs.

The Personality and Style of George Herbert Walker Bush

Commentators often focus on Bush's patrician background and his extensive insider experience in both business and government (Shogan, chap. 10; Barber, chap. 14). Bush grew up in a wealthy Connecticut family that traced its lineage back to the British Royal Family. His father was a powerful Wall Street investment banker and a Republican Senator from Connecticut. Bush attended the elite schools of Phillips Academy and Yale. Like his father, Bush was a member of the prestigious Yale secret society, Skull and Bones, which self-consciously trained its members for national leadership. Bush went on to be a teenage naval aviator during World War II, an independent Texas oil company executive, a local Republican Party chairman in Texas, a congressman from Texas, a candidate for the Senate from Texas, an ambassador to the United Nations, a chairperson of the Republican National Committee, an envoy to China, a director of the CIA, and vice president.

Several analysts attribute aspects of his personality and style in politics to his upbringing in patrician social circles. Bush had a reserved and proper style and was uncomfortable in public and mass events. Discussing Bush's strict childhood rearing and spartan educational experience at Phillips Academy, Shogan concludes that:

> In the case of George Bush this background endowed him with traits such as self discipline and perseverance that helped him fulfill his ambition. But by repressing his personality, it also produced an individual whose excessive body language, tendency to speak in sentence fragments, and use of euphemisms like "doo-doo" have made him vulnerable to the most devastating weapon that can be used against a public man, ridicule. (1992, 274)

Nonetheless, in smaller settings, Bush was an affable person who often built personal friendships or at least acquaintances with the numerous leaders and activists he met in his career in business, politics, and government. Bush was famed for his penchant for dropping thousands of thank-you notes along this path. Loyalty to this network of family, friends, and co-workers was a mark of Bush's career. Evan Thomas attributes Bush's emphasis on loyalty to his socialization in Skull and Bones, which "taught to an exaggerated degree the virtues of loyalty and male bonding" (1990, 33). Bush once explained his own emphasis on loyalty in the following terms: "I make friends. I believe in 'hands on.' I believe in staying in touch with people. And I learn from them. Loyalty goes two ways, to them and from them. I pride myself on that" (Shogan 1992, 272).

His long and varied experience in business and particularly government allowed him to build an extensive insiders' network which then formed the basis for his governing style. Rockman argued that Bush's leadership style was that of the quintessential insider.

> Insiders are likely to be consensus mongers and not "conviction politicians".... Moreover, they are likely to want to operate secretively, to cut deals in small groups, and to avoid rocking

boats. Further, they are likely to operate in incremental ways, to believe that the premises of the status quo provide the operative bases for future policy except under the most unusually compelling circumstances . . . . (18)

Most accounts emphasize Bush's tendency to make decisions in small informal groups by brokering the differences among the participants. An important part of this informal process is its secrecy. Bush had a significant aversion to public decision-making. A Republican insider suggested that Bush's desire for secrecy bordered on the obsessive:

A lot of the way the White House operates is based on the leaks thing . . . . I think you know how obsessed George Bush is about leaks. What you don't know is the fullness of the obsession. It's right up there as one of his core values. You know, service, family, religion, leaks."

(Campbell 1991, 208)

Bush's general affability, loyalty, and genteel manner were counterbalanced by a tendency to strike a pose of hostility and defiance when he was surprised, anxious, or frustrated. A series of incidents fit into this pattern, including his notorious televised dispute with Dan Rather, his "kicking ass" statement about the vice presidential debate with Geraldine Ferraro, his disparagement of Michael Dukakis during the 1988 campaign, his infamous tax dare ("read my lips"), his personal quest for the capture of Manuel Noriega, and his shrill attacks on "Bozo and the Ozone Man" (Clinton/Gore) during the 1992 campaign.

Many of these angry episodes may be connected to Bush's life-long attempt both to live up to his father's example and to prove his manhood. Barber sees Bush's teenage enlistment during World War II, his migration to the Texas oil fields, and his entrance into Texas politics all as attempts to prove his independence of and parity with his father (Barber 1992, 468–470). Barber also sees in Bush a need to take on missions as proof of his own worth (459). Bush only decided to adopt pit bull campaign tactics in 1988 after aides Ailes and Atwater showed him tapes of the Democratic Convention. Bush was angered by these mocking attacks of his political persona. Bush's aides knew that "it was easier to get him down-and-dirty if you persuaded him that he was wronged and the manly thing to do was to fight back" (Rockman 1991, 35).

Worldview is another important component of political personality. Bush was often criticized for lacking a basic set of political beliefs; this lack, in turn, made it difficult for him to articulate a vision for the nation. This common charge needs to be considered more carefully. Bush's desire to solve problems through quietly brokering incremental, prudent decisions among like-minded political elites undoubtedly resulted in the popular conclusion that he had no strong political beliefs. In terms of a standard left-right notion of political ideology, Bush appears quite nebulous. The many stages of his long political career seem to consist of frequent oscillations between the conservative and moderate wings of the Republican Party. When asked to classify himself as conservative or moderate in 1980,

Bush responded, "I don't want to be perceived as either" (Shogan 1992, 259). He has also failed to maintain consistent positions on central political issues of his time such as abortion and civil rights.

But if one looks at Bush's beliefs about social relationships and his general values, a pattern is more apparent. Several authors classify Bush as an American Tory (Rockman 1991; Campbell 1991). Tories place a significant value on the status quo and the maintenance of social harmony, but are willing to accept social change in the face of stark empirical evidence. However, short of that overwhelming evidence, they will be very skeptical of large governmental programs, favoring instead incremental adjustments to maintain the status quo and social harmony. Bush's belief in the need to protect proper procedures may also be linked to his Toryism. As already shown, Bush strongly believed in loyalty, civility, elite accommodation, and secrecy.

Finally, there is a set of values that seem to stretch back to Bush's family and patrician background.

> Bush is the product of a culture that prized not only good breeding and proper manners but martial virility and moral certitude. As a child Bush was taught to play fair, but was also taught to punch the bully in the nose. The concept of a 'just war' was taught, along with charity and faith, in morning chapel at Andover.
> (Thomas 1990, 33)

On domestic politics, a sense of *noblesse oblige* flows from these demands of fair play, moral certitude, and charity. One sees this side of Bush in his Inaugural Address:

> Are we enthralled with material things, less appreciative of the nobility of work and sacrifice?... We cannot hope only to leave our children a bigger car, a bigger bank account. We must hope to give them a sense of what it means to be a loyal friend, a loving parent, a citizen who leaves his home, his neighborhood, and town better than he found it....
> America is never wholly herself unless she is engaged in high moral principle. We as a people have such a purpose today. It is to make kinder the face of the nation and gentler the face of the world.
> ("Inaugural" 1989, 208–209)

Yet not surprisingly, after listing off a series of social calamities—homelessness, abused children, inner city drugs and welfare, crime, and unwed mothers—that call for programs illustrating that domestic moral purpose, Bush concluded in his inaugural that government programs could not solve these problems and that, in any case, the federal deficit made any large governmental response impossible. Instead, Bush called for a thousand points of individual light. Tory skepticism of large social change and a belief in individual duty and charity limit the possibilities for significant government response.

On the international front, Bush the patrician view saw the United States as the preeminent world power, which must be willing to use force to protect the national interest as well as to protect peace and stability around the globe. In his inaugural, Bush pledged: "To the world, too, we offer new engagement and a renewed vow: We will stay strong to protect peace. The 'offered hand' is a reluctant fist; once made, it is strong and can be used with great effect" ("Inaugural" 1989, 210).

Thus, though Bush's belief system could not readily and consistently fit into standard ideological categories, some basic precepts that did seem to guide his approach to public leadership. There was a belief in a moral responsibility to protect domestic and international harmony, but that responsibility was constrained by a Tory skepticism toward large and rapid change. There was also a confidence in meeting challenges to the status quo with prudent, incremental solutions arrived at through confidential bargaining with other elites. Procedural values of civility, fair play, loyalty, and secrecy must also be maintained.

The Bush Institutional Presidency

The institutional dimension of the Bush presidency resulted directly from Bush's personality and leadership style. An essay that detailed Bush's White House organization was appropriately titled "In Bush's Image" (Solomon 1990, 1642). As Greenstein and Burke suggest, we need to think of the institutional presidency as operating on two tracks: the formal and the informal. At the formal level, Bush's White House was quite hierarchically organized (Campbell 1991, 197–199; Pfiffner 1996, 131–137). In terms of Johnson's categorization scheme, it appeared to be a formalistic organization. John Sununu sat at the top of the organizational chart as the White House chief of staff. Responsibilities for policy making were divided among three cabinet councils: a National Security Council (NSC), a Domestic Policy Council (DPC), and an Economic Policy Council (EPC). The staffing and administration for each council was coordinated by a White House advisor (National Security Advisor Brent Scowcroft for the NSC and Domestic Policy Advisor Roger Porter for both the DPC and the EPC). Each council was divided into working groups on specific topics within that council's domain. Furthermore, each council had three levels: a working group at the staff level gathered background information, a deputies committee (cabinet officials at the deputy secretary level) made preliminary policy recommendations, and a formal council (cabinet secretaries) made the final recommendation.

But the formality of this arrangement was undercut by a variety of factors linked to Bush's own governing style. The administration was amply stocked with Bush loyalists and friends at both the cabinet and sub-cabinet levels of the administration. The two primary criteria for Bush administration appointments were competence and loyalty to Bush (Pfiffner 138). Both because of Bush's inclinations to stay personally in touch and because so many of the first- and second-level officials were former associates, Bush often skipped over the formal process to speak directly with officials outside the White House. This often broke down the potential isolation of a formal system and limited the influence of Sununu as chief of staff and presidential gatekeeper (Pfiffner 134 and Solomon 1644).

Executive department authority was quite extensive in the Bush administration for several reasons. Bush chose some of his closest friends for cabinet positions (Baker at State, Mosbacher at Commerce, and Brady at Treasury). Bush also allowed them to choose their own subcabinet aides and gave them a reasonably free hand to make departmental policy. Moreover, though Sununu had a considerable amount of power to control access to Bush, cabinet secretaries with a past relationship to the president were readily able to see him.

While on paper the policy council system appeared to be the dominant decision-making process in the Bush administration, reality was a bit more complicated. On narrower concerns, departments often had the authority to make policy. The formalized process of the policy councils handled more complex issues that went beyond the purview of a single agency. But issues that were politically volatile or of particular interest to White House operatives were often pulled out of the policy council system and handled informally in the White House (Solomon 1647).

The informal White House decision process had several characteristics. It was very collegial, no doubt partially the result of the homogeneity of the people working in the Bush White House. Solomon noted that the use of the extensive personal Bush network produced a certain "sameness" in the Bush White House personnel. "They're mainly affable white men in their 30s or 40s who are experienced in Washington's ways and hew to few ideological principles beyond pragmatism" (1644). Furthermore, Bush emphasized that personal confrontation and competition would not be appreciated in his administration. Rewards (thank-you notes and social invitations) and penalties (ostracism) were readily used by Bush to encourage collegiality (Solomon 1643).

Much of the most important decision-making in the White House was done in small informal groups. On domestic policy, the key decision-makers were Sununu and Darmen (Budget Director). Their access to Bush was unparalleled. They often reached their own private accord and then pushed their joint position by the adroit use of the media and outside policy actors. Many administration dissidents demurred on a dispute rather than get into a futile battle with the two (Solomon 1645). Other White House actors often sought to influence policy by using informal meetings or conversations with Sununu or Darmen before decisions were taken.

Nonetheless, on issues about which individuals felt intensely, there was a tendency for the White House to broker compromises among the departments before the dispute reached the president. Moreover, while Sununu often acted as a policy advocate in front of Bush, most participants acknowledged that he also was a fair broker of ideas, allowing opponents reasonable access to Bush.

Bush played a more consistently active role in foreign policy, but the process was informal here as well (Crabb and Mulcahy 1991, 194; Berman and Jentelson 1991, 99–103). Important foreign policy decisions were made in an informal small group that usually included Baker, Scowcroft, and Richard Cheney (Secretary of Defense). As in the domestic arena, the decision-making process was marked by collegiality. All of the major participants knew Bush and each other from previous Republican administrations. Unlike in many administrations, there were amicable relations between the National Security Advisor and the Secretary of State (Crabb and Mulcahy 198). Baker and Scowcroft were close personal friends. They readily divided roles. Baker handled external relations with foreign powers, Congress, and the media, while Scowcroft managed the internal policy process.

Like Sununu, Scowcroft was not simply a neutral custodian of the policy process. He also acted as close advisor and confidante to the president, but as with Sununu there was little evidence that Scowcroft sought to control the advisory process to his own advantage. Scowcroft, reacting to the politicization of the National Security Council under Reagan, sought to enhance the technical capacity of the NSC to support presidential decision-making. However, the many hours Scowcroft spent in Bush's company acting as confidante and companion affected his ability to manage the flow of paper and information that needed to be processed by a well-functioning NSC (Hoffman 1989, 6).

Secretary of State Baker also acted as a close advisor to Bush on foreign policy decisions. Like Scowcroft's, Baker's leadership of his own organization also led to problems with information processing. Baker heavily centralized the decision-making capacity at the State Department (Crabb and Mulcahy 199–200). Baker (and Bush) distrusted the professional Foreign Service at the State Department, and as a consequence Baker kept decision-making power within the Secretary's Office. This was filled with aides who had personal connections to Baker but who, in general, were young and inexperienced in foreign policy-making.

Bush favored an extremely informal style of foreign policy decision-making. He thought nothing of getting on the phone to seek out information from acquaintances in the government. His phone searches for information on foreign policy extended internationally. Often his response to an international problem was rolodex diplomacy: personal phone calls to the relevant heads of state to gather information, to request advice, or to attempt persuasion. Furthermore, few formal meetings of the NSC or formally presented options by staff from State or Defense preceded key decisions. Instead, Bush would meet casually with a few key confidantes, Baker, Scowcroft, and Cheney, to hash over decisions with little systematic consultations from experts in the government. Apparently, Bush's fear of leaks kept him from calling larger formal decision-making meetings with subcabinet officials. The result was a more *ad hoc* style of decision-making. This was apparent both in Bush's spur-of-the-moment, weekend creation of a new European security policy announced at NATO's May 1989 meeting and in Bush's uncertain response to the abortive Panamanian coup of October, 1989. (Even after Bush had announced his administration's intention to see Noriega deposed, no formal contingency plans had been created in the event of a coup in Panama.)

A useful summary of the Bush foreign policy-making style was provided by an administration source describing White House decision-making during that abortive Panamanian coup:

> For ten months, they've [Bush, Baker, Scowcroft, and Cheney] had this collegial, informal atmosphere . . . . They just continued as they had. They took in facts as they needed them. They shut out the bureaucracy. The flow of information into them should have been more organized. There should have been a central collection point. There was never a point when someone said, "Let's call a meeting."

Wandering in the Arabian Desert with George Bush 117

That's not the kind of thing you do if it's just the boys.... You just say, "Let's go talk."

(Hoffman 1989, 6)

LEADERSHIP AND DECISION-MAKING DURING THE PERSIAN GULF CRISIS

Given the stunning military victory of the allied forces, most early appraisals of Bush's performance during the Persian Gulf crisis were quite positive. With Saddam Hussein's retention of political power and his horrific repression of the Kurds and Shi'a, some later evaluations were less positive. However, the purpose of this paper is not simply to judge the quality of Bush's leadership, but rather to evaluate the impact of personality, organization, and bureaucracy on Bush's leadership behavior, both successful and unsuccessful, during the Persian Gulf crisis.

Prelude to War

In hindsight, Bush's leadership in the pre-invasion stage of the Persian Gulf crisis has been sharply criticized. A number of incidents in 1990 indicated that Iraq had aggressive intentions in the Persian Gulf in general, and in Kuwait in particular. On February 24, 1990, at a meeting of the Arab Cooperation Council, Saddam Hussein denounced United States hegemony in the Middle East in the aftermath of the collapse of the Soviet Union. He demanded a reduced American influence in the region. At that time Hussein began his demand for monetary support from the Gulf states. He demanded that Kuwait and Saudi Arabia forgive Iraq's $30 billion war debt and provide an additional $30 billion in grants. On several other occasions, Hussein was reported to have suggested to other Arab leaders that they join him in a coalition to carve up the Arabian peninsula and its oil riches (Mathews 1991, 56).

As the spring and summer progressed, Hussein continued to escalate his demands upon Kuwait, including reducing Kuwaiti oil production to drive up world prices, ceding forty-five miles of disputed border territory between the two nations, ceding part of Kuwait's Rumaila oil fields, and providing a long-term lease for two Kuwaiti Islands, which would give Iraq unrestricted access to the Persian Gulf.

In addition, the FBI arrested Iraqi agents as they illegally tried to export electronic triggers for nuclear weapons in late March. In early April, Hussein announced Iraq's acquisition of binary chemical weapons and threatened to incinerate half of Israel if it became aggressive. A few weeks later, British intelligence prevented Iraqi agents from shipping to Iraq sections of a barrel for a huge supergun capable of inexpensively hurling chemical and nuclear weapons a thousand miles.

In mid-July, American intelligence agencies were aware of Iraqi troops massing on the border of Kuwait. By July 30, the Iraqi force had reached 100,000. Despite all these provocations, Bush continued to pursue a relationship of detente and subsidized trade with Iraq. As late as July 31, the Bush administration argued against a congressional bill to impose trade limitations on Iraq. At no time did the Bush administration clearly indicate that it would militarily defend (or liberate) Kuwait. In his testimony at a July congressional hearing Assistant Secretary of State John Kelly articulated the administration's standard line. He maintained that while the United States was committed to peaceful resolutions of conflicts in the Middle East, "We have no defense treaties relationship with any gulf country ... We have not historically taken a position on border disputes" (quoted in Waas 39). On August 1, Iraq invaded Kuwait and captured the entire country in a matter of hours.

Several factors help explain the failure of the Bush administration to deter Iraq. From a bureaucratic perspective, there were problems in the relationship of State Department experts in the Foreign Service to Secretary of State Baker and indirectly to Bush. As noted before, Baker centralized authority among young inexperienced aides in the Secretary's Office at the State Department. This approach limited access to foreign policy expertise and limited the number of issues that could be handled at any one time. Baker and his close aides were so focused on the issues of the uniting of the two Germanies and the dissolution of the Soviet Union that they had insufficient time to consider adequately the situation in the Persian Gulf. A senior administration official conceded, "We were essentially operating without a policy. The crisis came in a bit of a vacuum at a time when everyone was focusing on German reunification" (Sciolino and Gordon 1).

Though there were periodic attempts to review the administration policy of detente toward Iraq in 1990, none of them received the primary attention of Baker, and consequently the reviews floundered amid bureaucratic squabbling and inertia (Freedman and Karsh 36). Departments like Agriculture and Commerce opposed diplomatic or trade sanctions in order to protect the economic interests of their clients. Furthermore, many of the mid-level policy analysts warning about Iraq's growing aggressiveness in 1990 had previously raised the possibility of working with moderates in Iran in the late 1980s. The Iran Contra scandal in the Reagan Administration was an indirect result of that policy advice. That scandal, in turn, reduced the bureaucratic influence of those mid-level policy analysts in the Bush administration (Gigot 5).

At the institutional level in the White House, a similar inability to focus sharply on the rapidly deteriorating situation was evident. As usual in the Bush administration, the Persian Gulf situation at this stage was handled informally. None of the various accounts mentions any formal National Security Council meeting in the months preceding the invasion in which contingencies were discussed for an Iraqi invasion of Kuwait. Perhaps, if such contingencies had been more carefully considered, the recognition of the high cost of a military liberation of Kuwait would have driven the administration to strengthen the comparatively less expensive option of deterring Iraq's behavior.

These contingencies probably weren't discussed, however, because the likelihood of an Iraqi invasion of Kuwait was not taken seriously by the White House. One factor that may have contributed to this overly optimistic appraisal was Bush's preferred style of information gathering: informal conversations with other elite leaders. In this case, much of his information about Sadam Hussein's intentions came from moderate Arab leaders like President Mubarak and King Hussein. Ultimately their "trustworthy" elite assurances that Hussein was merely negotiating with Kuwait overrode the growing evidence that Hussein was about to make an aggressive move into Kuwait. Careful, systematic evaluation of the evidence may have been short-circuited by an institutional predisposition toward *ad hoc* gathering of information.

Cognitive factors also played a role in the rejection of the possibility, until almost the last moment, that Iraq was about to overrun Kuwait. The drive toward cognitive consistency conspired to make the invasion seem improbable. In the aftermath of Iraq's nine-year war with the radical Iranian regime (1980–88), two principles dominated conventional wisdom in American foreign policy circles. It was now assumed that Saddam Hussein and Iraq were willing to play a moderating role in regional affairs as a balance to the extremist position of fundamentalist Iran. Furthermore, it was assumed that Iraq was too devastated both physically and economically to take aggressive actions in the region. It only made sense that Iraq would focus on internal reconstruction, not external aggrandizement (Hoffman 1990, 9–10).

Iraq's demands in the spring of 1990 for financial assistance from the Gulf states could be fit into a reconstruction interpretation. Even when Iraq began to mass troops on the Kuwaiti border, the assumption about Iraq's intentions was salvaged by a long-held Western stereotype of Arab behavior. One administration official explained that "Iraq and Kuwait had been playing cat and mouse for 30 years: Iraq clawed periodically, then Kuwait bought it off" (Mathews 56). Hence in the third week of July, the 30,000 Iraqi troops on the border were merely perceived as Iraq's opening bid in an Arab economic and political bazaar.

Further evidence for the impact of striving for consistency can be seen about ten days later when an additional intelligence argument for believing that Iraq did not intend to invade Kuwait emerged. Even though Iraq's troop strength on the border reached 100,000 at the end of July, Iraq had not moved sufficient support, munitions, communications, and logistics capacity to the border for an invasion. Yet when satellite reconnaissance identified that invasion support capacity on August 1, many analysts failed to reevaluate Iraqi intentions. As *Newsweek*'s Tom Mathews explained:

> Noting that he [Hussein] had done nothing to disguise his moves, the U.S. intelligence community assumed it was a bluff to bully Kuwait into a more compliant oil policy. It was a classic case of making intelligence fit the policy, instead of making policy fit the intelligence. The CIA, the Defense Intelligence Agency and the State Department Bureau of Intelligence all concluded there was little serious danger. (57)

A number of factors thus combined to reduce the likelihood that the Bush administration would offer a consistent policy of deterrence toward Iraq. An overcentralized bureaucratic structure in the State Department made it difficult for Middle East experts to have ready access to Baker. Furthermore, the small coterie of Baker insiders at State had difficulty focusing on the Gulf while other crises were brewing in Europe. The *ad hoc* style of decision-making in the White House was not able to compensate for the failings at State. Bush depended excessively on his informal conversations with Arab leaders. Moreover, few attempts were made to think ahead systematically about the implications for American interests of an Iraqi invasion. Finally, assumptions about Iraq's dire post-war situation and stereotypes of inter-Arab political bargaining made it more difficult for the Bush administration to recognize the danger of an Iraqi invasion. Consequently, Bush failed to take a leadership role in deterring Iraq from its adventures in Kuwait.

Decision-Making on the War

Bush's leadership after the invasion has received many accolades. In particular, he has been praised for his prompt decision to respond to the Iraqi invasion and his ability to construct a complex international coalition to roll back Iraqi aggression.

Bush was informed of the Iraqi invasion on the evening of August 1, 1990. Early Thursday morning, August 2, Bush, by executive order, froze Iraqi and Kuwait financial assets in U.S. banks. An NSC meeting was then held at 8 a.m. to discuss the invasion. At this meeting, General Norman Schwarzkopf outlined a series of military options available. The most significant option, based on an existing contingency plan (Operations Plan 90-1002), would involve 100,000–200,000 troops, and would take several months to put into place. But Schwarzkopf doubted that Arab nations would allow such a large contingent of U.S. troops on their territory. Most at the initial meeting saw little opportunity for U.S. military intervention and consequently much of the discussion of options focused on diplomatic and economic sanctions. Nonetheless, Bush ended the meeting with the conclusion: "This must be reversed" (Mathews 58).

After another inconclusive NSC meeting on Friday morning, Bush sent Cheney and Powell to brief the Saudi ambassador on Op. Plan 90-1002. The ambassador thought that in light of the possible threat to Saudi Arabia, the royal family might agree to the deployment. He suggested that a high level delegation be sent to Saudi Arabia to convince King Fahd. At 5 p.m. that evening the NSC met again. The intelligence agencies reported that Iraqi troops were moving toward the Saudi border and they feared that Iraq would take the eastern oilfields. While some in the meeting doubted this analysis, Bush seemed to agree. General Colin Powell suggested using American troops to "draw a line in the sand" to let Hussein "know that if he attacks Saudi Arabia, he attacks the United States" (Mathews 58). Bush asked that more precise military options be presented to him the next day, but he ended the meeting with the words, "I believe we go" (Woodward and Atkinson 8).

On August 4, at Camp David, Cheney, Powell, and Schwarzkopf outlined an expanded version of Op. Plan 90-1002 to Bush. The plan now had two components, one to defend Saudi Arabia and the other to liberate Kuwait. Schwarzkopf indicated that the first would require about 200,000 troops and take about seventeen weeks to deploy, whereas the second would require another 150,000 troops and take eight to twelve months to accomplish (Woodward 248). The meeting ended without any conclusion being reached. The following day Bush sent Cheney to Saudi Arabia with instructions to persuade the Saudis to accept the troops.

On Sunday afternoon Bush flew back to the White House in an angry mood. He was having trouble convincing King Fahd to accept the American troops, and King Hussein of Jordan had publicly attacked the United States position on the Gulf crisis. As Bush departed his helicopter, TV reporters asked for his reaction to the crisis. He angrily retorted: "This will not stand. This will not stand—this aggression against Kuwait" (Mathews 59). That evening another NSC meeting was held. Powell, sensing that Bush had already committed himself to an intervention, emphasized that considerable ground, naval, and air forces would be needed to project a credible deterrent and fighting force in the region. Bush simply told him to do whatever it takes to get the job done (Woodward 262).

Cheney's meeting with Fahd went well, and by Monday, August 6, Bush agreed to a massive deployment of troops to Saudi Arabia. Bush had approved the defensive component of Op. Plan 90-1002. At this point, no one had recommended an offensive strategy to free Kuwait, and Bush did not approve one. The president had adopted a multi-pronged strategy. The 200,000 troops being sent to the Gulf would be sufficient to protect Saudi Arabia, but not to push Iraq out of Kuwait. However, it was hoped that international economic sanctions approved by the United Nations on August 6 in combination with the troops would convince Hussein to withdraw from Kuwait. Within days of the invasion, Bush also directed that a covert plan be developed to destabilize Iraq and eventually remove Hussein from power (Atkinson 6; Woodward 237).

As American troops poured into Saudi Arabia over the next two months, Iraq increased the pressure on the United States and its coalition partners by taking western hostages in Iraq, trapping U.S. diplomats in the Kuwaiti embassy, plundering Kuwait, and increasing its military forces in and around Kuwait. By late September the pressure on the Bush administration was substantial. Intelligence indicated that the economic blockade, despite its effectiveness, was not likely to force Iraq out of Kuwait in the near to mid term. One senior administrative official remarked that "There was a sense of drift. Saddam seemed to have the initiative. We felt we had to do something to get it back" (Friedman and Tyler 12).

General Powell feared that the nation might be drifting into war. Bush continued to make bellicose public statements against Hussein, but little in the way of formal options were being presented, compared, and discussed in the White House. Powell believed that the sanctions option was still viable. In an early October informal meeting with Bush, Cheney, and Scowcroft, Powell indicated that either the current containment policy or an offensive strategy would eventually force Iraq out of Kuwait. Bush was not inclined toward the containment strategy. "I don't think there's time politically for that strategy," he responded (Woodward 42). Powell never indicated his preference for containment at the meeting. Within days of this meeting, Bush asked Scowcroft to have the Pentagon develop an offensive option for the White House to review.

On October 24, in a meeting with Cheney, President Bush agreed in principle to an increase in troop deployments for Saudi Arabia. On October 31, Bush met with Baker, Cheney, Powell, Scowcroft, and Sununu to go over the Pentagon's plans for Phase II. Bush approved the plan, which would add 200,000 American troops and take until about January 15 to be completed. Bush felt that "the only thing Saddam understands is force or the credible threat of force" (Devroy and

Balz 8). They also agreed to seek a United Nations resolution endorsing the use of force if Iraq failed to withdraw from Kuwait. All five thought there was a reasonable chance that the increased American forces backed by a United Nations mandate would lead Hussein to pull out of Kuwait without a fight. However, if Iraq did not peacefully withdraw, Phase II included a war plan and schedule. A massive air campaign against Iraq and its forces would begin about January 15 and the ground phase would come sometime in February. They decided not to announce this new troop deployment until November 8, two days after the 1990 elections.

The United Nations passed the enforcement resolution in late November, but Iraq refused to pull out of Kuwait. Phase II was implemented as planned. The air campaign began on January 17 and the ground campaign on February 23. Within four days Bush called off the offensive and accepted Iraq's request for an armistice.

Presidential Decision-Making Style and Decisions on the War

Leadership can be thought of as having two basic components: the ability to make a careful, balanced decision about the response to a problem and the ability to persuade other necessary actors to support that decision. Let us first look at the issue of balanced decision-making. Several of the institutional and personal factors that have been previously discussed may help explain the remarkable series of decisions that led to the largest American military intervention since the Vietnam War. The institutional structure of the White House decision process during the Persian Gulf crisis played an important role in the policy-making that led to the war. On its surface, the structure appeared formal, yet critical decisions were often handled quite informally. A Deputies Committee led by Robert Gates from the NSC and which included chief deputies from State, Defense, Joint Chiefs of Staff, CIA, Justice, Treasury, and Commerce formed the foundation of the decision process (Freedman and Karsh 208). One level above was a committee made up of the core agencies from the Deputies Committee (NSC, State, Defense, Joint Chiefs, and CIA). This core committee met several times a day and drafted most of the background papers which were then to be considered by the next level of decision-making, the "Gang of Eight" made up of Bush, Quayle, Sununu, Scowcroft, Baker, Cheney, Powell, and Gates.

Nonetheless, a careful analysis of the various accounts of the decision process indicates that key decisions were often made without detailed formal consideration of options developed at the lower levels of the hierarchy. Instead, there was a pattern of informal *ad hoc* decision-making throughout the Persian Gulf War. Several of the participants expressed surprise and dismay at the informality and lack of comprehensive consideration in the decision process.

For instance, the Saturday, August 4 meeting in which General Schwarzkopf presented an expanded version of Operations Plan 90-1002 ended without a conclusive decision. General Powell first realized that a decision to intervene militarily had been made when he heard on Sunday that Bush had sent Cheney to Saudi Arabia to convince King Fahd to accept the U.S. troop deployment on Saudi territory. Later that Sunday, Powell, as was his habit, watched Bush on CNN, hoping to gain insights into the president's thinking on policy. Powell heard Bush angrily state: "This will not stand. This will not stand—this aggression against Kuwait." With these new comments, Powell felt that policy had been irrevocably changed. In a public statement, the president had now indicated that his goal was no longer the defense of Saudi Arabia but the expulsion of Iraq from Kuwait. This was a shift in policy from the Saturday discussions that focused on the military defense of Saudi Arabia. Without consulting either Powell or the NSC, Bush had committed the U.S. to liberating Kuwait (Woodward 259–260).

That same Sunday evening, another NSC meeting was held. Powell, recognizing that military intervention was inevitable, pushed for a rapid and large deployment. Bush readily agreed and told Powell to do whatever it took to get the job done. After the meeting, Baker was struck by the casual way that a momentous decision to commit troops had been taken. All its implications had been neither discussed nor evaluated. Force levels had not been discussed with any precision. "The deployment had been decided by George Bush; the level of force was being decided by Operations Plan 90-1002" (Baker, quoted in Woodward 262). There is little evidence that diplomatic options were carefully and systematically weighed against a variety of military options during these early stages of the decision process.

Similarly, on October 24, Bush and Cheney came to an agreement in principle that troop levels would have to be increased significantly. This initial decision would eventually lead to more than doubling the American troop commitment and set the stage for the shift from Desert Shield to Desert Storm. Powell found out about the decision only when Cheney appeared on television news interview shows the next day to announce that American troops could be increased by 100,000. Neither Powell nor the NSC had been consulted at this point. No systematic discussion of the costs and benefits of sanctions versus military intervention ever took place in the NSC.

Not all informal decision-making led to escalations. The Bush decision to seek a late meeting between Baker and Saddam Hussein was apparently the result of casual conversations among Bush, Sununu, and Scowcroft in late November, 1991 in Monterey, Mexico. In order to protect the element of surprise and drama, the decision was taken with little consultation among Bush's diplomatic advisors or the State Department (Duffy and Goodgame 158). Bush announced his peace plan on November 30, the day after the United Nations authorized the use of force against Iraq. Bush made this decision for several reasons. He was anxious to have the opportunity to communicate to Hussein directly that Iraq had no choice but to leave Kuwait or face military attack. Bush also wanted to prove to the American public that he was willing to go the extra mile in the search for peace.

Unfortunately, the announcement had several detrimental consequences that had not been fully considered before taking the decision. Coming the day after the United Nations force resolution, Bush's offer seemed to reduce much of its threat. Some have argued that the announcement caused Saddam Hussein to doubt whether the United States would actually use its military forces. Moreover, it frightened Arab allies, who also thought the United States was now pulling back, leaving them exposed to Iraq's wrath (Freedman and Karsh 236; Duffy and Goodgame 158–159). Lastly, Bush had not clearly thought through the dates for the meeting between Baker and Hussein. The range of dates he extended to Hussein was too broad. Hussein was able to accept and specify a date within Bush's offer that was so late that Bush felt it was simply being used as a delaying tactic. Bush was then put in the embarrassing position of turning down an acceptance that was in compliance with his own offer. One would have to believe that a more systematic staffing process would have caught such an obvious error in the initial proposal.

Management of the Institutional White House and Decisions on the War

The management style of the policy-making process in the Bush White House also played an important role in decisions on the Persian Gulf War. Most scholars argue that someone must be responsible for managing the flow and presentation of information into the policy-making process to insure a balanced consideration of competing perspectives. Under most circumstances, that role of neutral custodian for foreign policy is played by the NSC advisor. But there is little evidence that Scowcroft (or anyone else) performed that function during the Persian Gulf crisis. Instead, he acted as confidante and counselor to Bush rather than as manager of the decision process.

This led to attempts to persuade the advisory system to adopt positions that Bush and Scowcroft favored rather than the careful presentation of a comprehensive range of options. For instance, after the initial meeting with the NSC on Thursday, August 2, both Bush and Scowcroft were disappointed that most in the meeting were focusing on the limits to military intervention rather than on the necessity of reversing the situation. Bush and Scowcroft agreed that Scowcroft would seek to rechannel the next NSC discussion toward an activist response (Woodward 235). Scowcroft opened the Friday morning meeting with a call to action: "We have to begin our deliberations with the fact that this is unacceptable. Yes, it's hard to do much. There are a lot of reasons why we can't do things but it's our job" (Woodward 237). Bush indicated his agreement with his National Security Advisor. Participants at the meeting later told Woodward that Scowcroft's opening "changed the entire focus" and "was a plea for the cabinet to unify, to fall in line" (Woodward 237). At a Friday evening meeting, Bush called for the Defense Department to present its deployment options to him the following day. Bush ended the session with the words, "I believe we go" (Mathews 58).

The October decision-making that culminated in the decision to double American forces in preparation for an offensive operation was also not well managed. As October approached, General Powell feared America was drifting toward war (Woodward 41–42, 297–307). Bush was making exceptionally bellicose statements toward Hussein in public. Without careful consideration, these might become *de facto* policy. Powell was disappointed in the NSC meetings. They resembled convivial gatherings of old pals rather than carefully constructed group considerations of policy options. "Positions and alternatives were not completely discussed. Interruptions were common. Clear decisions rarely emerged" (Powell, quoted in Woodward 302).

Powell believed that the containment approach, using sanctions and the defensive deployment of troops, should be given more time before moving to an offensive military option. He made this argument individually to Cheney, Scowcroft, and Baker. Both Cheney and Scowcroft thought sanctions were inadequate and would leave Kuwait in Iraqi hands. Scowcroft concluded: "The President is more and more convinced that sanctions are not going to work" (Woodward 301). Nonetheless, in early October Cheney arranged a meeting for Powell with Bush, Cheney, and Scowcroft. In this conference, Powell told Bush:

> There is a case here for the containment or strangulation policy. If you do not want to make more military investment, here is the alternative... This is an option that has merit. It will work someday. It may take a year, it may take two years, but it will work someday. (Woodward 42)

But Powell never informed Bush that he favored the containment option. Powell waited for one of the others in the room to indicate some support first. They never did. Nor did anyone ask Powell for his opinion. Powell then asked Bush for his view of containment. Bush replied, "I don't think there's time politically for that strategy" (Woodward 42). Powell left the meeting believing that containment had not been absolutely eliminated as an option. But Powell's reading was probably in error. Within days of the meeting, Bush asked Scowcroft to have the Pentagon develop an offensive option for the White House to evaluate. Bush believed that Hussein would not evacuate Kuwait unless the United States posed a credible offensive threat. Within weeks, an increase of over 250,000 troops would be formally approved in the White House.

There are several problems with the management of this conference. There was no attempt to balance the presentation and discussion of options. No background papers on the containment and intervention options were presented. Powell was invited to a meeting in which no other support was available. In particular, Baker, who was most sympathetic to the containment strategy, was absent from the meeting. This situation made it difficult for an even-handed discussion to take place. Furthermore, no one sought to draw Powell out on his policy preference. Thus, Powell never explained why he felt the containment option was preferable. Finally, the meeting ended without a clear conclusion. Powell left believing that containment had not been completely eliminated. Had he realized that Bush was about to eliminate the containment option, Powell might have made his policy preference and its rationale known to Bush. In any case, this meeting was indicative of the informal structure and loosely managed decision process in the White House during the Persian Gulf crisis.

Cognitive Factors and Decisions on the War

Other factors beyond the structure of the Bush White House are important for understanding the Persian Gulf War decision-making. Several cognitive dynamics played important roles. The two most prevalent seemed to be the use of historical analogies and the practice of bolstering.

Analogies of War

World War II. Two historical analogies were frequently raised by decision-makers in the Bush administration. The first was World War II. Bush continually made references to its events, personalities, and concepts. Many commentators noted Bush's frequent comparisons between Saddam Hussein and Adolf Hitler (U.S. News and World Report 174). His brother William explained that Bush "was convinced that Saddam has the same sort of objectives and character as Hitler, the same willingness to use blatant aggression and to brutalize a country" (Dowd 1991, 45). But his use of the World War II analogy was much more detailed than the mere presence of an aggressive dictator. In his speech to the nation on August 8 announcing the deployment of U.S. troops to Saudi Arabia, Bush described the Iraqi tank attack as a "blitzkrieg." He then went on to offer a history lesson. "But if history teaches us anything, it is that we must resist aggression, or it will destroy our freedoms. Appeasement does not work. As was the case in the 1930s, we see in Saddam Hussein an aggressive dictator threatening his neighbors" ("Bush Announces" 2614).

Bush had been reading Martin Gilbert's *The Second World War* and was struck by Churchill's view that World War II could have been avoided if Hitler had been stopped in the Rhineland before he became too powerful (Goodgame 23). Bush saw America as the only power that could stop Hussein before he grabbed Saudi Arabia and its oil, held the western industrial economies hostage and then declared a holy war against moderate Arab states, Israel, and the West.

Bush used the concept of appeasement as a cause of World War II to explain the need for rapid United States military intervention in the Persian Gulf. In the very first NSC meetings, Bush drew parallels between the Persian Gulf and Europe in the 1930s, arguing that the Saudis had to be persuaded to reject "the appeasement option" (U.S. News and World Report 72). In the first month of the crisis while vacationing in Kennebunkport, he remarked to a friend, "We are going to try to do this without war. But if the choice were war or appeasement, I would opt for war and risk losing the '92 election" (Wayne 39). In a public address at the Pentagon on August 15, Bush noted that "A half century ago, our nation and the world paid dearly for appeasing an aggressor who should and could have been stopped. We are not going to make that mistake again" (Smith 133).

> An aide noted the power of the appeasement concept for Bush: He is deathly afraid of appeasement. His generation had to fight a war over it and he feels that if he blinks today, he will be leaving a real mess for the next generation to clean up. You have an aggressor and if you let him take over Kuwait, he will take over Saudi Arabia and become the paramount power in the Middle East.
>
> (Wayne 39)

Moreover, as the Iraqi occupation of Kuwait continued, Bush saw further analogies to World War II. He kept a copy of Gilbert's book on Air Force One, comparing it with an Amnesty International report on Iraqi atrocities in Kuwait. He was convinced that the Iraqi atrocities were "hauntingly similar" to the actions taken by Hitler's Death's Head regiment during the invasion of Poland (Mathews 64). This seemed to reinforce his comparison of Hussein and Hitler. After reading the Amnesty International report, he came to see Hussein as an evil force that had to be stopped. In an October 23 speech, Bush commented: "I'm reading a book, and it's a book of history, a great big thick history about World War II. And there is a parallel between what Hitler did in Poland and what Saddam Hussein has done in Kuwait" (Smith 195).

Bush generally saw the Persian Gulf situation as equivalent to World War II. Discussing the Persian Gulf in December of 1990 with David Frost, he said: "It's that big. It's that important. Nothing like this since World War II. Nothing of this moral importance since World War II" (Smith 238). Bush believed that Iraq's naked aggression, much like Germany's in the 1930s, forced civilized nations to recognize the need for collective action to protect world order (U.S. News and World Report 142). Thus, it was no accident that when presidential spokesman Marlin Fitzwater announced the commencement of the bombing of Baghdad on January 16, he proclaimed, "The liberation of Kuwait has begun." The phrasing was a conscious attempt to parallel Eisenhower's D-Day announcement (Dowd 1991, 46).

Vietnam. If the historical analogy of World War II seemed to push Bush toward the decision to intervene militarily, another historical analogy both reinforced that inclination to intervene and influenced the strategic decisions which shaped that intervention. Unlike the World War II analogy, which seemed primarily to affect Bush, the "lessons" of Vietnam were much more widely dispersed within both the Bush administration and the military.

From almost the first day of the crisis, Bush and Scowcroft had desired both to avoid the mistakes of Vietnam and to end the Vietnam Syndrome (Diane 6). The very discussion of a so-called "Vietnam Syndrome" (a hesitance to use U.S. forces in a protracted conflict) indicates that the meaning of a historical event may be contested among segments of society. Competing interpretations of the same historical event often provide different understandings of a policy problem. Scowcroft saw the military's hesitance to offer effective military options for the Persian Gulf at the early meetings as indicative of their falling prey to the Vietnam Syndrome. From Scowcroft's perspective, the military mistakenly blamed the failure of Vietnam on inadequate domestic political support, and consequently, the military now sought an unreasonable amount of support in Congress and the public before committing to a military intervention. Scowcroft believed this approach would make it impossible for the United States to use the military option as a valid foreign policy tool and that the Persian Gulf crisis posed a critical test for American foreign policy (Woodward 230). "Can the United States use force—even go to war—for carefully defined national interests, or do we have to have a moral crusade or galvanizing event like Pearl Harbor?" he asked (Scowcroft, quoted in Goodgame 26). The decision by both Bush and Scowcroft to have the National Security Advisor take charge of the August 3 NSC meeting by demanding that the group recognize the necessity for intervention was intended to combat the Vietnam Syndrome within the Pentagon and to enable the government to use force for carefully defined national interests.

Bush, too, was concerned with the Vietnam Syndrome. Before the Gulf crisis, in his January, 1989 Inaugural Address, he decried the dissension rampant in the country:

> It's been this way since Vietnam. That war cleaves us still. But friends, that war began in earnest a quarter of a century ago; and surely the statute of limitations has been reached. This is a fact: The final lesson of Vietnam is that no great nation can long afford to be sundered by a memory.
> ("Inaugural" 210)

After moving to an offensive deployment in November 1990, Bush sought to reassure the nation that they were not about to enter another ill-conceived venture like Vietnam:

> On the same day as the speech, Bush used a very similar argument "to try to convince congressional leaders to support his policy of rapid escalation: '. . . No hands are going to be tied behind backs. This is not Vietnam . . . . I know whose backside's at stake and rightfully so. It will not be a long, drawn out mess'"
> (Bush, quoted in Woodward 339).

There is an important connection between Bush's understanding of World War II and his concern about the Vietnam Syndrome. For Bush, the most important lessons of World War II were the need to restrain international aggression promptly and to build a civilized international order. The United States had played a central leadership role in that struggle. In a 1988 foreign policy address, Bush argued that World War II set the foundation for the country to "fulfill its historic mission. We defeated the Nazi tyranny and from the rubble of a war built a new international order" (Devroy and Balz 8). Bush saw these issues raised once more by Iraq's invasion of Kuwait.

> We stand now at a singular moment. The civilized world is now in the process of fashioning rules that will govern the new world order beginning to emerge in the aftermath of the Cold War. The history of this century shows clearly that rewarding aggression encourages more aggression. If the world looks the other way in this first crisis of the Post Cold War era, other would-be Saddams will conclude, correctly, that aggression pays.
> ("Why" 29)

The Vietnam Syndrome with its debilitating affect on American foreign policy had to be overcome to allow the country to play its proper leadership role in this international crisis. Thus a successful U.S. intervention would not only pave the way for a new world order, but for the U.S. to play its essential international role as world leader. Responding to public celebrations after the overwhelming military victory, Bush exclaimed: "By God, we've kicked the Vietnam syndrome once and for all" (Cloud 52).

The lessons of Vietnam also affected decision-making on the military strategies chosen. Most of Bush's national security advisors were very sensitive to the failure in Vietnam. Consequently, one can see in the decisions being made both in August and in October an explicit attempt to correct for the perceived errors of Vietnam. The primary problem, as they saw it, was the use of gradual escalation of force, which allowed the North Vietnamese time to adapt. As the United States stepped closer to an offensive phase in the fall, Bush made it clear that errors of Vietnam had to be avoided. One top official stated: "The president has told us not to give him another Vietnam" (Atkinson and Woodward 6). In a speech given on September 12, Cheney stated that President Bush belonged to "the don't screw around school of military strategy." He went on to say that the administration sought certain victory in the field and that "it would be morally irresponsible for us to send out men and women into battle without every advantage we can give them" (Atkinson and Woodward 6). The Bush administration developed an alternative strategy based on the use of immediately overwhelming firepower to guarantee quick success on the battlefield (Atkinson and Woodward 6). Some of the principles of this new strategy had been developed in Operation Just Cause when the United States deposed Manual Noriega in Panama in December, 1989. Three basic principles formed the foundation of Operation Just Cause: secrecy, the rapid destruction of the command capacity of the opponent, and "the crushing shock of combat power intended to be so formidable as to prove invincible" (Atkinson and Woodward 6). With the success of the operation in Panama, Pentagon officials noted that these principles were raised to the level of a catechism within both the military and the Bush Administration.

Not surprisingly, then, one can see these principles in the development of Operations Desert Shield and Desert Storm. If war were to come in the Persian Gulf, the administration wanted the capacity to apply overwhelming force. One senior administration official said:

> There are five men [Bush, Cheney, Powell, Scowcroft, and Baker] who believe in their heads and hearts that the remedy is to present maximum firepower. The critics can debate the impact of the sanctions or the diplomacy or the timeliness of United Nations resolutions, but that maximization is the engine driving the train. Period. (Atkinson and Woodward 6)

The impact of this Vietnam lesson is apparent in the decisions taken for both the defensive and offensive phases of deployment. Powell and Schwarzkopf asked for overwhelming force capacities and Bush readily acceded to their requests for massive escalation. Bush's willingness to defer to the Pentagon on military strategy was also supported by a second lesson of Vietnam: avoidance of civilian micro management of the military. The military was to be given a free hand to run the operations in their best professional judgment. As Baker observed, "The deployment had been decided by George Bush; the level of force was being decided by Operations Plan 90-1002" (Woodward 262).

The World War II and Vietnam analogies appeared to have several important impacts on the decisions taken. In the eyes of George Bush, the World War II analogy provided the moral imperative for the military intervention. The strategy for that intervention, in turn, was partially shaped by the Bush administration's understanding of the lessons of Vietnam. Most important, Vietnam drove them to adopt a strategy of massive military escalation. Their perceptions of the lessons of Vietnam—that gradual escalation more easily allowed the adversary to adjust to United States efforts or even to take the initiative and that it immorally tied the hands of American soldiers—were so clear and powerful in their minds that the Vietnam analogy may have hindered the Bush administration's ability to recognize the limitations of the massive escalation strategy. There seemed to be little sensitivity to the dangers of massive escalation. In particular, inadequate consideration was given to the tension between the difficulty of maintaining a large overseas troop deployment for a long period of time and the risk to American international influence if that large overseas troop contingent was removed without the complete accomplishment of its goals. As a result, the massive escalation strategy raised the stakes for the United States in the confrontation, shortened the time available for conflict resolution, and made the use of military force as a solution more likely. The combination of a moral imperative with massive escalation made the risk of war even greater. The analogy to the moral imperative in World War II made intervention necessary and compromise very difficult, whereas the Vietnam analogy led to massive escalation that greatly reduced the time available for non-military solutions to be effective.

CATEGORICAL ARGUMENTS AND BOLSTERING

Another cognitive dynamic played an important role in decision-making during the crisis. Bush had a propensity to use categorical arguments that left little room for balanced considerations during decision-making. In particular, there was a tendency for Bush to see the conflict in absolute terms. From the very beginning, Bush portrayed Saddam Hussein as a diabolical and evil force that must be stopped. As will be considered below, these early categorizations of evil may have been evidence of Bush's anger at the situation. But the later uses of absolute and moralistic categories seem to be a case of bolstering: minimizing the disadvantages of a chosen course of action while exaggerating its advantages.

In this case, Bush seems to have used these categorical perceptions to conclude that he had no choice but to intervene militarily. Any costs of intervention were overridden by the absolute need to avoid an unacceptable consequence. At times Bush would contrast the civilized possibilities of the new world order to the chaos of international aggression. For instance, in a December 18 interview with Time, when asked about his personal reaction to bringing the country to the brink of war, Bush responded:

> I am not churning about it. Because I know what has to be done. And I know the promise of a new world order if it is done right. I know the devastating effect on the world if it is done wrong, if we fail, if the United States is unwilling to back the newest,

most helpful peacekeeping mission of the United Nations since 1948.

(Muller and Stacks 32–33)

At other times Bush would use moral arguments. After a Christmas break, at his first meeting with key advisors in 1991, he explained his decision to initiate an attack against Iraq if necessary. Bush told them that he had come to terms with the problem and had a clear conscience. Participants at the meeting recall Bush making a clear moral argument. "It's black and white, good vs. evil. The man has to be stopped" (Dowd 1991, 46). "For me it boils down to a very moral case of good versus evil, black versus white . . . If it's right, it's gotta be done" (Mathews 65).

Bush appears to have used this stark construction of the situation to become comfortable with his own decision to initiate the attack on Iraq. His depiction of the consequences left him little choice but to attack. Bush visited American troops in Saudi Arabia over Thanksgiving and seemed troubled by the impending war. Bush then spent Christmas vacation at Camp David. While there, he carefully read the Amnesty International report on the Iraqi occupation of Kuwait. It was on the basis of this report that Bush apparently came to his decision that he would have no choice but to initiate a military attack if Iraq failed to withdraw from Kuwait. He announced his decision to his advisors at the first meetings in January, 1991. His advisors noted that he now seemed at peace with his decision (Mathews 64–65). In an interview, Bush noted that "I've got it boiled down very clearly to good and evil. And it helps if you can be that clear in your own mind" (Wayne 40).

There is also an interesting connection between Bush's use of moralistic argument to bolster the decision to attack and his use of World War II as a historical analogy. Bush saw the same moral imperative at work in both World War II and the Persian Gulf crisis. In a late December interview with Hugh Sidey, Bush reviewed his comparisons of Iraq's atrocities in Kuwait and Hitler's Death's Head Regiment in Poland. Bush then described World War II: "It was good vs. evil . . . The evil was epitomized by Adolf Hitler and Emperor Hirohito. There was never any second guessing, never any rationalization about what we might have done differently" (Sidey 14). Bush reasoned that the absolute requirement to stop evil in both World War II and the Persian Gulf left decision makers no choice but to intervene.

Emotive Factors and Decision-Making on the War

There was an emotive dimension to Bush's decision-making during the Persian Gulf crisis. As noted previously, George Bush had a tendency to react with hostility and defiance when he faced public surprises and challenges. Evidence of Bush's sustained anger at Iraq's invasion of Kuwait and the series of actions that ensued is abundant. Almost all the news accounts of his famous August 5 public commitment: "This will not stand—this aggression against Kuwait" note Bush's anger (Mathews 59, Woodward 260, and *U.S. News and World Report* 79). When the reporters there pressed him about whether the U.S. would use force, Bush seemed to take it as a challenge and responded: "Just wait. Watch and learn." (Woodward 260). A close Bush aide present at this informal press conference thought, "This is a fight George Bush has been preparing for all his life . . . Saddam Hussein doesn't know what he is in for" (Mathews 59).

In the next months Bush continually made derogatory public comments about Hussein. In September, after both meeting with the Emir of Kuwait and going over intelligence reports about Iraqi atrocities in Kuwait, Bush's mood was described as marked by "suppressed fury and disgust" (Freedman and Karsh 217). House Majority Leader Richard Gephart (D., MO) remarked that Bush was "visceral" in his anger over Iraq's holding U.S. diplomats hostage in the embassy in Kuwait (Devroy and Balz 9). By December, Bush told congressional leaders that if it came to war, Saddam "is going to get his ass kicked" (Smith 232).

The causes of Bush's anger were undoubtedly multi-dimensional. Bush felt personally betrayed by Hussein. By most accounts, Bush relied upon a personal Tory code of diplomatic conduct that Hussein had clearly violated. Hussein had given direct assurances to both Ambassador Glaspie and Arab leaders like Mubarak and King Hussein that no invasion would be forthcoming and these assurances had been passed on to Bush. Bush was later quoted as saying: "The guy lied to his own Arab colleagues. Why should I ever believe him? He's a lying SOB" (Nelson 12).

Bush also held certain Tory notions about civilized international behavior. These, too, were violated by a large nation overwhelming a smaller one, by the refusal to accord American diplomats in Kuwait with proper protections, by the taking of foreign hostages, and by the atrocities of the Kuwaiti occupation. Furthermore, Bush was politically exposed by Hussein's decision to overrun Kuwait. The Reagan and Bush administrations had consistently tilted toward Iraq. Bush had continued this policy even after Hussein's rhetoric and actions had become more aggressive in 1990. Bush had fought Democratic congressional attempts to impose trade sanctions in response to these recent Iraqi actions. For Bush, there clearly could be a partisan political price to pay for Hussein's betrayal (Mintz 609).

Janis suggests that policy makers often invoke a variety of emotive decision rules to relieve emotional stress (1989, 69–85). Two of these seem apparent in Bush's behavior: the use of a gut decision to make the decision quickly rather than agonize over it and the choice of a high-risk option to avoid the appearance of a lack of nerve. Such emotive decision rules may, however, reduce cognitive efficiency.

Many of the descriptions of Bush's decision to intervene note that it was a gut reaction on Bush's part. Thomas Friedman noted that "by all accounts it is President Bush's gut instincts that drove the rapid American commitment of forces to Saudi Arabia" (Renshon 85). In a later interview with *Time*, Bush stated that he had made an "almost instantaneous" judgment that the United States would have to intervene after Iraq occupied Kuwait (Duffy and Goodgame 140). Administration sources made the same assessment to *U.S. News and World Report* reporters (48). These accounts are lent further credence by the efforts of Bush and Scowcroft from the very beginning to compel the NSC to reject its original inclination for a passive response and instead to accept the necessity for intervention, no matter the difficulties.

Similarly, one can see a tendency in Bush to lean toward risky escalatory options at almost every stage of the decision process. Bush's "this will not stand" is indicative of his inclination toward risky policy. As noted previously, this casual public comment was made only a day after a more formal meeting had made a safer commitment only to the defense of Saudi Arabia. Wayne argues that this spontaneous statement was typical of an impulsive streak in Bush when he felt his decisiveness and strength were publicly challenged (35–36).

Moreover, throughout the decision process, Bush sought to speed up the pace of the decision-making and the American commitment to a definitive outcome. Before August was over, Bush began to discuss an offensive military option with close advisors (Duffy and Goodgame 156). By October, Bush was highly impatient and feared that Hussein had recaptured the initiative. He told Powell that there was no longer time for the containment option to work. He pushed the Pentagon and Schwarzkopf to come up with plans for an offensive phase that led to more than doubling the U.S. troop deployment. In mid November, Bush told CNN, "There is a ticking of the clock . . . I don't think this matter is going to go on forever. As far as I'm concerned it's not" (Smith 207). By late December, in a meeting with congressional leaders, he left the impression that he was becoming impatient and now accepted the likelihood that the U.S. would initiate a military attack to end the crisis (Smith 207–208).

This evidence of impatient escalation could have several interpretations. The fear of an impending collapse of the anti-Iraq coalition may have led to a desire for rapid closure. Furthermore, the widespread belief in the application of invincible force as opposed to gradual escalation could drive parts of the decision process more rapidly. This belief system explanation is ultimately a less convincing interpretation, however, since two of the strongest proponents of invincible force (Powell and Schwarzkopf) were willing to pursue the containment strategy for a significantly longer period.

Finally, there may have been emotive factors at play. Under high levels of stress, decision-makers may seek to bring a crisis to quick closure. There was evidence of this closure dynamic in accounts of the Cuban Missile Crisis (Blight and Welch 128–131). But in addition, there seemed to be a tendency toward risky decision-making during the Gulf crisis. Key White House decision-makers perceived less risk than did others. A particularly good example of this is the decision to double the troop commitment in October. The White House did not see the risk in this strategy. They were taken aback by the domestic political uproar over the escalation. One Bush aide explained, "The public thought it meant war was inevitable. We saw it as part of the Big Bluff" (Mathews 83). Bush was unwilling to be outwitted by a two-bit Third World dictator. Bush raised the ante, confident that Hussein would fold. Of course, given the momentum of the escalation and the intransigence of Hussein, the public may have had a better sense of the implications of this bet. It did mean war.

This inclination toward risky decision-making may have been intertwined with another emotive factor: Bush's tendency to personalize the conflict in the Gulf. As we have seen, Bush, unwilling to be bested in any way in a global conflict with Hussein, tended to focus much of his anger about the Gulf situation onto a demonic Hussein. In another context (his analysis of groupthink), Irving Janis suggests that the demonizing of an adversary and choice of risky options can often be linked together. In this case, Bush continually escalated the pressure in his unbending effort to defeat unconditionally the Iraqi tyrant.

The emotive constraints on some of the decision-making came at a cost. Bush's gut reaction to intervene decisively, combined with the *ad hoc* style of decision-making in the administration, made it very difficult for alternative options and their consequences to be carefully considered. Moreover, the anger toward Hussein and the willingness to engage in a risky game of chicken with him built an escalatory momentum that made it very difficult to solve the crisis in the Gulf without a war.

Contrast John Kennedy during the Cuban Missile Crisis with Bush in the Persian Gulf. While Kennedy took a highly active military response to the placement of the missiles with a naval embargo and the preparation for airstrikes in a short period of time, there was great care to provide paths by which Krushchev could de-escalate the confrontation without losing face. (For instance, Kennedy clearly left open the possibility for future negotiations with Krushchev about U.S. missiles in Turkey once Russia removed the Cuban missiles.) Thus the application of military pressure combined with an open style of diplomacy defused the crisis. In the Persian Gulf, on the other hand, little effort was made to provide Hussein with a graceful way out of the crisis. The best example of Bush's diplomatic approach was his letter to Hussein, which Baker carried to the Geneva meetings. Essentially the letter was a call for Hussein's unconditional surrender, with a threat of punishment should he refuse. "We prefer a peaceful outcome. However, anything less than full compliance with United Nations Security Council Resolution 678 and its predecessors is unacceptable. There can be no reward for aggression. Nor will there be any negotiation. Principle cannot be compromised" ("White House" A20). Sometimes decisively humiliating an opponent is a rational thing to do. Bush's letter also warned that the U.S. would not tolerate any use of chemical or biological weapons, the destruction of Kuwaiti oil fields, or the use of terrorism against coalition partners. "You and your country will pay a terrible price if you order unconscionable acts of this sort" ("White House" A20).

This aggressive stance was not surprising, given Bush's view of the conflict with Hussein. He discussed the issue of allowing Hussein to save face in a November CNN interview: "When you rape, pillage, and plunder a neighbor, should you then ask the world, hey, give me a little face? The answer is no, there isn't going to be any compromise with this kind of naked aggression" (Smith 208). There did not seem to be any recognition within the Bush White House that this combination of a massive military escalation and hardline diplomatic approach made the risk of war significantly higher.

Presidential Style and Persuasive Leadership

Having looked in some detail at the decision-making component of leadership, one should now turn to persuasion as leadership during the Gulf War. An exploration of the role of presidential style provides useful insights in a comparison of

Bush's persuasion of allied nations to join his diplomatic and military coalition against Iraqi aggression with his attempt to persuade the American public and Congress to support those same efforts.

Persuasion of the International Coalition

Bush's efforts to construct a remarkable coalition of western allies, the Soviet Union, and Arab nations were extraordinarily successful. By one count, Bush made twenty-three calls to twelve different leaders in just the first five days after the invasion (Dowd 1990, A17). Bush's efforts here were based on a strength of his insider style of governance: informal, private persuasive conversations with other members of elites. Bush's prior experience in foreign policy positions and his rolodex style of diplomacy in those positions had enabled him to build personal relationships with a large number of international leaders. He then used these very astutely to build the alliance against Iraq.

PERSUASION OF THE AMERICAN PUBLIC

But these persuasive powers were less well used both with the American public and Congress. Bush's problems with the public were endemic to his style of governance. He had previously shown little talent for capturing the public's imagination through mass communication and little that he did during the crisis would reverse this impression. Two things seemed to cause Bush the most trouble in this regard. The first had to do with the "vision thing." As Bush often conceded, he had difficulty portraying his public goals and their rationales to the public. Though there was some use of the ambiguous phrase "new world order," little was done to explain it carefully to the public. More important, the Bush administration was never clear about the purposes of either Desert Shield or Desert Storm. Bush often personalized the conflict; Saddam Hussein was portrayed as an international outlaw whose aggression could not be appeased if international order was to be maintained. But at other times Bush and his cohorts offered a wild melange of competing rationales including restoration of legitimate government in Kuwait, the defense of Saudi Arabia, the liberation of western hostages in Iraq, the cessation of Iraq's rape of Kuwait, the protection of Western access to its economic lifeline of Gulf oil, and, finally, the nullification of Iraq's access to weapons of mass destruction. Bush's own pollster found in October that the public had been badly confused by the multiple rationales (Freedman and Karsh 222). The result was declining public support for Bush's handling of the crisis. About 80% of the public supported Bush in August; by October it was hovering around 50%.

In addition, Bush's penchant for secrecy failed to prepare the public, or Congress for that matter, for the escalation of troop strength by over 250,000 in the transition from Desert Shield to Desert Storm. That particular decision had been made at the end of October, but had not been made public until November 8, two days after the 1990 mid-term elections. The announcement set off a political firestorm from both the public and Congress. For the first time since the crisis Bush's popularity dropped below 50%. The administration was taken aback by the public reaction. One Bush aide said, "The public thought it meant war was inevitable. We saw it as part of the Big Bluff" (Mathews 64). Administration spokespersons were sent across the country to reassure the public and to explain the rationale for American efforts. But the result was a continued jumble of uncoordinated and differing rationales. One of Bush's public relations specialists conceded that "It was an embarrassing display. Very few people were fooled" (Mathews 64). Bush's public support continued to fall.

Persuasion of Congress

Congress was also surprised by the increased troop commitment. Little effort was made to consult with important congressional leaders during the troop escalation. Senator Sam Nunn (D, GA), the most influential Senator on military affairs, was notified of the new deployment only an hour before Bush announced it to the public. He later complained, "I was not consulted, I was informed" (Mathews 64).

Two primary factors seem to account for Bush's failure to consult with Congress. One was the ever-present Bush predilection for secrecy. Decision-making on Desert Storm was extraordinarily tightly controlled in both the White House and in the Pentagon. Most within those institutions were unaware of the decisions being contemplated. Bush was unlikely to risk the loss of secrecy by including members of Congress in the decision process. In addition, Bush had a strong belief in presidential prerogative on foreign policy and did not hold not Congress in high regard in this area. Bush argued that he had the authority to initiate hostilities in Desert Storm as commander in chief without congressional approval (Woodward 326).

This style of governance consistently resulted in the underestimation of the domestic political reaction to decisions.[4] These political reactions, in turn, forced the administration to redirect its attention to the domestic arena. Angered by his exclusion, Nunn held a series of public hearings in which national security experts and former officials questioned the wisdom of an apparent rapid shift in strategy away from sanctions and toward a ground war. In reaction to these hearings and the continued loss of public support, Bush announced on November 30 that he would send Baker to Iraq to meet with Hussein in a last attempt at a diplomatic solution. When this effort fell through in early January, Bush offered to send Baker to Geneva to meet with Iraq's foreign minister.

Bush's failure to prepare the public and consult with Congress came at a great cost. The Nunn hearings not only fed the public's already existing fear that Bush was leading the nation toward an unnecessary war with Iraq, but it undoubtedly strengthened Hussein's belief that the United States did not have the political will and unity to pursue a war in the Gulf successfully. Similarly, Bush's two diplomatic counterplays frightened Arab coalition partners and bolstered Hussein's confidence, since both interpreted Bush's move as a sign of political weakness. The end result undercut Bush's attempt to convince Hussein that the United States was serious about using its military to free Kuwait and ironically made the use of force more likely.

Conclusion

Presidential leadership requires both high quality decision-making and effective political persuasion to build the necessary support to implement those decisions. This paper has attempted to evaluate the effectiveness of both the decision-making and the creation of political support by the Bush administration. It has also sought to explain the variations in the quality achieved in these two components of presidential leadership.

As shown previously, a high quality decision process (HQDP) has several dimensions: a comprehensive survey of the objectives at stake, broad review of the options available, a careful analysis of the costs and benefits of the available options, an intensive search for information, and careful consideration given to the implementation of the chosen option under different contingencies. The application of these HQDP criteria would result in a mixed evaluation of the Bush administration's performance during the Persian Gulf crisis.

The pre-invasion period of the decision process was highly flawed. There is little evidence that the Bush administration met any of the criteria for an HQDP. There was no careful consideration of the issues at stake, and neither was the necessary information about the situation intensively sought. Not only was a careful consideration of the available options absent, but there was no consideration of contingencies if the mild diplomatic efforts failed to deter the Iraqis.

The highly centralized decision-making in the Baker State Department was incapable of handling a potential crisis in the Middle East while primarily focusing on the collapse of the Soviet empire in eastern Europe. This incapacity was exacerbated by the tendency for *ad hoc* decision-making in the Bush White House. Without the engagement of top-level State Department and White House officials, decision-making became bogged down in lower-level bureaucratic politics among a variety of national security and commercial agencies with different interests at stake in Iraq. Furthermore, the information available and its interpretation were skewed by the tendency of Bush to rely excessively upon his informal conversations with Arab leaders, as well as by a stereotypical view of Iraqi interests and behavior. Cognitive seeking of consistency led to benign reinterpretations of the aggressive Iraqi acts in the summer of 1990.

The quality of the decision-making in the post-invasion phase was higher, though problems were still evident. Accounts of the process indicate that the Bush administration did directly consider the interests at stake. Bush, in particular, sought to bring these out with his early question to the NSC: "What if we do nothing?" A reasonable series of options also came up for early discussion, including doing nothing, diplomacy, embargo, covert operations, a token military response, a defensive military response, and an offensive military response. But from the beginning, Bush and Scowcroft pushed the group to adopt a decisive military intervention. In this drive for an initial military response, little indicates that the costs and benefits of different military intervention strategies were carefully analyzed. Nor was there a systematic comparison of the advantages and disadvantages of an embargo versus a military offense as the decision was made to shift to an offensive option. Throughout the crisis, experts (both in and out of the government) were rarely used to explore the likely political, diplomatic, and military consequences of the various options. Instead, crucial decisions were often handled informally among Bush and his closest advisors: Scowcroft, Cheney, and Baker. One result may have been to underestimate the momentum for war that was created by the combination of rapidly escalating American military deployments and the country's unbending diplomatic stance.

With the current available information, the adequacy of contingency planning is a bit difficult to judge. The military component of the decision was so successful that one cannot readily evaluate whether adequate back-up plans had been made for the variety of military problems that might have occurred. Nonetheless, some successful contingency planning was apparent. For instance, careful diplomatic and military precautions were taken for potential Iraqi missile attacks on Israel. These precautions helped stabilize the allied coalition when those attacks took place (Friedman and Tyler A1). However, the Bush administration seemed quite unprepared for Hussein's political ability to survive his decisive military loss. Nor had they developed useful contingency plans to respond to Hussein's internal actions after the war. The United States seemed to be caught quite off guard by Hussein's attacks against both the Shi'a and Kurds. World opinion and televised accounts eventually forced the administration to seek some relief for the Kurds, but only after weeks of indecision.

The flaws in the decision process in the post-invasion period can be attributed to several factors. A couple of institutional features contributed to the problems. Bush's personal style of decision-making was quite informal. Consequently, White House decision procedures were created to be compatible with Bush's preferences. In addition, Scowcroft acted predominantly as a counselor to Bush, rather than as a custodian of the decision process. The result was to limit the degree to which the decision process was comprehensive and systematic.

Psychological factors also came into play. The use of World War II and Vietnam as historical analogies decisively shaped the administration's understanding of both the moral imperative for intervention and the choice of the strategy of intervention. Finally, Bush's anger at Saddam Hussein affected his decision-making about the crisis. The result was a strategy that dangerously combined a massive military intervention with an intransigent diplomacy.

The evaluation of the second dimension of presidential leadership—building political support—was also mixed. Bush did an excellent job of building his complex international coalition to support both the embargo and the military intervention. However, he showed less ability in building that support in Congress and among the American public. The great disparity in Bush's international and domestic political success seems attributable primarily to his style of governance. His closed insider style worked very well as he constructed his international alliance through one-on-one personal contacts with other international leaders. However, his desire to work in great secrecy with other members of elites and his inability to communicate clearly with the public made it much more difficult to build support there or with Congress. Unfortunately, Secretary of State Baker, who was quite skilled at building domestic political support coalitions, was unable to compensate for Bush's weak domestic political skills during the crisis, as his time was committed to keeping the international coalition intact.

Some scholars have begun to argue that the criteria for successful decision-making that have been developed in the social sciences are too stringent for real world conditions (Welch; Renshon). Thus, they might argue that the analysis presented here has been excessively critical of the Bush administration. Undoubtedly, decision analysts must guard against the application of unrealistic 20-20 hindsight criteria for "perfect" decision-making. Nonetheless, as some observers have noted, a number of fortunate factors may have magnified the apparent success of the United States in the Gulf crisis. If Iraq had pushed into Saudi Arabia in the days immediately following the Kuwaiti invasion, or attacked the Saudi ports, or kept its tanks mobile rather than digging them in, or partially withdrawn from Kuwait before the American counterattack, United States decision-making would have been more sorely tested (Pfiffner 1993, 16–17). In a sense, the Bush administration was given a simpler (though not simple) problem to solve (Hybel 77–79). More careful decision-making and more astute construction of domestic political support would have been necessary, if Hussein had acted differently. As we have seen, factors related to the structure of the Bush White House, the governing style of Bush, and his personality and belief system might have limited the ability of the administration to construct a better decision process.

Notes

[1] It should also be acknowledged that Johnson examined the possibility of building mixed systems of management to compensate for the weaknesses in each of the pure models. He does not, however, make the distinction between organizational structures and procedures.

[2] Neustadt's analysis of bargaining and George's analysis of multiple advocacy are two interesting attempts to examine presidential strategies to deal with bureaucratic politics.

[3] See Stanley Renshon's "Good Judgment and the Lack Thereof During the Gulf War" for a different interpretation of Bush's anger.

[4] Woodward maintained that Baker recognized the costs of a sudden announcement of a major change in policy without building public support and consulting with Congress. But his efforts to build a viable international coalition often kept him out of the country while these decisions were made. He was in the Soviet Union on November 8th. See Woodward 323.

Works Cited

Allison, Graham. *Essence of Decision*. Boston: Little, Brown, & Co, 1971.
Atkinson, Rick. "If War Comes, What Is Our Goal?" *Washington Post National Weekly*, 27 Aug.–2 Sep. 1990: 6–7.
Atkinson, Rick, and Bob Woodward. "The Doctrine of Invincible Force." *Washington Post National Weekly*, 10–16 Dec. 1990: 6–7.
Barber, James. *Presidential Character*. Englewood Cliffs, NJ: Prentice-Hall, 1992.
Berman, Larry, and Bruce Jentleson. "Bush and the Post-Cold War World." *The Bush Presidency*. Ed. Colin Campbell and Bert Rockman. Chatham, NJ: Chatham House Publishers, 1991.

Blight, James, and David Welch. *On the Brink.* New York: Noonday Press, 1990.
Braybrooke, David, and Charles Lindblom. *A Strategy of Decision.* New York: Free Press, 1963.
Burke, John. *The Institutional Presidency.* Baltimore: Johns Hopkins Press, 1992.
Bush, George. "Inaugural Address." *The Election of 1988.* Ed. Gerald Pomper. Chatham, NJ: Chatham House Publishers, 1989.
———. "Bush Announces Deployment of Forces to Saudi Arabia." *Congressional Quarterly,* 11 Aug. 1990: 2614.
———. "Why We Are in the Gulf." *Newsweek,* 26 Nov. 1990: 29.
———. "Bush Defends Gulf Buildup." *Congressional Quarterly,* 1 Dec. 1990: 4010.
———. "White House Releases Bush Letter to Saddam." *Cleveland Plain Dealer,* 13 Jan. 1991: 20-A.
Campbell, Colin. "The 'Lets Deal' President." *The Bush Presidency.* Ed. Colin Campbell and Bert Rockman. Chatham, NJ: Chatham House Publishers, 1991.
Cloud, Stanley. "Exorcising an Old Demon." *Time,* 11 Mar. 1991: 52–53.
Crabb, Cecil, and Kevin Mulcahy. *American National Security.* Pacific Grove, CA: Brooks/Cole Publishing, 1991.
Devroy, Ann, and Dan Balz. "George Bush: Unwavering, Unbending from the Start." *Washington Post National Weekly,* 21–27 Jan. 1991: 8–9.
Dionne, E. J. "Drawing Lessons from History." *Washington Post National Weekly,* 13–19 Aug. 1990: 6.
Dowd, Ann. "How Bush Decided." *Fortune,* 11 Feb. 1991: 45–46.
Dowd, Maureen. "The Longest Week: How Bush Decided to Draw the Line." *New York Times,* 9 Aug. 1990: A17.
Duffy, Michael, and Dan Goodgame. *Marching in Place.* New York: Simon and Schuster, 1992.
Freedman, Lawrence, and Efraim Karsh. *The Gulf Conflict, 1990–91.* Princeton: Princeton University Press, 1993.
Friedman, Thomas and Patrick Tyler. "From the First, U.S. Resolve to Fight." *New York Times,* 3 Mar. 1991: A1.
George, Alexander. *Presidential Decision Making in Foreign Policy.* Boulder, CO: Westview Press, 1980.
Gigot, Paul. "A Great American Screw-Up." *National Interest,* 1990/91 Winter: 3–11.
Goodgame, Dan. "What If We Do Nothing?" *Time,* 7 Jan. 1991: 22–26.
Greenstein, Fred, and John Burke. "The Dynamics of Presidential Reality Testing," *Political Science Quarterly* 104, 4 (1989–90): 557–80.
Hoffman, David. 1989. "The Politics of Timidity." *Washington Post National Weekly* 23–29 Oct. 1989: 6–7.
———. "Blinded by the Light in Iran, the U.S. Didn't See the Fire in Iraq." *Washington Post National Weekly,* 27 Aug.–2 Sep. 1990: 9–10.
Hult, Karen. "Advising the President." *Researching the Presidency.* Eds. George Edwards, John Kessel & Bert Rockman. Pittsburgh: University of Pittsburgh Press, 1993.
Hybel, Alex Roberto. *Power over Rationality.* NY: SUNY Press, 1993.
Janis, Irving. *Groupthink.* New York: Houghton Mifflin, 1982.
———. *Crucial Decisions.* New York: Free Press, 1989.
Janis, Irving, and Leon Mann. *Decision Making.* New York: Free Press, 1977.
Johnson, Richard. *Managing the White House.* New York: Harper & Row, 1974.
Jones, Christopher. "American Prewar Technology Sales to Iraq: A Bureaucratic Politics Explanation." *The Domestic Sources of American Foreign Policy.* Ed. Eugene Wittkopf. New York: St. Martin's Press, 1994.
Kellerman, Barbara. *The Political Presidency.* New York: Oxford University Press, 1984.

Kellerman, Barbara, and Ryan Barilleaux. *The President as World Leader.* New York: St. Martin's Press, 1991.
Khong, Yuen Foong. *Analogies at War.* Princeton: Princeton University Press, 1992.
Mathews, Tom. "The Road to War." *Newsweek,* 28 Jan. 1991: 54–65.
Mintz, Alex. "The Decision to Attack Iraq," *Journal of Conflict Resolution* 37, 4 (Dec. 1993): 595–618.
Muller, Henry, and John Stacks. "Determined to Do What Is Right: Interview with George Bush." *Time,* 7 Jan. 1991: 32–33.
Nelson, Jack. "Bush Is Described as Calm but Angry and Determined to Destroy Saddam." *Akron Beacon Journal,* 17 Feb. 1991: A12
Neustadt, Richard. *Presidential Power and the Modern Presidents.* New York: Free Press, 1990.
Pfiffner, James. "Presidential Policy Making and the Gulf War." *The Presidency and the Persian Gulf War.* Eds. Marcia Whicker, James Phiffner & Raymond Moore. Westport, CT: Praeger, 1993
———. *The Strategic Presidency.* Lawrence, KS: University Press of Kansas, 1996.
Renshon, Stanley. "Good Judgment and the Lack Thereof during the Gulf War." *The Political Psychology of the Gulf War.* Ed. Stanley Renshon. Pittsburg: University of Pittsburg Press, 1993.
Rockman, Bert. "The Leadership Style of George Bush." *The Bush Presidency.* Ed. Colin Campbell and Bert Rockman. Chatham, NJ: Chatham House Publishers, 1991.
Salinger, Pierre, and Eric Laurent. *Secret Dossier.* New York: Penquin Books, 1991.
Sciolino, Elaine (with Michael Gordon). "U.S. Gave Iraq Little Reason Not to Mount Kuwait Assault." *New York Times,* 23 Sep. 1990: A1
Sheehy, Gail. *Character.* New York: William Morrow & Company, 1988.
Shogan, Robert. *The Riddle of Power.* New York: Penguin Books, 1992.
Sidey, Hugh. "History Lessons." *Time,* 31 Dec. 1990: 14.
Sifry, Micah, and Christopher Cerf, eds. *The Gulf War Reader.* New York: Times Books, 1991.
Smith, Jean Edward. *George Bush's War.* New York: Henry Holt & Co., 1992.
Solomon, Burt. "In Bush's Image." *National Journal* 7 Jul. 1990: 1642–1647.
Stein, Janice. 1992. "Deterrence and Compellence in the Gulf, 1990–91," *International Security* 17, 2 (1992): 147–179.
Steinbrunner, John. *Cybernetic Theory of Decision.* Princeton: Princeton University Press, 1974.
Strong, Robert. *Decisions and Dilemmas.* Englewood Cliffs, NJ: Prentice-Hall, 1992.
Thomas, Evan. "The Code of the WASP Warrior." *Newsweek,* 20 Aug. 1990: 33.
U.S. News and World Report. *Triumph without Victory.* New York: Times Books, 1992.
Waas, Murray. "Who Lost Kuwait?" *Village Voice,* 22 Jan. 1991: 30–38.
Wayne, Stephen. "President Bush Goes to War: A Psychological Interpretation from a Distance." *The Political Psychology of the Gulf War.* Ed. Stanley Renshon. Pittsburgh: University of Pittsburgh Press, 1993.
Waterman, Richard, ed. *The Presidency Reconsidered.* Itasca, IL: F. E. Peacock, 1993.
Welch, David. "Crisis Decision Making Reconsidered," *Journal of Conflict Resolution* 33, 3 (1989): 430–445.
Woodward, Bob. *The Commanders.* New York: Simon & Schuster, 1991.
Woodward, Bob and Rick Atkinson. "Launching Operation Desert Shield." *Washington Post National Weekly,* 3–9 Sep. 1990: 8.

An Odyssey In Black Leadership: Joseph Gomez, a Bishop in the African Methodist Episcopal Church

Annetta Louise Gomez-Jefferson

The Black church in the U.S.A. has been and remains the convergent point of the Black community. It serves not only the spiritual requisites of its members, but, as C. Eric Lincoln and Lawrence H. Mamiya point out in *The Black Church in the African American Experience,* the church:

> ... has no challenger as the cultural womb of the black community. Not only did it give birth to new institutions such as schools, banks, insurance companies and low income housing, it also provided an academy and arena for political activities, and it nurtured young talent for musical, dramatic and artistic development. (1980, 8)

The minister of such an institution is required to be multi-faceted in his or her approach to leadership in order to be effective. This was especially true for Joseph Gomez, whose career took him from a mission charge in Bermuda in the early 1900s to the pastorate of large urban churches in the United States between 1919 and 1948. Later he moved up in the African Methodist Episcopal Church's structure as Prelate of the 10th (Texas), 13th (Kentucky and Tennessee), 4th (Indiana, Illinois, Michigan, Ontario in Canada), and 17th (Zambia in Central Africa), until he retired at the age of 82. During all these years, in ever-widening arenas, he fought for the well-being of his people on many fronts, including housing, education, the arts, and politics.

The "Little Giant," as he was affectionately called, began his odyssey in 1890 in Willikies, a remote village on the island of Antigua in the Caribbean. He was the first son of Rebecca Richardson, of African descent, and Manoel Gomes, a Portuguese merchant. Although Joseph revered his Catholic father, from the very beginning it was his mother's African heritage and her love for the Methodist Church with which he most identified. He never thought of himself as anything other than Protestant and Black.

In the eulogy at his funeral in 1979, Bishop Hubert N. Robinson described Gomez as "small in stature," but a leader whose "compatriots had to look up to see him, for his heights of vision and his ideals made him lofty in stature." He was never noted for doing anything in a small or ordinary way. For instance, on June 18, 1914, he graduated from Payne Seminary at Wilberforce University, Wilberforce, Ohio, was ordained a minister, married Hazel Thompson of Toledo, Ohio, and was sent to his first charge in Bermuda, all on the same day.

Gomez manifested his leadership in various ways. His primary but not exclusive concern was with the spiritual well-being of his congregation. Since the African Methodist Episcopal Church (the first Black autonomous denomination) was founded by Richard Allen in 1787 as a protest against the status of slaves in the white Methodist Church ("African Methodist" 1947, 11), Gomez believed that it must play a vital role in uplifting his people. Second, he felt that the civil and economic rights of Negroes had to be fought for on every front. One way to do this was through political involvement. He maintained that "no element in the American body politic [was] more entitled to the rights and privileges guaranteed by the constitution than the Negro." The Negro's participation in every war and especially the World Wars had enabled him to lift "the Negro problem out of the narrow confines of American Provincialism," and present its "case before the world's tribunal" (Gomez, "New Negro" 1920). Third, he believed that Negroes must claim and take pride in their rich heritage and must continue to develop their own culture while contributing to American and world culture. "Each race should be given fullest opportunity to develop its particular genius, and make its distinct contribution . . . the real history of any race is the record of its distinctive contributions," he wrote in the *A.M.E. Review* of April 1931.

Most important, he saw all of these elements as interdependent and interrelated. His mentor, Bishop Reverdy C. Ransom, had so often told him, "You cannot preach God to an empty stomach or to a person who feels he has no pride in or power over his own destiny." This became Gomez's creed.

As a religious leader, Gomez was not a fundamentalist. He was more interested in the symbolic truths of the Bible than any literal interpretation. He had little use for theological treatises that did not address themselves to the human condition. As he said at the Fifth Seminar of Judaism in Cleveland, January 25, 1940, he hoped the day would come "when basic religion would have a common and compelling channel of expression." If people would examine carefully all religions, they would discover "much that is wholesome and beautiful in all religions . . . common religious connotations, the essential morality of religions . . . a larger and more comprehensive definition of our common heritage" ("Address" Fifth). His sermons were not of hellfire, brimstone, and damnation, but of love, compassion, and healing. However, though there was an earthiness in his sermons, there was also an air of mysticism in his message. He believed that all true spiritual leaders were prophets who affirmed the omnipresence of God in the affairs of women and men.

On May 2, 1968 at the A.M.E. General Conference in Philadelphia, he preached that just as the Son revealed God's grace to his followers in His day, Christ's Holy Spirit yet operates in the lives of leaders and that "divine healing is not quackery but the legitimate function of the church and ministry." Gomez affirmed that the same Spirit was revealed to the Civil Rights leader, Dr. Martin Luther King Jr. In his "I Have A Dream" speech at the March on Washington in 1963, King's vision was made clear. Just as the Biblical John saw "a new heaven, a new city, a new society, a new community of God," King eloquently affirmed that a new American society was being born. The fulfillment "was for an appointed time. Though it tarry it [would] come. It [would] surely come" ("New Society" 1968).

At the age of twenty-nine, in 1919, Gomez was sent to his first American pastorate, Bethel A.M.E. Church in Detroit, Michigan, a church that had a membership of over two thousand. Never before in the history of American Methodism had a minister that young been given such a prestigious charge. Initially, the congregation referred to him sneeringly as "the boy preacher and his baby wife." Nevertheless, before a year had passed, Gomez had increased the membership of Bethel to over three thousand, had to open up a second Sunday morning service, and had started plans for the building of a "Greater Bethel" to accommodate the rapidly growing congregation ("Minutes Thirty-Fourth" 1920).

In his Christmas message for that year, he reminded his members "of the truth historical, that the steps upward have always been marked by tears and blood. This mystery of Pain is the root of Progress" (Gomez, "Christmas" 1919). His message was prophetic. By 1925, despite the threats and cross burnings of the Ku Klux Klan, and the disapproval of other white groups, the members of Bethel marched from Napoleon and Hastings, the heart of the Negro ghetto called the Black Bottom, to Frederick Street in a white neighborhood, and entered their new home. At the Michigan Annual Conference in September 1925, Gomez's Presiding Elder, Rev. T. H. Wiseman, called the new church "the fulfillment of a dream. The realization of a vision splendid which represented the tremendous possibilities of a people." He concluded that "there is not a greater or finer church in the United States among our people, nor is there a greater field of constructive work [being done] anywhere among our people" ("Minutes Thirty-Ninth" 1925).

Even more important, while at Bethel, Gomez organized a much needed Social Service Department to help find jobs and lodging for the influx of Blacks who were migrating from the South. In *A Study of Housing Conditions of Negroes in Detroit* by the Research Bureau of Associated Charities (1919), Forrester B. Washington, secretary of the Detroit Urban League, describes the housing conditions in this manner:

> The majority of Negroes are living under such crowded conditions that three or four families in an apartment is the rule rather than the exception. Seventy-five percent of the Negro homes have so many lodgers that they are really hotels. Stables, garages and cellars have been converted into homes for Negroes. The pool-rooms and gambling clubs are beginning to charge for the privilege of sleeping on pool-room tables.

The task of finding housing for the in-coming Blacks seemed impossible, but Gomez's Social Service Department was responsible for placing hundreds of Negroes in homes and jobs. *The Detroit Contender* of November 13, 1920 called the work being done there "splendid." In return for the help they had received, many of these Blacks became active members of the church and the department, assisting other migrants to adjust to urban life. For example, when Charles Diggs, Sr., his wife, and brother arrived in Detroit, they had $6.35 among them. Gomez persuaded a Negro physician, Dr. Rainwater, who owned a building on the corner of St. Antoine, to let the family stay in one of the apartments for a month, rent free. Later Diggs became a prominent funeral director and a Michigan State Senator; his son, of the same name, became a United States Congressman (Lockett 1987).

From the time of his earliest ministry in Bermuda, Gomez was determined that Negroes should have a decent place to bury their dead rather than in a remote woods or the corners of white cemeteries. In Detroit he had the opportunity to take concrete action. On June 17, 1925, he and twelve other prominent Negroes purchased sixty acres of land in Warren Township, Macomb County. They became the founders and first Board of Directors of the Detroit Memorial Park Association (Articles 1926). Gomez often boasted that his investment in the cemetery was the only stock from which he received steady dividends. Though small in amount, they represented far more to him than mere money. They were symbolic of the Negro's struggle to have power over his or her own destiny.

Throughout his ministry, Gomez was an active participant in civic affairs, and his churches were used as forums where American leaders of all races were given an audience. At Bethel Detroit, the controversial A. Philip Randolph and Chandler Owens, co-editors of *The Messenger*, were often invited to speak despite their socialist views (Owens 1920). Bethel church bulletins listed other speakers such as Eugene Kinckle Jones of the National Urban League, James Weldon Johnson of the National Association for the Advancement of Colored People, and W. E. B. DuBois, editor of the NAACP's *Crisis Magazine*. When Gomez was assigned to St. James, Cleveland, Ohio, as pastor (1936–48), he also became the Director of the Literary Forum, where, among others, Harry S. Truman, Margaret Webster, Langston Hughes, Carter G. Woodson, Ralph Locher, Frank Lausche, and Eleanor Roosevelt were heard. Every Sunday afternoon at 4 p.m., an overflow crowd gathered in the sanctuary to address the vital issues of the day. Those arriving late were unable to find even standing room (Minutes St. James 1936–1948). After the church burned down on January 2, 1938, *The Cleveland Press* of February 18, in its campaign to help raise funds for a new building, referred to the church as the "center of spiritual activity and civic ferment in Cleveland," and added that the "St. James Forum had served for 11 years as a sounding board for the continuous discussion of public affairs by some of the ablest men in this city and in the nation, both white and Negro."

When Gomez had arrived in Detroit in 1919, he learned that the Council of Churches barred Negroes from its organization. *The Detroit Independence* on October 10, 1923 came out with an exposé, criticizing the Council for its refusal to take issue with the Ku Klux Klan. Gomez promptly wrote an open letter congratulating the paper for noting "the base betrayal of faith by those men of [the] city clergy who, in recent session of the Detroit Council of Churches, voted to table a resolution condemning the Ku Klux Klan." He pointed out that this was the second offense of its kind. Gomez reminded his readers that two years ago when he was President of the Colored Detroit Interdenominational Alliance, his group passed a resolution asking the City Council and the Council of Churches to join ranks with the Alliance in condemning the Klan and prohibiting them from conducting open exhibitions within Detroit's corporate limits. This the City Council did. However, instead of acting on the request, the Council of Churches referred it to the Committee on Social Relations, and nothing further was heard of the matter. Gomez noted that now once again, by their silence, the Council of Churches was "aiding the Klan, an organization that under the guise of 'one hundred percent Americanism' goes forth to murder and plunder, reducing our American institution to a state of lawlessness" ("Open Letter" 1923). The Council of Churches was furious with Gomez for his castigation of their venerable organization, but Black ministers of the city applauded him for his daring.

Just as had been the case in Detroit, the Kansas City Chapter of the Council of Churches also excluded Negro ministers from its membership. As pastor of Allen Chapel A.M.E. Church during the early thirties, Gomez was determined to address this problem. He had his opportunity on February 3, 1930 when he spoke before the white Ministerial Alliance at the Locust Street YMCA. He related again the story of the Detroit Council's refusal to condemn the Klan. He declared that the present day pulpit was weakened by such silences, especially when compared to the boldness of the Fathers of Protestantism. This "growing apostasy," he said, accounted for the number of Negroes who were now flocking to the Catholic Church. "Either the Bible—its teachings of brotherhood—was practicable and workable or else it was a lie," he concluded ("Address" Ministerial 1930). The Protestant Church would have to make its choice.

Gomez was a convincing speaker, a passionate believer in the rightness of the causes he championed. He was often able to sway people who had strong opinions. In an editorial, "Talking it Over," that appeared in the *Kansas City Call* February 7, 1930, Roy Wilkins, later the Executive Secretary of the NAACP, noted that after the speech at the YMCA, the Executive Committee voted to admit colored churches to the Kansas City Council of Churches.

> The tact, the diplomacy, the irrefutable logic, the telling persuasion, the uncompromising reasoning, the fluent citations of ecclesiastical history and the stirring plea for the practical application [of Christian] principles to the problems of the day, made the eloquent minister of Allen Chapel A.M.E. Church hold its listeners spellbound. . . .

The Kansas City American of February 6, 1930 called the speech "an acme of eloquence, a challenge to the sponsors and followers of the Master." Whenever he had the opportunity, Gomez attacked the hypocrisy of religious organizations and schools that preached the brotherhood of man and yet practiced discrimination based on race, color, creed and/or economic status. While pastor for St. Paul A.M.E. Church in St. Louis (1930–36), Gomez and Rev. John F. Moreland from the A.M.E. Zion Church petitioned Eden Seminary to admit them to their graduate seminary. Eden, a school governed and supported by the Evangelical Synod of North America, was located at Webster Grove, a suburb twelve miles from the center of St. Louis. After much pressure from the two ministers, the Negro press, and some white supporters, Moreland and Gomez were finally admitted. On June 7, 1934, they became the first members of their race to receive a degree from Eden Seminary, thus opening the door for other Negroes who would come after them. During a banquet at the Pine Street YMCA following the graduation, Gomez told the audience that in order for Negroes to get those things to which they were justly entitled, they "must find some way to unite . . . forces" just as he and Moreland had done, even though they were from different denominations ("Address" *St. Louis* 1934). On June 5, 1964, Gomez, by then a Bishop in the African Methodist Episcopal Church, delivered the Commencement Address at Eden Seminary and was given an Honorary Doctor of Divinity (Eden 1964).

Soon after the United States entered World War II in 1941, Gomez became embroiled in another controversy. The Red Cross refused to accept Negro blood in its blood banks. Sloan Colt, director of the Red Cross drive, said on December 30th that "the Red Cross is now about to obtain from white donors enough blood to keep all the processing plants fully occupied so that the total amount of blood plasma available to the armed forces is not lessened by our inability to accept Negro donors" (*Cleveland Call and Post* 11 Jan. 1942). As pastor of St. James, Cleveland, and President of the Cleveland Methodist Ministers' Union, Gomez called for concerned Negroes to meet at St. James on January 8, 1942. The result was a formal complaint sent to the Red Cross which called the policy of not accepting Negro blood "unjustifiable and unscientific . . . an unwarranted assault upon racial as well as national morale." They asked that the policy be altered so the Red Cross would accept "any and all human blood" (*Cleveland Call and Post* 11 Jan. 1942).

From his pulpit every Sunday and in letters to friends and congressmen, Gomez lashed out at the Red Cross' insult to Negroes. All over the country he and other Negroes exerted so much pressure on the federal Government to intervene that finally in February, 1942 the Red Cross announced that it would accept Negro blood, but it would be stored separately. Gomez found this equally unacceptable and urged Negroes to continue to protest until the practice was eventually abandoned (*Cleveland Call and Post* 25 Feb. 1942).

As a graduate of Wilberforce University in Wilberforce, Ohio and as trustee on the Church and State Boards at various times during the 30s and 40s, Gomez became involved in the fight to prevent the State of Ohio from dictating the policy of the Church University. In 1888, the State had entered into an agreement with the A.M.E. Church whereby it set up an Industrial Department on the campus to "aid Negro citizens of Ohio to equip themselves for service in the industrial society that called for skilled performances." Later it extended its offering to include Teacher Training. All the other departments of this liberal arts university were operated by the Church. For years there had existed two Boards of Trustees, one representing the A.M.E. Church and the other the interests of the State of Ohio. Initially, the Church had sufficient representation on the State Board. Nevertheless, in 1947, the Ohio Legislature introduced Bill 258, which would increase the number of appointees on the State Board to eight, leaving only one member to represent the Church. Since the state was by far the richer of the two, it could then dominate all the university's policies (Walker 1947 4–5).

Gomez, Bishop Reverdy Cassius Ransom (Bishop of the 3rd which included Ohio), and D. O. Walker, former President of Wilberforce, and other prominent representatives of the A.M.E. Church went to Columbus to attempt to prevent the bill from passing the Senate. The Church was firmly convinced that what the State had in mind was to establish a separate state school for Negroes at

Wilberforce so that when they applied for admittance to Ohio State University, they would be told there was a school for them at Wilberforce (Walker 16). Along with Walker, Gomez became a spokesman for the Church's position.

The *Cleveland Call and Post*, April 26, 1947, recorded the essence of Gomez's speech before the Legislature. In it, he warned Senator Albert L. Daniels of Green County, the strongest proponent of the bill, that neither he nor anyone else who thought like him would ever "operate a college apart and separate for Negroes, not while free men shall live and speak." The bill was passed despite the strong objection of the Church. Charles Wesley, the president of Wilberforce, who had supported the bill, was fired by the Church Board. The State retaliated by setting up a separate university on the land where the Industrial Department had been housed before, calling it Central State, and appointing Wesley president. Though he and the others had fought as hard as they could, Gomez always felt that this was one fight the A.M.E. Church had lost, but that in losing it had maintained its integrity by refusing to be a part of a segregated school. There still are two universities in Wilberforce, Ohio.

Gomez's second fight on behalf of an A.M.E. educational institution was more successful. When he was elected to the bishopric in 1948, he was appointed to the Texas Diocese. As bishop, he also became Chancellor of Paul Quinn, an A.M.E. college located in Waco. When he arrived he found a two-room administration building obscured by grasses and weeds; a fortress-like three-story brick building used as a library, classroom facility, and men's dormitory; a women's dormitory which also housed the Home Economics Department; a long barn-like building called the George B. Young Auditorium; a two-story apartment for faculty; a nursery; and two other houses, formerly used as dormitories, that would become the President's House and the Episcopal Residence. The college had been founded in Austin, Texas in 1872 by a small group of A.M.E. circuit riding ministers for the education of Blacks after the Civil War. It had moved to Waco in 1881, where it occupied twenty-two acres of the old Garrison Plantation (*Encyclopaedia* 1947 461–462).

Gomez found himself head of a college that had no major accreditation. It was poorly staffed with a faculty and administration who had few graduate degrees. The student records were not up-to-date and were kept in cardboard boxes on the floor of the administration building; the outdated catalogue listed courses that had not been taught for years; the financial records were in disarray. In general, it was a glorified high school rather than a college.

Waco resembled a small town in the Deep South, although it was in Texas. The train station had separate waiting rooms, drinking fountains, and toilet facilities. Downtown the restaurants were closed to Negroes, as were the drugstore and ten-cent store counters. In the department stores, they could not try on certain clothes. Negroes had to sit at the back of the city buses, and Baylor, the Baptist University, was closed to Black students. There was little communication between the races. Segregation was an established way of life. This was the environment that faced Gomez when he arrived.

Before he left eight years later, he had erected an administration building, a women's dormitory, a chapel, a dining room/student union, and a gymnasium; he upgraded the faculty, so that everyone had at least a Master's Degree and most a Ph.D. More important, the racial climate between the city and the college had greatly improved. He became one of the first Negroes to speak at Baylor University on November 8, 1949. The occasion was World Community Week, which was sponsored by the United Council of Church Women. He spoke of a world community of "moral suasion and convictions of deepest spiritual meanings... which would unconditionally and uncompromisingly recognize God as our Father, Jesus as our Elder Brother, and all mankind as brothers." This speech marked the beginning of a spirit of cooperation between Paul Quinn College and Baylor University ("Speech" *Christian Recorder* 1949). In addition, Gomez convinced the Waco Appeals Review Board to raise $200,000 for the expansion of Paul Quinn, and the ministers and laymen in his district to match the amount (*Waco Tribune-Herald* 3 May 1953).

In March 1956, the Association of Texas Colleges commended Paul Quinn for its improvement of faculty, reorganization of curricula, development of an effective general education program, and accuracy of records. Soon after, the college received a "yes" from the State Commissioner of Education for its right to prepare teachers according to the revised teaching standards passed by the Board in consequence of the Supreme Court's school desegregation ruling in 1954 (Jackson 1956). Changes had not come easily. After much controversy, Gomez had to remove from office the President, who he felt was impeding the progress of the school. Her dismissal was not popular among some of the ministers, who considered him and the president he appointed to be outsiders—northerners. Nevertheless, his decision proved to be the correct one. Before he had left Texas for a new diocese, the *Waco News-Tribune* hailed him as the "Saviour of Paul Quinn College" in an editorial and noted that "the old Negro school was near extinction when he came...." Gomez, the writer said, "was the 'principal architect' of all that had been accomplished in Waco in terms of the college and racial cooperation." He was a man of "rare qualities of leadership, of eloquence, of understanding" ("Editorial" 28 Aug. 1956).

Further proof of his effective leadership in racial cooperation had occurred in August, 1951 when the Annual Texas A.M.E. Congress met on the campus. The Mayor of Waco proclaimed the week "Paul Quinn Week." Thursday night was designated as Interracial Night. In addition to several other prominent business and civic leaders, guest speakers included A. M. Goldstein of Goldstein Migel Department Store and Dr. W. R. White, President of Baylor University. During the same week, Gomez was able to get the Waco Transit Company to drop its segregated seating and to name the downtown loop intra-city bus after the college (*Waco News-Tribune* 17 Aug. 1951). Later in 1955 when the Bishops' council held its session on campus, Gomez persuaded the city to open up all its hotels and restaurants in the downtown area to accommodate the visitors who had come from all over the United States, Africa, and the Caribbean (*Waco Times-Herald* 25 Feb. 1955).

In 1953, Gomez was one of the representatives of eleven different denominations who met to form the Texas Council of Churches. Dr. M. E. Sadler of the Christian Church was elected President, and Gomez was elected First Vice President, the first Negro to hold an elected office in any Texas state religious organization (*Dallas Morning News* 5 May 1953). This seemed an impossible feat in the early '50s, since it was well in advance of the '60s Civil Rights Movement.

An Odyssey in Black Leadership 151

At the first annual meeting, President Sadler was ill, and Gomez presided over the Council. In his introductory remarks, he called upon the Church to "exert itself before it [lost] possession of its soul as leader in the affairs of the nation." He considered the new Texas Council to be a giant step, which would succeed if its members learned to "disregard the false standards of race, color or creed" ("Speech" Texas 6 Jan. 1954). At the close of the conference, he was given a standing ovation, and many urged him to accept the presidency for the coming year. He refused because of his other obligations and because he did not feel that some of the churches in the Council were ready yet for a Negro president. By presiding over the gathering, he made the point that Negroes were indeed more than capable. Now it was up to the council to alter its outdated, narrow way of thinking.

Before Gomez left Texas, many changes had taken place, and many more would occur before he visited again. In terms of the A.M.E. Church, he had urged the ministers in his district to return to seminary and seek further knowledge. The quality of ministers improved greatly. He also made it a rule that both the minister and his wife had to live in a parsonage in the community in which they pastored. He put in place a budget plan that enabled each church to meet its obligations. As far as Waco was concerned, it was one of the cities that found desegregation during the '60s easier than many others in the South; this was largely the result of the progress Gomez had already made in race relations during his tenure there.

The golden years of his ministry and marriage came while he was Prelate of the 4th Episcopal District which included Indiana, Illinois, Michigan, and Ontario, Canada. He strongly urged his ministers to register and vote during the 1960 election, stating that no man had "a right to campaign against segregation, discrimination and bigotry in Alabama and come to . . . cities of the North and not register to vote" ("Minutes Illinois" 1960 345–346). To him, this was hypocrisy of the highest order. He joined the Crusade for Freedom Movement headed by Dr. Martin Luther King, Roy Wilkins of the NAACP, and A. Philip Randolph, which had as its aim the registration of an additional one million Negro voters ("Minutes Illinois" 345–46). On January 2, at a Summit Meeting of his district, he gave an address entitled "To the Summit with Christ," in which he challenged those present to return to their churches and give financial, physical, and spiritual aid to the various protest movements. "Freedom will not be won by abstract theorizing or beautiful words. It will only be won by day to day pressure on the opponent. Freedom has never been given to the oppressed—never in the history of the world" ("To the Summit" 1961).

In August 1961, he was a delegate to the 10th World Methodist Conference in Oslo, Norway (Delegate List). That same year in November he attended the World Council of Churches meeting in New Delhi where he had an opportunity to converse with Vice President Radhakrishnan of India; Bishop Shot K. Mondol of Delhi; American Ambassador to India, John K. Galbraith; Clifton R. Wharton, a Negro from Norway; and other church leaders from around the world, including some from the Soviet Union (Gomez, "Special" Nov.–Dec. 1961). In August of the following year, he was honored by the National Association of Colored Women's Clubs along with Robert Kennedy, Arthur Goldberg, Walter Reuther,

Dr. Jonas Salk, Henry Ford, A. Philip Randolph, Senator Phil Hart, and other distinguished figures who had made outstanding contributions in their fields (*Christian Recorder* 28 Aug. 1962).

During the July, 1963 NAACP National Convention held in Chicago, he and 18,000 others paraded to Loop Grant Park with Mayor Richard Daley; Rev. J. H. Jackson, head of the National Baptist Convention; Roy Wilkins, Executive President of the NAACP; and Senator Paul Douglas. When they reached the park, Daley and Jackson were booed from the platform because of unpopular statements they had made during the convention. When it was Gomez's time to speak, he told the crowd, "These are times when men must show courage as well as the understanding necessary to properly guide the millions of people who don't quite [comprehend] the urgency of the times." He reminded them of how the history of the A.M.E. Church and its beginnings reflected "the very mood of the present day struggle for freedom." Upon completion of his speech he was "given a rounded ovation" (*Indianapolis Morning Tribune* 5 July 1963).

On November 13, 1964, 3,000 people gathered in the ballroom of the Sherman House in Chicago to celebrate the Gomezes' fiftieth wedding anniversary and fiftieth year in the ministry. Mayor Ralph Locher flew in from Cleveland and Mayor Daley of Chicago left his daughter's wedding reception to attend. James Gomez came all the way from Trinidad to present his brother the Golden Jubilee Medal on behalf of Mayor Edward Taylor of the island. This was the first time the medal was awarded to a leader from outside Trinidad (*Trinidad News* 28 Nov. 1964). The entire Gomez family was present, the daughters, sons-in-law, and grandchildren.

When asked for a response to the celebration, part of what Gomez said was:

> The shifting patterns of life are always sources of fruitful study and understanding of men and things. Looking across the half century of public life and sifting gold from dross, I come up with buoyant faith in the Providence of God and the worthwhileness of life. The shadows which I experienced were so many opportunities to probe for life and the deeper meanings of the universe, to discover good and choose that good as against evil.
> (*Christian Recorder* 29 Dec. 1964)

He had not run from any of life's "shadows," but saw both the dark and bright hours as occasions to expand his understanding of God's will for him in his ministry.

Throughout all his many activities, Gomez had always remained a family man—the ideal father, grandfather, and husband. So, after saluting his daughters and their families at the close of his response to the anniversary celebration, he turned to his wife. "What more can I say of this woman—my Hazel T.—who for fifty years . . . breasted the storms . . . cheered my successes, gave wings to my dreams, allayed my fears." She had been his "companion, friend, critic, team-mate, mother, and wife" (*Christian Recorder* 29 Dec. 1964).

Gomez' last district was in Zambia, in Central Africa. At the age of 80, he realized his dream of setting his feet on the continent from which his mother's

An Odyssey in Black Leadership 153

people had originated. If he had been a younger man, he said, he would have stayed there. He saw democracy being practised as in no other place he had been: whites and Blacks living together harmoniously. He embraced Zambian President Kenneth Kaunda's unique definition of "humanism," which reached out to all peoples. As Kaunda said in his address to the National Council at Mulungushi, "Our society has in the past and must continue now and in future to place the right value on man. That fact that this man is there—God's noble creature, the creature of creatures—is all that matters and our task is to serve him selflessly, and without distinction of any type at all" (1969, 7). Kaunda's "humanism" recognized the equality of all people and God as the center of all being.

When Gomez returned to the United States in 1972 at the age of 82, he retired from the A.M.E. Church, lived in Cleveland for a few years, then moved to Wooster, Ohio to reside with his younger daughter. On April 28, 1979, he died of a heart attack after dining with his family and a friend. His funeral was held at Bethel A.M.E. Church in Detroit, and he was buried at Detroit Memorial Park, the cemetery he had helped to found in 1925. Rev. John Hunter, who had been Gomez's Assistant Pastor at St. James in Cleveland, said at his funeral that he was:

> a great Biblical preacher . . . a preacher every day of the week . . . a prince of pastors. He had few scholastic equals in contemporary Christendom. He developed leaders as he led. If you would see his living monument in leadership—look around, all around.

His odyssey had brought him from the tiny island of Antigua to major centers the world over. He had visited the White House during the administrations of Kennedy and Johnson, had had an audience with the Pope, could claim friendship with many prominent leaders, including Speaker of the House of Representatives Sam Rayburn; Governor of Michigan G. Mennon Williams; and the Archbishop of Cape Coast, Ghana, West Africa, The Most Reverend John Kodwo Amissah. But he never lost the common touch. He was equally comfortable with the Aunt Sues, who sat on the front pews and could neither read nor write, as he was with the Ph.D.'s, who found it more fashionable to sit in the balcony. He was generous to a fault, but was also quick of temper and could rise up in righteous indignation. He was a dynamic preacher, scholar, teacher, and leader, an uncompromising fighter for the rights of his people. Most of all, he had a huge appetite for living. Each age for him had its "own compensation," so that when his sun set, "all the gathered beauty and brilliancy of a long march [was] poured out in blended tones, softened and hallowed by the touch of approaching night" (Gomez, "Sunset" 1917).

WORKS CITED

"African Methodist Episcopal Church 1897–1947." *Encyclopaedia of African Methodism.* 2nd ed. comp. R. R. Wright. Philadelphia. A.M.E. Sunday School Union, 1947.
Articles of Incorporation of the Detroit Memorial Park Association. 1926.
Christian Recorder. 28 Aug. 1962.

Christian Recorder. 29 Dec. 1964.
Cleveland Call and Post. 11 Jan. 1942.
Cleveland Call and Post. 25 Feb. 1942.
Cleveland Call and Post. 26 Apr. 1947.
Dallas Morning News. 5 May 1953.
Delegate List. 10th World Methodist Conference. Oslo, Norway. 18 Aug. 1961.
Detroit Contender. 13 Nov. 1920.
Eden Seminary Commencement Program. 5 June 1964.
"Editorial." *Waco News-Tribune*. 28 Aug. 1956.
Encyclopaedia of African Methodism. 2nd ed. comp. R. R. Wright. Philadelphia. A.M.E. Sunday School Union, 1947.
Gomez, Joseph. "Address." Fifth Seminar of Judaism. Cleveland, Ohio. 25 Jan. 1940.
———. "Address." Ministerial Alliance. Locust Street YMCA. Kansas City. 3 Feb. 1930.
———. "Address." *St. Louis Argus*. 15 June 1934.
———. *A.M.E. Review*. Apr. 1931.
———. "The New Negro Is Here." *The Detroit Contender*. 30 Oct. 1920.
———. "The New Society of God." Thirty-Eighth Session of the A.M.E. General Conference. Philadelphia. 2 May 1968.
———. "Open Letter." *The Detroit Independence*. 15 Oct. 1923.
———. "Special to *The Cleveland Call and Post*." New Delhi, India. Nov.–Dec. 1961.
———. "Speech." *Christian Recorder*. 10 Nov. 1949.
———. "Speech." Texas Council of Churches. Austin. 6 Jan. 1954.
———. "Sunset." *Voice of Missions*. May 1917.
———. "To the Summit with Christ." *The Michigan Chronicle*. 7 Jan. 1961.
Gomez, Joseph, and Mrs. Gomez. "Christmas Message." 1919.
Hunter, John. "Eulogy of Bishop Joseph Gomez." Rec. 2 May 1979. Audiotape. Bethel A.M.E. Church. Detroit, Michigan.
Indianapolis Morning Tribune. 5 July 1963.
Jackson, Reid E. Letter to Joseph Gomez. 25 March 1956. Paul Quinn College. Waco, Texas.
Kansas City American. 6 Feb. 1930.
Kaunda, Kenneth. *Zambia's Guidelines for the Next Decade*. Lusaka, Zambia: Zambia Information Service, 1969.
Lincoln, C. Eric, and Lawrence H. Mamiya. *The Black Church in The African American Experience*. Durham: Duke University Press, 1990.
Lockett, Cora. Personal interview. Spring, 1987.
Minutes of the Illinois Annual Conference of the A.M.E. Church. Champaign. Sept. 1960. 354–346.
Minutes of the St. James Literary Forum. 1936–1948. Cleveland, Ohio.
Minutes of the Thirty-Fourth Annual Session of the Michigan Conference. Fort Wayne, Indiana. Sept. 1920. 46.
Minutes of the Thirty-Ninth Annual Session of the Michigan Conference. Jackson, Michigan. Sept. 1925. 49–50.
Owens, Chandler. Letter to Joseph Gomez. 15 Feb. 1920. Detroit.
Robinson, Hubert N. "Eulogy of Bishop Joseph Gomez." Rec. 2 May 1979. Audiotape. Bethel A.M.E. Church. Detroit, Michigan.
Trinidad News. 28 Nov. 1964.
Waco News-Tribune. 17 Aug. 1951.
Waco Times-Herald. 25 Feb. 1955.
Waco Tribune-Herald. 3 May 1953.

Walker, D. Ormond. "The Struggle to Control Wilberforce University." St. James Literary Forum. Cleveland. 27 April 1947.
Wilkins, Roy. "Talking It Over." *Kansas City Call.* 7 Feb. 1930.